If the skies were made of parchment...

If all the trees were made into pencils...

If all the oceans were filled with ink...

If every person on this planet became a skilled scribe...

...the story of the Holocaust would still remain untold.

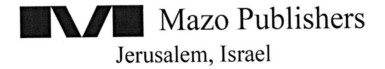

Not To Forget Impossible To Forgive

by

Dr. Moshe Avital

WITH BEST WISHES

Dr. Moshe Avital

Mazo Publishers

Jerusalem, Israel

Not To Forget
Impossible To Forgive

ISBN 978-1-936778-57-7

Published by:
Mazo Publishers
Chaim Mazo, Publisher
P.O. Box 36084
Jerusalem 91360 Israel

Website: www.mazopublishers.com
Email: mazopublishers@gmail.com

USA Tel: 1-815-301-3559
Israel Tel: 054-7294-565

Maps used in this book have been reprinted from *McMillan Atlas Of The Holocaust*, © 1982, by Martin Gilbert, published by The Jewish Publication Society, with the permission of the publisher, The Jewish Publication Society.

A Memorial

"Oh (how I wish) that my head were waters, and my eyes a fountain of tears, that I might weep day and night for the slain of my poor people." (Jeremiah 8:23)

With this book, I wish to create a memorial to the pure souls whose remains are strewn on the fields of Poland, Russia, and Germany. May the Almighty avenge their innocent souls.

My father, Rabbi Joshua (Yehoshua) Doft.
My mother, Pearl Doft.
My sister, Leah Hirsh and her five children.
My sister, Sarah, her daughter and her husband, Aba Weinberger.
My brother, Chaim Leib.
My brother, Nachum Uri.
My brother, Joseph.
My 200 relatives in our extended family.

May their memory be blessed.

"Earth, conceal not the blood shed on thee."
(Job 16:18)

Table Of Contents

Part 4

From The Gates Of Hell To The Gates Of Hope – 167

Part 5

Reflections And Analyses – 225

Part 6

Educating Today's Generation About The Holocaust – 305

Acknowledgments

I wish to express profound gratitude to my dear wife Channah, and my precious daughters, Leora, Sheara, and Reva, who convinced me to record my testimony for future generations. Without their assistance, this volume would have never been completed.

Special thanks to my daughters: Sheara and Reva, for their computer skills and input into this undertaking, turning a massive collection of papers into a manuscript for publication; to Leora for being the liaison with the publisher in Israel.

I would also like to thank my son-in-law, Ilan Slasky, for his great help in matters concerning the book's publication. Ilan's acumen has been a major component to this manuscript becoming a finished book.

Also, special thanks to my dear wife Channah, for her insight into the text and assistance with the editing and proofreading, and her support, which was great solace to me as I relived, while writing, the pain of those trying years.

Thanks to the *Memorial Foundation for Jewish Culture* for the partial grant to help with the publishing of this book.

My sincere thanks to Rabbi Herschel Schacter who, as Chaplain of the American Army in Buchenwald after liberation, comforted me and gave me spiritual strength to heal my wounds and for allowing me to use some of his photographs from the Army and Buchenwald.

Many thanks to my dear friend Sam Bloch for his help.

Thanks to Dr. Judith Hemmendinger for allowing me to use the photographs of the train of the Children of Buchenwald en route to France for recuperation, and a partial list of the children survivors of Buchenwald.

Thanks to Dr. Jerry Weinberg who provided a number of photographs of an American soldier who liberated Buchenwald.

About The Author

Dr. Moshe Avital

Dr. Moshe Avital was born Moshe Doft in Bilke, a village in the eastern part of the former Czechoslovakia called Ruthenia, now Ukraine. Brought up in a traditional Jewish home and in a Jewish environment, he received his early secular education in the Czech public school system and his Jewish education in the Jewish schools in his hometown.

In 1939, Czechoslovakia was torn apart by Germany. The German Reich annexed the Sudetenland, Moravia, and Bohemia. Slovakia became an independent Fascist state, a satellite of Germany. Ruthenia had been ceded to Hungary. Thus his former homeland in the very heart of Europe came to an end.

During the Holocaust, he was imprisoned in Ghetto Berehovo (Beregszasz in Hungarian). From there he was deported with his entire family to Auschwitz, Poland, transferred to Plaszow, then to Gross-Rosen, then to Bolkenheim, then to Reichenau, and finally to Buchenwald, Germany. There the United States Third Army liberated him on April 11, 1945. After weeks in a makeshift hospital in Buchenwald, he was sent to Ecouis, a village in Normandy, in northwest France to recuperate.

In July 1945, he joined the *Aliyah Beth* movement, which was an illegal immigration to Palestine, conducted by the *Jewish Brigade* of Palestine. He was taken to a secret port in France where he boarded a freight boat which was renamed *Yaldei Buchenwald*, the Children of Buchenwald. The ship was intercepted by the British Navy, ordered to the Haifa Port, where he was forcefully removed from the ship and escorted to *Atlit,* a detention camp near Haifa.

He was liberated one night by members of the *Hagannah*, a Jewish military underground in Palestine. He later joined the Hagannah and was fully mobilized after the United Nations passed a resolution to partition Palestine. He fought in the War of Liberation, 1947-1950, mostly in the Jerusalem area. He also fought in the 1956 War and served in the Israeli Army (I.D.F.) for another six months.

Dr. Moshe Avital in his study at home.

In November 1950, he first came to the United States for his sister's wedding, who had also survived the Holocaust.

Dr. Avital pursued his higher academic and Judaic studies at Yeshiva University where he graduated with honors and received a B.A., M.S. and Ph.D. in Hebrew Literature.

For 40 years he served in various educational positions, the last 12 years as the director of education and culture of the Jewish Agency for Israel American Section.

Dr. Avital is a steady contributor to the Hebrew Press in America and in Israel. He writes about the Holocaust, Israel, Zionism, Jewish Education, American Jewry, Commentaries on the Bible and Jewish Prayers, on Jewish personalities and Jewish Holidays.

He speaks half a dozen languages and is a translator. He has translated 10 ancient Hebrew Kabbalah books into English.

Dr. Avital was the official Hebrew to English translator for the ABC Network during the proceedings of Egyptian President Anwar Sadat's historic visit to Israel and the proceedings in the Israeli *Knesset,* the Parliament, on November 18, 1977, and later on the press conference at the reciprocal trip to Alexandria, Egypt, by Israeli Prime Minister Menachem Begin.

Dr. Avital is the author of three books which were published in Israel; *The Yeshivah and Traditional Education in the Literature of the Hebrew Enlightenment Period*; *My Hometown Bilke Which Was – But Is No More*; and *For Our People and Our Country*, a series of essays about the Holocaust, Zionism and Israel, Jewish Education, Jewish Holidays and Commentaries on Prayer.

Dr. Moshe Avital with Rabbi Herschel Schacter (R) on the occasion of receiving the Abraham Friedman Memorial Prize in Hebrew Literature. (October 21, 2001)

Rabbi Schacter was the U.S. Army Chaplain who was among the liberators of the Buchenwald Concentration Camp and befriended Moshe as a young boy in the camp.

Dr. Avital is the recipient of the prestigious Abraham Friedman Memorial Prize in Hebrew Literature. It was awarded to him on October 21, 2001, by the Histadrut Ivrit of America, the organization for the advancement of the Hebrew language and culture in America, for his authorship of three Hebrew books and hundreds of articles in the Hebrew press in America and in Israel.

Dr. Avital is married to Anita (Channah) Hershman. They have three married daughters and ten grandchildren. The Avitals live in New York.

Introduction

A state of horror existed for 12 years, from 1933 to 1945, and enveloped all of Nazi-occupied Europe. Many of the natives of Germany, Poland, the Ukraine, Lithuania, Latvia, Estonia, and others collaborated in the annihilation of their peaceful neighbors, who had lived with them for many centuries.

The term most commonly used to describe this tragedy is Holocaust. It is derived from the Greek word meaning a sacrificial offering that is consumed entirely by flames. More commonly, it is used to define a total destruction by fire or a widespread destruction. The definition is inadequate and inappropriate, but it is the best we have. In Hebrew, we call this tragedy *Shoah*, which means catastrophe, destruction, or disaster. Sometimes people use the expression, the third destruction, following the destruction of the two Jewish States in the past. No matter what expression we use, it will never describe the real Jewish tragedy.

The Holocaust is a story of the hunted, the persecuted, and the murdered. It is also the story of the heroism of sainted martyrs, of the courage of the Jews who resisted and defied Nazi terror, and of the humanity of the all too few non-Jews who did not overlook or set aside their responsibility to their fellow human beings.

Of the approximately 8,300,000 Jews in Nazi Europe, more than 6,000,000 perished, of which 1,500,000 of these Jewish souls were children. Only some 2,000,000 Jews were left alive.

Of every three Jews, one survived, bereaved, and homeless... an empty shell.

People who did not go through the Holocaust cannot understand, and will never understand the survivor's frame of mind. For many years, like many other Holocaust survivors, I avoided speaking about what happened to me and my family during the dark years of the Holocaust. For most survivors, talking about that time became a painful journey back to a time that we wanted to erase from our memories.

I feel compelled to tell my story of the Holocaust because I was one of the lucky ones who survived. Only by relating my story will people begin to understand the anguish and fear that permeated every moment of my daily life during that horrible time, watching family, friends, and acquaintances disappear or die while I remained helpless.

Lately, many survivors have realized the importance of telling their painful recollections, so others will have the opportunity to learn from these experiences. I feel that new and future generations should hear our testimonies so they may protect themselves and avoid future calamities.

As the Psalmist said, "I shall not die, but live and tell the wonders of the Lord." (Psalm 118:17) We, the survivors, together with our brethren, have an obligation to continue carrying the banner of our faith of Jewish *Hemshechiyut*, the continuity, the unbreakable bond that joins our generation with the previous ones and the generations to come.

One can impart the Holocaust legacy, not only with factual knowledge, but also by moral meaning. I will bring the positive values in the behavior of our brethren during the Holocaust. I will tell of the courage, nobility of spirit, and sense of group responsibility with which young people can identify. Just as we teach about the destruction of the Temple in Jerusalem and what *Tisha B'Av*, the 9th day of the Hebrew month *Av*, represents in Jewish life, so should we teach our children about the Holocaust, the Shoah, and what *Yom Hashoah* means to our people. It is a *Yom Zikaron*, a *yahrzeit*, a memorial day, which teaches our children to affirm hemshechiyut.

In preparing this book, I struggled with a formidable problem – how much to include of this ghastly record. What happened to our people in Europe has no parallel in the history of mankind. It is a very difficult task to convey those horrible years of the Holocaust. No matter how talented a person may be, there are not enough fitting words to describe or explain what happened to the Jews of Europe during those tragic years.

This book is an eyewitness account of the events I experienced as a youngster in the ghetto, in Auschwitz, and in other concentration camps, until my liberation by the American Army in Buchenwald. I present this book, not only as a victim of Nazi tyranny, but also as an educator.

I will give you some important highlights and will point out to you some of the implications the Holocaust has for Jews today, and the lessons we should

The borders of the European countries *before* World War II.

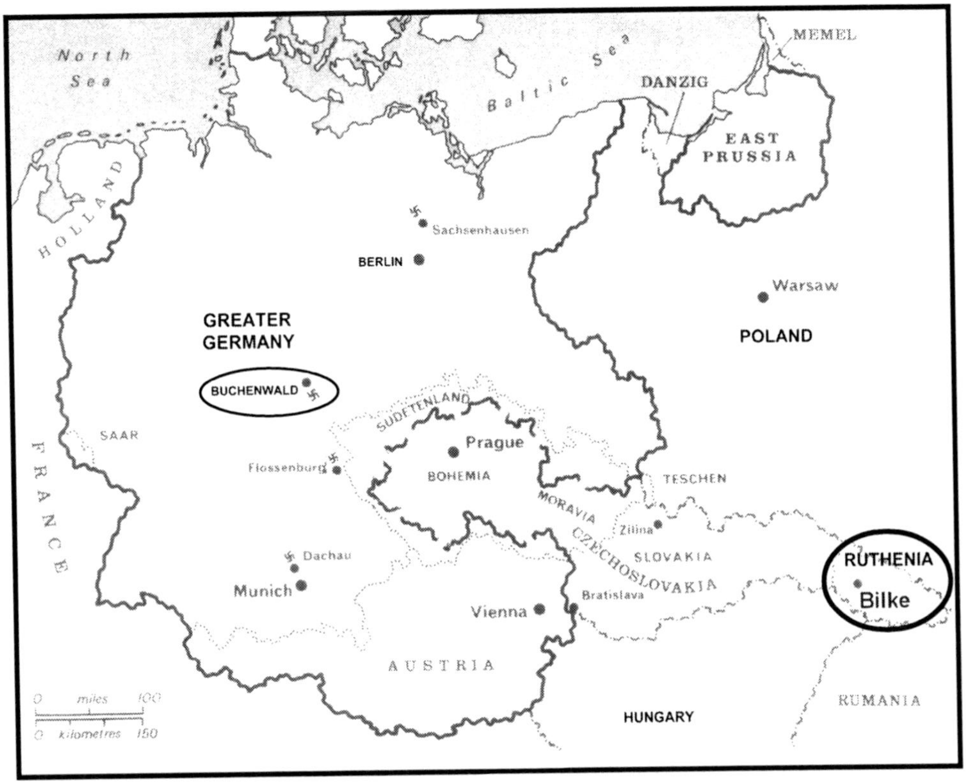

Reprinted from *McMillan Atlas Of The Holocaust*, © 1982, by Martin Gilbert, published by The Jewish Publication Society, with the permission of the publisher, The Jewish Publication Society.

learn from our tragedy.

In this book, I tell the reader what happened and try to explain why it happened. However, it will take many generations until all the atrocities that were committed by Hitler, his followers, and their collaborators are fully discovered.

As a victim, I tell my story of agony for posterity. As a witness to the Holocaust, I want to make sure the world knows what happened during those tragic years; the horrific events I witnessed and experienced, along with the catastrophic events that resulted in the murder of 6,000,000 Jews. The Holocaust must not be forgotten. It must not happen again.

In this book, I tell about our town, the rich and vibrant spiritual and cultural life that lasted for more than 300 years through 15 generations. In this book are accounts of the calamity that befell our people during the six years of persecution and annihilation. I, who miraculously survived, describe the agony and suffering we endured during captivity under inhuman conditions, which the Germans, the Hungarians, and other collaborators inflicted upon us.

During the Holocaust, we harbored in our hearts a deep Jewish pride, which we carried with us wherever we were driven by the Nazi beasts. When the trumpet of freedom was finally sounded, we survivors were transformed into builders of a new Jewish life. We rebuilt our lives, established new families, and forged new links in the long chain of Jewish history.

As survivors, we are a symbol to future generations of how remnants of the death camps who were almost lifeless heaps of bones, turned into creative Jewish individuals. The answer to the incisive question of the Prophet Ezekiel, (37:3), "Will these bones live again?" was given by the survivors, an unequivocally positive answer. Out of the heap of helpless victims of the rule of terror, we became the carriers of a new Jewish life. After our liberation from the death camps, we, the survivors, applied ourselves to the revitalization of the dry bones.

The destruction of European Jewry during the Holocaust posed the most radical, philosophical, moral, and theological problems ever faced by the Jews. It raised very difficult questions. But no matter how difficult the subject of the Holocaust is, it is of utmost importance that our young people learn the lessons of the Holocaust and their consequences.

The Holocaust and the restoration of Jewish independence in the Land of Israel are two major events in our time that have drastically changed the course of Jewish history. Today, we cannot understand Jewish life without thorough knowledge of these two watershed events of the Jewish people. It is, therefore, essential that we transmit to our people the significance of the Holocaust and the establishment of the State of Israel.

I strive with this book to ensure in our hearts, in our conscience, and hopefully in the hearts of the coming generations, that the imperishable hope and prayer and yearning of those who died in despair, helpless and forsaken, will be remembered forever.

Dr. Moshe Avital

Not To Forget
Impossible To Forgive

Part 1

The Doft Family

"Mercy and truth met together; righteousness and peace have kissed each other." (Psalm 85:11)

As dark clouds covered the skies of Europe and Satan got a free hand to unleash destruction, the fate of the Jewish community of Bilke in the Carpathian Mountains was sealed.

Since permission was given to the evil forces, they did not distinguish between the wicked and the just.

Rabbi Joshua Doft

During sleepless nights, the image of my father, of blessed memory, appears before me as it was engraved in my mind and on my heart. I absorbed a great deal of knowledge and learned proper ethical behavior from my father, qualities that direct my life until this very day. Over the years, I realized the great influence he had on my character as it was forming and developing. I will keep his memory in my heart and I shall preserve my deep admiration for him until the end of my days.

All these years, I cannot get the images of my father, mother, brothers, sisters, and other dear family members out of my mind, who in life and death were not parted. The terrible Holocaust, which befell our people, uprooted our beloved ones.

Rabbi Joshua Doft

Rabbi Doft perished in Auschwitz on May 25, 1944. This picture was taken in the 1930s.

Rabbi Joshua Doft was a shining light in the darkness of the town of Bilke. He was the Cantor and the *Shochet*, the ritual slaughterer. He devoted his entire life to serving his community.

Rabbi Joshua Doft, the son of Shlomo Dov and Miriam Eidel Doft was born in 1880 in the city of Zidachov, Poland. Rabbi Joshua was a descendent of a famous family of judges and *Shochatim*. At the age of five, he and his family moved to Polyne, a town in the Carpathian Mountains where his father was appointed Shochet.

Rabbi Joshua married Pearl, the daughter of Rabbi Abraham and Rachel Yitte Lipschitz of Zalizshe in the Carpathian Mountains. Rabbi Abraham was the son of Rabbi Shabsai Lipschitz, the chief judge of Irshava, who was a famous scholar and author. Mrs. Rachel Yitte was a descendent of the *Noda Beyehudah*, Rabbi Ezechiel Landau, Chief Rabbi of Prague.

Pearl was a true woman of valor and a great homemaker. She was beautiful, had a pleasant personality, was righteous and a great help to her husband. Rabbi Joshua adored his wife and treated her like a queen. She had 11 children and raised them. Their children and other members of the family revered her.

In 1905, Rabbi Joshua was appointed Cantor and Shochet in Bilke,

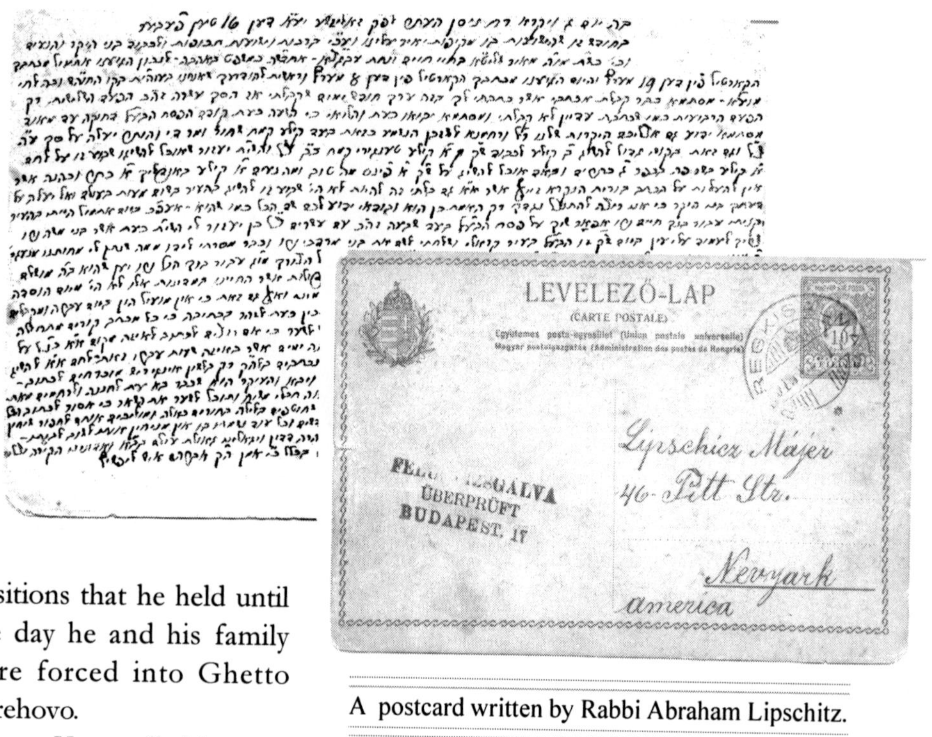

A postcard written by Rabbi Abraham Lipschitz.

positions that he held until the day he and his family were forced into Ghetto Berehovo.

He excelled in every aspect of his undertaking. He was a remarkable blend of talent, compassion and integrity, leaving an indelible imprint on the Bilker community, which he served until the last minute before his deportation to the ghetto. He was revered by all of his constituents for his behavior and his way of life. His

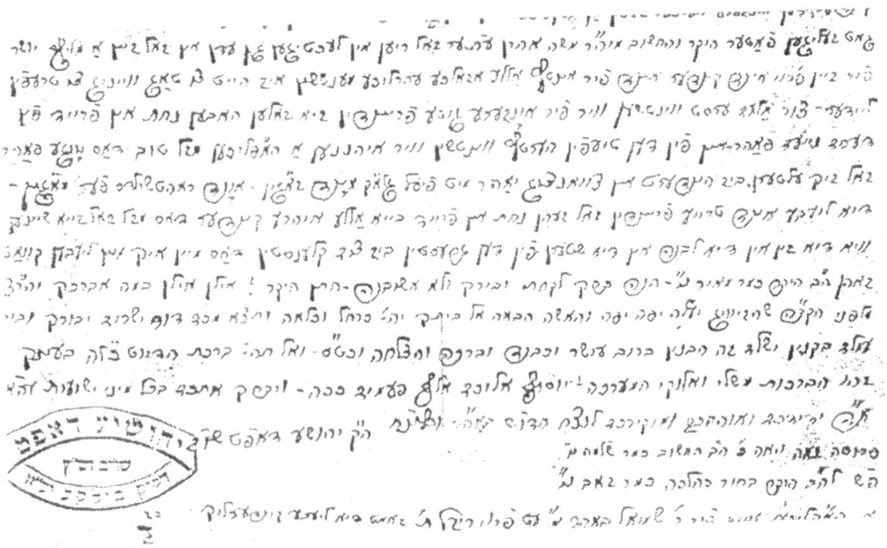

The Hebrew handwriting of Rabbi Doft.

humane behavior, his love and devotion to the members of the community, and especially his concern for people, created the image of a popular and beloved personality in Bilke and its environs.

Rabbi Joshua served as the Cantor in the Great Synagogue in the center of Bilke, which served as the focal point of the Jewish spirit. Rabbi Joshua was approached many times by larger and more affluent Jewish communities with tempting offers to serve as their Cantor. These offers he refused. His concern for the Bilker community prevented him from improving his economic situation. All who came in contact with him felt an extraordinary marvel, a special spirituality that emanated from his personality. His spiritual strength and extraordinary character uplifted and strengthened those of the Bilker community who needed encouragement and support.

Rabbi Joshua was a representative of a special generation that disappeared during the Holocaust. When Rabbi Joshua walked on the path from his house to the main Synagogue with his *Talit* and *Tefillin* bag under his arm, the passersby looked at him with great admiration, as if they were saying, "Here passes Rabbi Joshua, who is the pillar of the community, and who is the epitome of *Derech Eretz*, of honor and respect." He was the Beacon who illuminated the darkness of the town, who spread heavenly light and spirit into the lives of his constituents. He possessed many good and special qualities of the admired Jew. He had many talents, which enhanced his aristocratic personality. He was a G-d-fearing person, a *Chasid*, and at the same time, a deep, caring person to his fellow human beings. He loved peace and pursued it. He was a great scholar with a vast amount of knowledge in the Talmud, Bible, Midrashim, Oral Law, and many other books in Judaica. He was a pleasant person and remained so until his last days. He lived and breathed Judaism. Deep in his strong personality was embedded a soft and sensitive soul. He was a deeply religious person who succeeded in imbuing in his constituency an uncompromising faith.

In addition to being the Shochet in Bilke and its environs, Rabbi Joshua had a great talent for writing in a pure and clear Hebrew handwriting with a special style. Each letter was like a pearl, and his letters were bright and soothing to the eyes. He wrote the *ketuboth*, marriage documents, for all the couples that were married in Bilke all those years. As a specialty, he wrote the entire scroll of Esther on a postcard, which he sent to the various branches of the family as *Shalach Manot*, gifts for Purim. He also prepared and edited the script of Rabbi Abraham Lipschitz, his father-in-law's book, *Yalkut Avraham*, since Rabbi Abraham became semi-blind after an operation. It was known that Rabbi Joshua produced and created things to perfection.

Rabbi Joshua always went out of his house immaculately and splendidly dressed. His beard was combed and his *payot*, sidecurls, were always curled. His face was bright and on his lips a pleasant smile. He had a delightful and lovely personality. He was all soul. His royal appearance, his radiant face and his extraordinary stature contributed to an honorable aura of awe that moved everyone with whom he came in contact. His wife, sons, daughters, grandchildren and in general all his larger family loved him and honored him. He loved children with all his being and was deeply devoted to his family.

On *erev* Shabbat, the Sabbath eve, Rabbi Joshua prepared the Shabbat candles in the candlesticks. After he secured the candles in the candelabra, he lit them for a moment, according to tradition, to make it easier for Mrs. Pearl to light the candles.

Rabbi Joshua came from a musical family, a talent that was passed on from generation to generation. He had three brothers and one sister. Rabbi Joshua had a very strong, sweet and pleasing voice. His three brothers also had beautiful voices. His brother Tzvi Hersh was a famous Cantor in Paris until he was deported to Auschwitz. Rabbi Joshua's voice had an unusual sweetness, which inspired his worshipers. His singing was exalted and heavenly, as if it came from above. His renditions and melodies were rooted in holiness, which one could compare to the music of the ministering angels, which rose all the way to heaven. Those who heard his singing felt a *taam Gan Eden*, a taste of paradise.

Rabbi Joshua stood in front of the *Aron Kodesh*, the Holy Ark, dressed in full Shabbat splendor, in awe, as if he actually stood in front of his creator. He lifted his heart and soul to produce sweet and pleasant sounds during the year-round Jewish calendar, on the Shabbat, *Rosh Chodesh* – the new month, the three festivals, the high holidays, special days, weddings, and other happy occasions as well as sad days on the calendar, each prayer for the right occasion, each prayer with its meaning, intention, and devotion.

The melody had a special meaning and a deep mystical expression for Rabbi Joshua. He said that one had to know how to gather in the various floating voices to compose them into a harmonic melody, which creates joy, and through it one penetrates the gates of heaven. He produced a very pleasant, soothing feeling with his voice. It was very clear this helped to heal and comfort broken hearts. In music, he saw strong human expression that could influence a person.

During the early hours of the morning at *Selichot*, the Penitential service, when he began *Haneshama Lach*, "The soul is thine…O Lord do it for Thy name's sake," a vibration, a tremble went through the worshipers, since each one felt as if his soul was attached to the creator. By his superb renditions, Rabbi Joshua gave his congregation a great deal of spiritual joy. He inspired his worshipers and at times he brought warm tears to their eyes. His prayers captured many hearts and thus strengthened the spirit of Jewish tradition, faith and Jewish values that sanctified G-d's name.

Whoever did not hear Rabbi Joshua lead his congregation in prayer did not hear prayers that came from a pure heart. His melodies were full of sensitivity, sweetness, and an outpouring soul. My brothers and I stood with our father. *Chaim Leib*, *Shmuel Tzvi*, and *Nachum Uri*, my father's older sons stood on his right. *Shlomo Yeshaya*, *Yosef*, and *I – Moshe Nechemya*, the younger sons, stood on his left, on the steps that led to the Aron Kodesh. Rabbi Joshua prayed with the *nusach*, the melody, which he learned from his father, who inherited it from previous generations. The worshipers listened with awe, and sat as if they were frozen from the great *nachat ruach*, spiritual joy, that Rabbi Joshua gave them by his renditions.

A number of his melodies were familiar to the worshipers and from time to time the congregation joined his singing, which was spiritually uplifting for them. From time to time, one of his sons sang a solo and the other brothers harmonized. Rabbi Joshua sang certain prayers with joyous melodies through which he expressed his happiness, his overflowing heart in order to give thanks to the Almighty. There were other prayers which he sang with a broken heart, with a sad melody, as if he was a distraught person. There was time when he hurried through a melody as if he were running to approach a king to present him with a gift.

When Rabbi Joshua began a festival *Maariv*, evening service, a feeling of awe and joy overcame the worshipers. When he reached the prayer *Vayedaber Moshe*, "Moses proclaimed the festivals of the Lord unto the children of Israel," (Leviticus 23:44), he raised his voice very high and thus filled the Synagogue with his sweet voice. On *Shavuot*, Pentecost, after the *Shacharit*, the morning service, before the Torah reading, Rabbi Joshua recited the poem *Akdamut*, which describes the greatness of G-d, with a special traditional melody. This melody, with its extraordinary flavor, was greatly favored and admired by the Jews of Bilke. This melody established the mood of the holiday. During *Hallel*, the selection recited during the important and minor festivals, Rabbi Joshua mesmerized the audience with his original melodies that captured the hearts of the worshipers. This was especially so when he reached the verse *Hodu lashem ki tov*, "Give thanks to G-d for He is good," and *Ana Hashem hoshia na*, "Please G-d save us. We beseech thee." The congregation stood motionless and listened to his loud voice. During the holiday of *Sukkot*, the Feast of Tabernacles, during the ritual of shaking the *lulav* and *etrog*, the palm branch and citrus, in all the directions, he expressed his acceptance of the rule of the kingdom of G-d to whom the universe belonged.

After the Shabbat meal on Friday night, Rabbi Joshua would review the portion of the week according to tradition, twice a verse of the Bible and then once the verse of the *Targum*, the Aramaic commentary. He was an experienced Torah reader. He read the Torah every Shabbat in the main Synagogue for all the years he was the Cantor. On Shabbat *Zachor*, the Shabbat before Purim, for *Maftir*, he read the section about the destruction of Amalek, the historic enemy of Israel. He read the passage, *Zachor et asher asah lecha Amalek,* "Remember what Amalek did to you." *Timche et zecher Amalek mitachat hashamayim. Lo tishkach,* "Erase the memory of Amalek under the heavens. Do not forget," (Deuteronomy 25:17-19) with great feeling and with a loud voice. Meyer Berger, one of the members who had a good sense of humor said, "Rabbi Joshua finished him now."

Rabbi Joshua was especially admired for his reading of *Megillat Esther*, the scroll of Esther, the Purim *Megillah*. He beautified the reading of the Megillah by adding special melodies. He intertwined cantillations from the various melodies of the *trop*, the cantillation, into the Megillah. There were times when he raised his voice high and other times when he lowered it. His voice rang out in the *shul*, the Synagogue, and one could hear every word clearly, even in the women's section upstairs. When he reached the four verses of redemption, he recited the melody of triumph and when he reached the verse of Haman's ten sons, he sang it powerfully in one breath. The verses *Asher hogla meyerushalayim*, when the Jews were exiled from Jerusalem and *Vehair Shushan Navocha*, and the city of Shushan was perplexed, were read with the melody of *Aicha*, Lamentations, the sad melodies which emphasize the suffering of the Jewish people in exile. The large crowd that filled the Synagogue listened tentatively with great interest, delight, and pleasure.

During the High Holidays, Rabbi Joshua and his six sons stood in front of the pulpit ready to begin the singing and chanting. It represented a special, holy and beautiful occasion. The melodies of the high holidays were special and were composed for that occasion. Rabbi Joshua was a devoted servant of G-d. He stood before the Almighty and asked forgiveness for his congregation on the Day of Judgment. His voice was pleasant and sweet and it captured the heart.

The members of the Jewish community of Bilke saw in their Cantor, Rabbi Joshua, their true and faithful ambassador who was capable of representing them before their creator with dignity. He always emphasized the prayers that had special meaning regarding the fate of the Jewish people. For example, at *Neilah*, the concluding service of Yom Kippur, *Yisrael Nosha Bashem*, "Israel shall be saved by the Lord with everlasting salvation." During the *Musaf*, the additional service, the section *Unesaneh Tokef*, he sang the words of this very meaningful passage with special accentuation raising and lowering his voice with coloratura, changing from a strong to a lyric voice with his sons harmonizing at various levels and cadences. At times, they acted as soloists and at other times as a choral group. The entire congregation listened with great attention as they felt great pleasure, joy, and satisfaction. During the *Aseret Yemei Teshuva*, the ten days of repentance, many Jews in Bilke hummed Rabbi Joshua's melodies especially *Kevakarat Roeh Edro*, as the shepherd musters his sheep.

At weddings, Rabbi Joshua used to welcome the *Chatan*, the groom, with the greeting, *Baruch Habah*, and *Me Adir Al Hakol*, with the accompaniment of his six sons. When the *Kallah*, the bride, circled the groom seven times, Rabbi Joshua sang, *Me Bon Siach*, he who understands the meditation of roses, the love of the bride, the joy of the loving groom will bless the Chatan and the Kallah. The unique poem was passed down in the family from generation to generation.

The family of Rabbi Joshua Doft was very special and became a sort of institution in the town of Bilke. They represented a solid, deep-rooted Jewish family. The family was the pride of the town. The family had a natural, noble and aristocratic posture, one of a kind. Rabbi Joshua and his wife Pearl had 11 children, five daughters and six sons: Leah, Sarah, Chaya Feige, Chaim Leib, Shmuel Tzvi, Nachum Uri, Miriam Eidel, Reise, Shlomo Yeshayah, Yosef, and Moshe Nechemya.

Rabbi Joshua, his family, and the entire Jewish community were driven from their homes into the Ghetto Berehovo and from there to Auschwitz and other death camps. Rabbi Joshua, his wife Pearl, their daughter Leah and her five children, their daughter Sarah and her daughter Malka, died in Auschwitz on the third day of *Sivan* 5704, May 25, 1944. Chaim Leib and Nachum Uri perished in labor camps on the plains of the Ukraine in Russia and Yosef perished in the Plaszow Concentration Camp in Poland. Sixteen dear souls of the immediate family perished in the terrible Holocaust. Chaya Feige, Miriam Eidel, Reise, Shlomo Yeshayah, and Moshe Nechemya miraculously survived. They settled in the United States where they raised families. Shmuel Tzvi made aliyah to Eretz Yisrael and established a family there. The sons and daughters of Joshua and Pearl continued the golden chain of their parents.

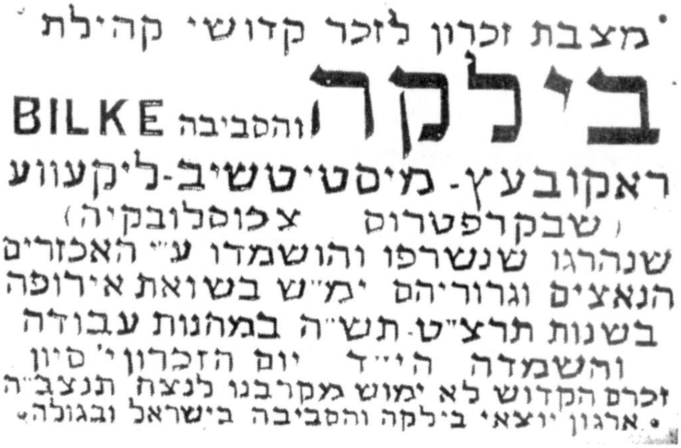
מצבת זכרון לזכר קדושי קהילת
בילקה
BILKE והסביבה
ראקובעץ- מיסטיטשיב-ליקעווע
(שבקרפטרוס צכוסלובקיה)
שנהרגו שנשרפו והושמדו ע״י האכזרים
הנאצים וגרוריהם ימ״ש בשואת אירופה
בשנות תרצ״ט-תש״ה במחנות עבודה
והשמדה הי״ד יום הזכרון י׳ סיון
זכרם הקדוש לא ימוש מקרבנו לנצח תנצב״ה
ארגון יוצאי בילקה והסביבה בישראל ובגולה

This memorial plaque to remember the Bilker community hangs in Jerusalem at the Cave of the Shoah on Mount Zion.

Until this day, the remnants of the survivors of Bilke who miraculously overcame the Holocaust, who settled in Israel and the United States, remember Rabbi Joshua, may his memory be a blessing, with great love and reverence, which has never left their hearts.

Mrs. Pearl (Lipschitz) Doft

My mother, Mrs. Pearl (Lipschitz) Doft, was born in Zalizshe Sub-Carpathia. She came from an illustrious background. Her father, Rabbi Abraham Lipschitz, came from a long chain of Rabbis. He was also a Talmudic Scholar and author of religious books. From her father's side she was a descendant of Ezra the Scribe. Her mother's name was Rachel Yitte Kahana, a descendant of Rabbi Ezechiel Landau, the *Noda Beyehudah*, the Chief Rabbi of Prague and from Rashi, Rabbi Shlomo Yitzchaki of France, the great Biblical commentator.

Mrs. Pearl (Lipschitz) Doft

Mrs. Doft perished in Auschwitz on May 25, 1944. This picture was taken in the 1930s.

She married Rabbi Joshua Doft, who was originally from Poland. They moved to Bilke in the Sub-Carpathian Mountains in 1905 and lived there until 1944 when the entire family was deported to Ghetto Berehovo and from there to Auschwitz, where she perished at the end of May 1944.

My mother gave birth to eleven children – six boys and five girls. She nurtured them with great love, both physically and spiritually. She was an unusual and special woman. She had a very difficult task. She had to take care of thirteen people day in and day out. Our home was always immaculate, especially when she made all the preparations for the Shabbat and Holidays. She

Rabbi Abraham Lipschitz

Rabbi Abraham Lipschitz, Moshe Avital's grandfather, was a *Dayan,* a Judge, and Shochet, in Bilke. He was a great Talmudic and Biblical scholar. He was the author of *Yalkut Avraham,* commentaries on the biblical interpretations of *Halacha,* Jewish law, and a guide to *Shochatim* and *Mohalim*. This picture was taken in 1920. He died in 1933 and was buried in the Jewish cemetery of Bilke in an *Ohel*, a mausoleum.

had a great ability to evaluate a situation. She had a fabulous gift of judgment. She had a very strong will, determined to reach any goal she set for herself. Her goodness, grace, and kindness was evident all over our home and she was a symbol of courage and tolerance. All of her life she was guided by one mission, by how to give, to whom to give, and when to give. She was steadfast and always found ways to accomplish tasks for her large family. She was a person with a mind of her own. She was a warm and caring mother instilling in us a love for people. She was rarely angry. My mother had a major influence on me, molding my personality throughout my childhood. In addition to being a devoted and loving wife, mother, and homemaker, she was also very concerned with the poor people of our town. She always looked after the needy and offered them help.

My mother was known in Bilke as a special homemaker. On Friday mornings and on the eve of holidays she would rise early in the morning to bake challot, two challot for each male in the family, bread for the entire week for 13 people and all kinds of pastries. The rest of the day she was busy with the cooking of fish, meat, chicken soup, noodle pudding, and compote. During the winter months

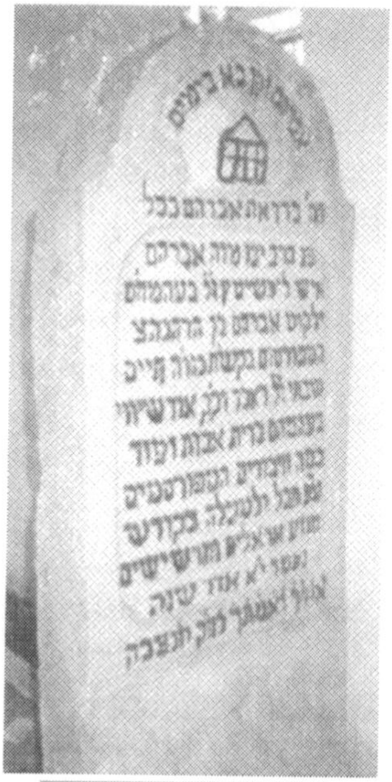

The *Matzevah* – the monument of Rabbi Abraham Lipschitz, in the cemetery of Bilke.

Moshe Avital is the seventh generation descendant of Rabbi Ezechiel Landau, who was the Chief Rabbi of Prague in the 17th century.

Rabbi Ezechiel Landau

she baked matzoth, which was broken into pieces to put in the chicken soup.

A few moments before the Shabbat was to be ushered in, she put on a white dress and a white scarf on her head, which was most fitting for the occasion. She looked like a queen. She lit 13 candles, one for each person in the family and covered her eyes with her hands. She made a few motions with her hands and recited the blessing over the candles, and recited silently in Yiddish the following prayer:

> "May it be Your will Almighty G-d, my G-d and G-d of my forefathers, that you show favor to me, my husband, my sons, my daughters, and all my relatives and that You grant us and all Israel a good and long life; that You remember us with a beneficent memory and blessing; that You cause Your presence to dwell among us. Privilege me to raise my children and grandchildren who are wise and understanding to illuminate their eyes in the ways of Torah and good deeds and that they should engage in the service of the Creator. Hear my supplication at this time, in the merit of Sarah, Rebecca, Rachel, and Leah – our Matriarchs, and Your light to illuminate our home that it be not extinguished forever and let Your countenance shine so that we are safe. Amen."

As the Shabbat was about to end, just before *Havdalah*, my mother stood with my sisters near the window facing the Great Synagogue reciting in a sweet, sad and subdued chant the prayer, *Goth Fun Avrohom*, G-d of Abraham, in Yiddish, because the Shabbat, the spiritual day of the week, which gave strength to the Jew was about to end, asking G-d for a successful and peaceful

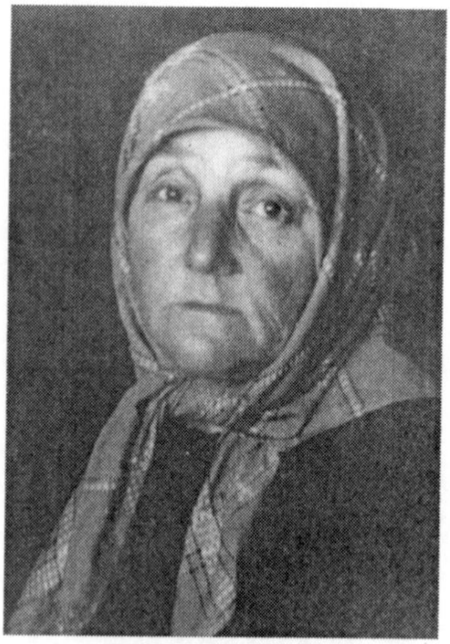

Rachel Yitte Lipschitz

Moshe Avital's grandmother Rachel Yitte Lipschitz, the wife of Rabbi Abraham Lipschitz, died in 1940 in Bilke and was buried in the Jewish cemetery of Bilke beside her husband. This picture was taken in the 1920s.

week. This is the prayer she recited:

"G-d of Abraham of Isaac and Jacob, protect Your people, Israel, from all evil in Your praise, as the beloved Holy Shabbat takes leave, that the coming week may arrive to bring perfect faith in scholars, love, and attachment to good friends, attachment to the Creator, Blessed is He, to have faith in Your Thirteen Principles and in the complete and close redemption speedily in our days, in the resuscitation of the dead, and in the prophecy of our teacher Moses, peace is upon him. Master of the universe, since You are the One who gives strength to the exhausted, give Your beloved Jewish children the strength to praise You and to serve only You and no other. May the week arrive for kindness, for good fortune, for blessing, for success, for good health, for wealth and honor, and for my children, life, and sustenance, for us and for all Israel. Amen."

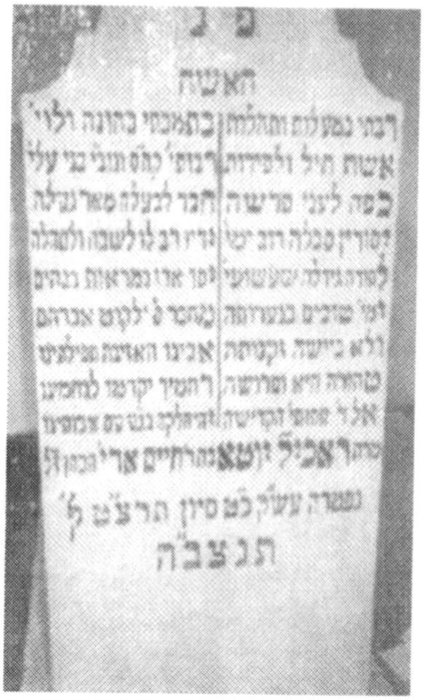

Grandmother Lipschitz's monument

Then she lit two candles and waited for the men to come home from the Synagogue.

She observed Rosh Chodesh, the beginning of the new Hebrew month, by not doing any exhausting work. It was a custom, which dates back to Biblical times and which was passed on from generation to generation that women do not do work on Rosh Chodesh, because in Biblical times it was like a minor festival. Also, on Chanukah, in the evenings after the lighting of the candles, she ceased working because it was a holiday in which women had a great share in the miracle that happened, so the break from work had a special meaning.

She wore a wig according to strict Orthodox Jewish tradition. On weekdays, my mother prayed at home mornings and evenings. Even though women are not required by Jewish law, my mother would recite the supplications which she loved. She never missed attending the services in the Great Synagogue on Shabbat and Holidays where my father was the Cantor. She, her daughters, and many other Jewish women of Bilke worshiped in the *ezrat nashim*, the women's section in the balcony.

Besides being an exceptional mother and great homemaker, she had unusual organizational ability, which helped her to master the preparations that had to be made for such a large family. She handed out various chores and responsibilities to the children. The girls helped her with baking, cooking, and cleaning the house. The boys did the more strenuous work. They fetched water from the neighbor's well for drinking, cooking and baking, and from the nearby stream they fetched water for washing, bathing, and watering the flowers and vegetable gardens in the back of the house. At that time in Bilke, there was no running water or electricity. The boys also chopped wood for heating the brick oven for baking, and the stoves for cooking, and for heating in wintertime. Especially when the holiday of *Pesach*, Passover, was approaching, my mother had her hands full with cleaning the entire house including the ovens, the stoves, to preparing the chicken fat for cooking and the potato starch for baking cakes. She made sure that everything in the house was done according to strict Jewish tradition.

When the holiday of Shavuot, Pentecost, approached, my mother baked for days. She baked all kinds of challot, rolls, honey cake, and especially cheesecakes, which is customary to eat on Shavuot. Also for the holiday of Purim, her baking was legendary. She prepared many platters to send *Shalach Manot*, gifts of food, to neighbors and friends. She made a huge braided challah, with raisins, which had *taam Gan Eden*, the taste of Paradise.

When my sisters got married, my mother planned and prepared everything for the affairs. In those days in Bilke, one could not buy a ready-made dress or suit; it had to be handmade. She went to the textile stores where she picked the most beautiful materials for the bride's gown, for the dresses of the other women in the family, and for the suits of the men in the family. My sister

Feige was a dressmaker; and so she sewed the dresses. They all were made according to the latest styles and in very good taste. In those days there were no caterers to cater affairs; the family of the bride had to prepare all the food for the wedding. My mother prepared a menu and made a list of all the ingredients she would need. She recruited all the women in the family, and also asked friends and neighbors to help her with the baking and cooking for a few hundred people. Their hard work paid off. The weddings were a great success.

Everybody was astonished to see the unusual variety of tasty foods and cakes. Even with her busy schedule and hard work, she did not forget to prepare a special table for the poor people of our town who were also invited to the weddings. It was in my mother's blood and character to always look out for the needy.

Not only in good times when we were home, and one could buy all kinds of products to prepare good food, did she succeed. Even during the most trying times when we were deported to Ghetto Berehovo, somehow she always prepared something warm and tasty to eat although supplies were extremely limited. She created miracles. In the ghetto, there was no such thing as being able to buy food. Under the most difficult conditions, under pressure and tension, she was cooking in the field near our shed. She cooked those meals on a makeshift and improvised cooking place made of stones and a piece of tin on top of them. It was heated with scraps of wood and branches, which the children gathered for making the fire. She made all kinds of goodies from the pieces of matzah, which we brought with us from home when we were driven to the ghetto.

Her devotion to her husband, children, and grandchildren and the extended family was a model and an example to many women in Bilke and in the ghetto. She was a beautiful woman, always dressed neatly in good taste. She was a real woman of valor with an unusually strong personality, a righteous and pious person, a great help to her husband and a very proud Jewess. The Jews of Bilke and vicinity greatly admired my mother. She was known as a very charitable person. She was very knowledgeable in tradition and in Jewish learning, which she imparted to us by practice and by teaching. My mother never complained about her responsibility of raising 11 children, or managing a big house, or about the day-to-day worries. She accepted her lot with love and understanding. Sometimes when I wouldn't eat what she gave me, or would ask for the impossible, she would say to me, "Moshe, don't sin, you should be happy with what you have." Later on, when I was starving in the concentration camps, I remembered my mother's words, and they added to my pain.

True, I was only a child when my mother gave me these moral talks, but in the camps it pained me that I did not appreciate what my mother was trying to teach me.

I learned a great deal from my mother, which has served me all my life. For example: caring for other people, to be considerate, devotion to family and to the Jewish people, cleanliness, punctuality, organization, thoroughness, love of learning, to search for the truth, to be truthful, to honor scholars and scholarship, and above all to be a *mensch*.

My father adored my mother and treated her like a queen. We, the children and the entire family, revered her and loved her dearly. I knew her for only 14 years, but during this time she gave me so much that it has lasted a lifetime. The last time I saw her was in Auschwitz when she and my sisters with their children were sent to the side of no return.

My Talented Brothers Who Perished

When black clouds covered the skies of Europe and the evil forces of Hitler and his helpers were let loose, the future of three of my brothers, as well as our entire family was in great danger. The Talmud says, "Since permission was given to the destroyer, he does not distinguish between the righteous and the wicked." (Tractate *Baba Kamah* 60A.) My fourth brother saved himself by immigrating to Palestine in 1937.

The four brothers who have passed on to the world to come, *Chaim Leib*, *Shmuel Tzvi*, *Nachum Uri*, and *Joseph* possessed many talents. During many sleepless nights, their images, which are engraved in my heart, appear before me. Because I was the youngest in my family, I was privileged to be influenced by all of my siblings. Each one of them invested in me their best talents, and contributed to my education and development. They guided me during childhood, and from them, I absorbed a great deal of knowledge and good attributes, which has directed me until this day. Only later did I realize the great influence they had upon me. I will always be grateful to them and keep their memory in my heart.

Each one of the four brothers was blessed with various talents; however, they were different one from another in their character. Each one of them made great efforts to achieve the goals they set for themselves. Whatever they did, it was done thoroughly and faithfully. Thoroughness was a family trait in our home, like a higher command to do everything perfectly. Just as my brothers were different, so they also died differently. Destiny was very cruel to each one in a different way.

Chaim Leib, the oldest of the sons in the family, was born in Bilke, Czechoslovakia in 1913. He received his early Jewish education in Cheder, the one room schoolhouse, and in the Bilker Yeshivah. He received his secular education in the public school. It was customary in our family that after Bar Mitzvah, at the age of thirteen, the boys attend famous Yeshivoth in Czechoslovakia, as Jewish tradition says: "Wander to a home of the Torah," (Sayings

Chaim Leib Doft-Lipschitz was taken by the Hungarians to the forced labor camps in the Ukraine. He perished on Pesach 1943 in the village Dorowitz near Davidkof in the Ukraine. He was only 30 years old. This picture was taken in 1940.

Chaim Leib Doft-Lipschitz

of the Fathers; 4:18) to go to a place where eminent teachers reside to benefit from their great scholarship. Chaim Leib went to study in the Insdorfer Yeshivah, in Slovakia. Many of these yeshivoth were modeled on the system of teaching used by the great scholar, Chatam Sofer.

My brother had a great thirst for learning. He was quick to grasp the deep ideas of the Talmud and its commentaries. He delved deeply into the various Jewish sources with great diligence. After a while he acquired expertise in a number of tractates of the Talmud and other traditional holy books. He was an excellent *Baal Koreh*, a Torah reader with the traditional cantillations. He had a beautiful voice, which he inherited from our father. Chaim Leib was a good Cantor and knew the traditional chants for the Shabbat and the holidays year-round. He also absorbed everything he learned from his parents, teachers and Rabbis, which was reflected in his behavior and his way of life. He was a young erudite scholar with knowledge and wisdom.

He wore a beard and payot, but his hair was always properly combed and appropriately cut. One could see he was very conscious of his dress and that he paid attention to his external appearance. He had a majestic look and his personality commanded respect. He was always dressed in good taste, without a speck on his clothing. He was a role model and example to all the young men of our town. Just by his appearance he brought joy and honor to people and to G-d. Many people wished they had such a son. They would say, "We wish we could have a son like Chaim Leib." Everyone predicted great and wonderful things for him, and a glorious future.

When he returned home after many years of study and graduate study in the Yeshivah in Insdorf, he saw it as his duty to contribute to the Jewish education of the young people in our hometown, Bilke. He also felt it was time for him to help the family financially. The leaders of the community appealed to him to undertake to teach two classes for boys who would study Talmud and commentaries and other Judaic subjects.

Teaching came to him naturally after so many years of study himself, especially in light of the rich experiences he acquired from his teachers and Rabbis. Within a few years, he became a master teacher and great pedagogue. Each lesson was planned and it was a masterpiece. He explained the subject to his students in an easy way of progression and with a system. The students in turn reacted favorably and were eager to learn. He used to delve into a topic or a problem by concentrating all his sources and his thinking. He was an overflowing treasure of learning and wisdom.

He was a unique and special type of person. He inherited from our father the love for his fellow man, which brought him close to all sufferers and the exploited. From our mother he inherited a strong personality, the strength for endurance and his devotion to idealism. He was a wonderful human being, appreciated by the people of Bilke. He earned their respect.

During the years he was home, he was my father's right hand in many ways. When my father became ill, he took care of him. He sat at his bedside day and night. He filled many of his community obligations. He was attached to our father spiritually and his soul was bound with his soul.

When Hitler, the great Demon, lit the great and terrible fire, the evil forces did not pass over Chaim Leib. In the beginning of 1940, the Hungarian Fascist forces decreed that all males ages 18 to 50 had to report to *Munko Tabor*, forced labor battalions. Chaim Leib, among the other Jewish males of Bilke, was taken into Hungary. From there the Hungarians dispatched battalion after battalion to the Russian front to help the German war effort. These battalions were organized into army-like units under the command of the Hungarian army. They dug tunnels and trenches, and built rail lines and fortifications. Many Jews of the forced labor battalions died from hard work, starvation, sickness, frostbite, enemy actions, and at the hands of the fanatic Hungarian anti-Semites.

In the beginning, we received a postcard from my brother from time to time, which was censored. However, in between the lines, we could read that his situation at the Russian front was grave. Once in a while, while we were still home, we were allowed to send him small packages of food. These packages slightly extended the lives of our brethren in a foreign land in the distant Ukraine and Russia. The forced labor battalions moved with the front line. From the beginning of 1942, we seldom received mail and then his voice fell silent. We did not know whether or not he was alive. Sad news, like in the book of Job, was spread in Bilke about these battalions and our home was filled with sadness and pain. But we still did not know what really happened.

After the awesome *Shoah* which befell European Jewry and our family among them, we learned from a survivor what happened to Chaim Leib, together with thousands of Jews from the forced labor battalions who worked for the Hungarians and the Germans near the River Don in the Ukraine. Thousands of Jews in these labor units were concentrated there under inhuman conditions. Thousands fell victim daily to hard labor, starvation, and sicknesses. Then came the big German retreat due to the Russian offensive. The Jewish forced labor battalions were also forced to retreat. This retreat brought even more death, especially because most of them became sick with typhoid. The Hungarians and the Germans concentrated the sick Jews in a horse stable in the village of Dorowitz near Davidkof in the Ukraine. Some 800 young Jews were lying in this stable with high fever and without medical care.

On Passover 1943, the German and Hungarian beasts set the stable on fire and all the Jewish slave laborers were burned alive. According to Shlomo Rosenberg, from a town not far from Bilke, who was among the Jews in the stable and who by a miracle crawled out of the fire with terrible burns, told us that the cries and screams of our brethren reached all the way to heaven. Thus were burned alive 800 precious Jews, among them my brother Chaim Leib, who was only 30 years old. May G-d avenge their suffering and their deaths.

Shmuel Tzvi, the second son in our family was a different type. Already during his youth, although he was raised in the same family and received an identical Jewish and secular education, he had a different ideal. From the time he was a youngster, the love of Zion, the Land of Israel, became a part of him. The stories and the legends about Jerusalem and the Land of Israel which he heard at home, in the Cheder, and in the Yeshivah, his study, and his immersing in various Jewish books, all these influences excited his imagination and strengthened his love and devotion to Eretz Yisrael.

While still a youngster, he would tell his friends that he felt the coming of Jewish sovereignty to Eretz Yisrael in the air. He claimed the time was ripe and should not be put off. His ideal and objective stemmed from a deep-rooted source in his soul. While he hardened his heart on the altar of his mission, he sacrificed everything; his family, his parents, friends, his hometown, and his homeland. He did not listen to reasonable explanations and arguments, and did not heed the preaching of morality by all those with whom he came in contact. He only listened to the inner small voice, which was bursting from a hidden place in his soul, which imposed on him the fulfillment of his Zionist messianic goal.

Shmuel Tzvi struggled very hard with his pious parents. Even with the

Shmuel Tzvi Doft-Lipschitz

hostile environment to the Zionist ideal in those days, he would not give in. He stood firm against threats and promises, because the Zionistic ideal became the goal of his life.

Shmuel Tzvi, born in Bilke in 1914, went through all the stages of Jewish traditional education in the Cheder and in the Yeshivah. With the establishment of the Czech Republic, of which Bilke became a part, he also studied in the Czech public school. Like his older brother Chaim Leib, he also left home to study in a Yeshivah in Novozami (New Heisel) in Slovakia in order to broaden his Judaic knowledge. After five years in the Yeshivah, he took a bold step and made a decision, which no other young man in Bilke dared. Without his parents knowledge, he decided to switch from the Yeshivah to *Hachsharah*, a place where young people were preparing through work and study, to live in Israel. When our father found out, he summoned him home immediately.

He had a difficult struggle with his parents, his extended family, the Rabbi of Bilke, and others who tried to convince him that he should return from his errant ways. But he proved his determination. He said, "An old love one does not forget." From the time he read in the Jewish paper, *The Moment*, that young men who studied the Talmud in a Yeshivah were being accepted to the Hebrew University in Jerusalem, a deep desire for a broader education, especially in a Hebrew atmosphere on Mount Scopus in Jerusalem, was awakened in him. Could there be a more noble desire than that, he asked? Also he had detected an undercurrent of anti-Semitism, which became evident even in Czechoslovakia in the 1930s.

Many obstacles stood in my brother's way. He needed documents about his education and letters of recommendation from the Yeshivoth where he studied in order to be accepted to the Hebrew University. The leadership of Yeshivoth in those days was anti-Zionist and they refused to issue the proper documents for him. They were hoping these obstacles would prevent my brother from going to Eretz Yisrael. He also needed 1,000 Kronen, Czech currency, (about $1,000 dollars in those days) in order to prepay his tuition fees to the Hebrew University before they would send him a certificate, which was a British permit to emigrate to Palestine. In addition, he needed a large sum of money to purchase a ticket on a boat that was sailing from Constanta, Rumania.

After many requests, pleading and begging, the Rabbis finally issued the proper documents and letters of recommendation for the Hebrew University in Jerusalem. My brother borrowed money from good neighbors of ours and from an uncle, Yitzchak Doft, my father's brother, who was a very liberal and kind person.

He received a very strong letter of recommendation from Abraham Newman, the leader of the religious Zionists in Bilke, addressed to the Zionist movement in Jerusalem.

This is what he wrote about my brother:

> "Before you is a member of ours, Shmuel Tzvi Doft, a faithful member of our movement who will need help to bring to fruition his lofty ideals. All of his life he has devoted himself to Zionist activities and would very much like to continue it in Eretz Yisrael, with his entire spiritual and physical strength. He was the first Zionist pioneer in our hometown and its preacher to many of us. He suffered greatly for his untiring devotion to Zionist pioneering. In spite of that, it did not weaken his strong will for fulfillment. On the contrary, the struggle strengthened his spirit even more." (Dated 23 *Nissan* 5697-1937.)

I will never forget those days. Twice he left home for Constanta, Rumania on his way to Eretz Yisrael. I was only a child of eight. One time after midnight, there was a knock on the door of our house. Everyone awakened, Shmuel Tzvi had returned because there was no more room on the ship. How tall my brother looked to me then. In my eyes, he was like a giant. I knew that he was the tallest in the family, but that night he looked even taller to me. My hands were hugging and squeezing his legs and did not want to let go of him.

When he left again, this time for good a few weeks later in order to sail to Israel, the farewell was heartbreaking and very emotional. How strongly he was pulled to Israel, to the land of our Fathers at a time when his parents and most of the family looked at the whole idea very unfavorably. There were good reasons for not wanting to part with such a young son. He was only 18 years old. He was going to a strange, faraway, desolate, and dangerous country.

Shmuel Tzvi was like a pillar of fire, a pioneer who led the way for the young people of Bilke. He climbed his way to the land and paved the road for the other pioneers from our town. When he arrived in the land of our Fathers,

From the day Shmuel Tzvi arrived in the land of our Fathers, Eretz Yisrael became something concrete and tangible in our home and to the Jews of Bilke.

he wrote very impressive letters. He described his difficulties during his voyage and his adjusting to the land. He toured the land and gave details, which were fascinating to us because even though we had never been there, the descriptions in the Bible which we knew well and his eyewitness reports made it come alive. He had a great talent for writing. He wrote home in three languages; Hebrew, Yiddish, and Czech. Even though so many in the family were against his aliyah, after the fact everyone was very proud of him. Each one of his letters consisted of many pages. His description of the holy places, the scenery, the accomplishments of the pioneers and the heroes of the Jewish underground were very interesting and wonderful. From the day Shmuel Tzvi arrived in the land of our fathers, Eretz Yisrael became something concrete and tangible in our home and to the Jews of Bilke. Because of him, within a short period of time, a number of young people made aliyah. He had a great influence on the young people while he was still in Bilke, but this time his influence came from a distance by his example.

Each *Oleh*, immigrant, from Bilke, knew that when he would arrive in Israel, there was an address to turn to. Shmuel Tzvi's apartment turned into a gathering place for all Bilker *Olim*. Each time a ship arrived and the British detained the Olim in the detention camp, Atlit, where the British kept the illegal immigrants, Shmuel Tzvi, made great efforts to free the Bilker Olim. If a Bilker arrived in Eretz Yisrael without informing him about his arrival, but found out about it from others, he immediately contacted him and reprimanded him for not informing him of his coming. He made efforts to help the Bilker Olim find work, apartments, and other things necessary to settle in the Land. He, himself, at first worked hard in all kinds of jobs in order to support himself in addition to his studies at the Hebrew University. He made great strides at the University. At the same time, he also devoted time to study at the Yeshivah of Rabbi Dushinsky in Jerusalem, as he promised our father.

When he arrived in Jerusalem in 1937, he brought regards from Czechoslovakia to the family of Rabbi Shamai Aksel, who lived in the Meah Shearim section. There he met Channah Ludmir, the granddaughter of Rabbi Shamai, and fell in love with her. She was a tall, young lady with a dark complexion. She was graceful and had a good appearance. Shmuel Tzvi became a part of the family in Rabbi Shamai's home. Mrs. Frumah Ludmir, Channah's mother, who was a widow, made him feel at home. After a short time, Channah and Shmuel Tzvi were married and raised a family. They had five children, two sons and three daughters. My brother wrote home to Bilke that he wanted to marry Channah Ludmir. He told us about the distinguished lineage of Channah on both sides, from her mother's and father's sides, who were honorable families. He sent us a picture of the bride and the entire family shared in his joy. On the wedding day, when all the Bilker Olim in Israel gathered in Jerusalem to participate in

Shmuel Tzvi and Channah
1940 in Jerusalem

Fruma Ludmir
Channah's mother

Rabbi Shamai Aksel
Channah's grandfather

Standing (L-R) Uri, Channah, Nili
Sitting (L-R) Efrat, Mordechai, Peninah

Shmuel Tzvi's family, after he passed away.

Shmuel Tzvi's and Channah's wedding, the family in Bilke made a wedding party in our home in honor of the wedding. Many friends and neighbors were invited. The picture of the bride and groom was passed around and everyone remarked what a fine couple they were. Refreshments were served and everyone joined in the latest Hebrew songs that were then popular, such as the song, which Chanah Senesh composed (who later parachuted into Yugoslavia to help save Hungarian Jews and was caught by the Hungarians and executed.) This song was: "My homeland is the land of Canaan, my destination is the *Kibbutz Sdoth Yam*," and many others which we learned in Bilke in the clubs of the Zionist movement. This party was later described in a letter to my brother and his bride Channah. Everyone in the family added good wishes to the letter that included my father, mother, brothers and sisters, and even I, the youngest wrote a few lines.

When Czechoslovakia was overrun by the Germans in 1938, the postal ties with Palestine became strained, and mail contacts became shaky. At first, we received a few censored post cards from my brother and his family. As a very devoted son to his family, he was greatly worried about our future. He made great efforts to send certificates at least to his brothers, but it was too late.

When it became known in Eretz Yisrael of the systematic destruction of European Jewry, among them the Jews of Bilke, his spirits plummeted and his health deteriorated. Because of family need, he interrupted his studies at the University, since his responsibility to his family came first. He held a position in the postal service administration. In 1954, he had a heart attack; then other complications developed. He struggled with his critical situation. On the 27th day of *Tamuz*, 5714-1954, his soul returned to his maker. He was only 39 years old. The destruction of so many of his family members in Europe dangerously affected his health and caused his death because he took our losses greatly to heart. At least he merited to leave five wonderful children. Because it was his strong determination, there is a continuation of his dreams. He also

Top Row, fourth from the left, circled: Nachum Uri Doft-Lipschitz
Middle Row, first from the right, circled: Miriam Eidel Doft-Lipschitz

Nachum Uri Doft-Lipschitz at the age of 15. He was taken by the Hungarians to forced labor camps behind the Russian front, where he was captured by the Russians. He died as a prisoner of war near Marshansk, south of Moscow in February 1943 at the age of 26.

merited to be interred on *Har Hamenuchoth*, the cemetery in Jerusalem that he loved so much. He lived in Israel in a time of crossroads in history at the peak of the struggle for Jewish independence in the land of our fathers. He merited to live a few years in a free Jewish state. However, I also considered Shmuel Tzvi to be a victim of the Shoah.

Nachum Uri

The third son in the family, Nachum Uri, was born in Bilke in 1917. He was a super person, gifted with many talents, and crowned with many attributes. He loved learning and was thirsty for knowledge. He searched for wisdom and delved into Jewish texts. He studied in Cheder from the age of three and a half, continued in the local Yeshivah and then to the greater Yeshivah of Selish, a city in Ruthenia. When he was growing up, the winds of the enlightenment movement also reached Bilke our hometown, via the three important Yiddish newspapers of that time, the *Heint*, *Tug*, and *Moment*, which were published in Poland. The younger generation turned not only to religious education; they also absorbed secular and Zionist education. The youth began to be active in youth organizations and became aware of what was going on in the various political and new movements which sprang up in Czechoslovakia.

Nachum Uri loved to read those papers. He would read them from beginning to end. He devoured whatever was written about the Jewish world. Many old timers looked unfavorably upon anyone reading these papers, not only because it was wasting precious time which could be utilized learning Torah, but also because of the fear that maybe these young people would adopt foreign, strange and dangerous ideas, and would adopt a new outlook on life which was not welcomed.

Rabbi Naftali Tzvi Weiss, the Rabbi of Bilke, in his sermons attacked the youth who leaned to Zionism and other modern movements, and strongly demanded from the parents, not to allow their sons and daughters to turn away from the traditional ways, but rather to continue to weave the traditional chain of our fathers. The sons of the Doft family belonged to the *Agudah*, and *Mizrachi Youth*, the religious youth movements. The older generation looked with suspicion even upon these movements. In these religious clubs, the young people conducted communal services, group learning of Torah, the study of the Hebrew language, reading of Jewish newspapers, and discussions about the events in the Jewish world, especially in Eretz Yisrael.

Nachum Uri was a member of the Mizrachi Youth, and was the backbone of the Jewish youth in Bilke. In our town and in the entire vicinity he was the most talented and well rounded young man. He had a warm Jewish heart that pulsated with love for his fellow man.

He had a colorful personality. He not only absorbed Jewish culture in its entirety but also dwelled on the secular culture on his own. He was known as an enlightened person and served as an example and a role model to many of the Jewish youth in Bilke. He never tried to impose his authority on anyone, and that was one of the reasons why everyone admired him. Actually, it was easy for the youth in Bilke to identify with him. He was very interested in Jewish history and he knew Hebrew perfectly. He was a gentleman, was well mannered and knew how to control himself. He had a noble demeanor that evoked great admiration from many people. He was successful in creating a synthesis of the old and the new, Jewish tradition and modernity in one. Greatness and wisdom existed in one personality. He had an unusually pleasing personality with many talents and attributes. Since he knew well realities of life, he showed tolerance and understanding even to those with different opinions. In one word, a thread of love was interwoven in all of his deeds and behavior. I can still see him as he was, standing in our living room, dining room, at the window facing the courtyard of the Great Synagogue reading the Jewish paper.

Like Chaim Leib, he too devoted himself to teaching the youth of Bilke. He saw in this a national mission as long as he was in Bilke. He faithfully followed the spiritual progress of his students. His diligence and steadfastness were wondrous. His lessons were prepared in a very orderly fashion and according to common sense. People would whisper and say, "In front of Nachum Uri an eternal light is lit." His words were living words, which emanated from his very nature and character. He was regarded by all as a very educated, prominent and distinguished person.

I, the youngest in the family, was privileged to study in his class for a short while. I loved to study in Nachum Uri's class. It was a pleasure to see how the young students listened to his words. His voice was clear, simple and hearty. His eyes were pure and sparkling with a smile. When his eyes looked directly at you, they seemed to be looking deeply into your soul. How profound, and at the same time how simple were the teachings of Nachum Uri. How sweet his voice was and at the same time touching the chambers of the heart. The light of the Torah and the light of wisdom dwelled in his soul. These were the kind of lights, which lit and also altered fellow men. During his classes he never sat down. Instead, he was fully alert and ready to approach a student who needed his help, his advice, or remark. He never used corporal punishment although in those days it was very much prevalent. His students admired him. They listened to him and longed for his love and respect.

Nachum Uri was the only one in our family who served in the Czech Army. He was a healthy and well-built young man and did not try to evade the draft. He wanted to fulfill his duty to the Czech Republic. As a religious man, from a family with a long chain of Rabbis, Judges and Shochatim, it was not easy to get along in a non-Jewish environment, to keep kosher and observe the basic Jewish commandments. However, with his steadfastness and his devotion to his ancestor's heritage, he was able to stand the test. His service in the Czech Army did not last very long because with the occupation of Czechoslovakia by the German Army, Horde's, the Czech Army, disintegrated and Nachum Uri returned home.

In the 1930s, the Jewish youth in Eastern Europe were aware of two basic facts. They knew there was no future for the Jewish youth in Eastern Europe. At the same time, they knew that their parents were against immigration overseas, to the new world or to Eretz Yisrael. Certain individuals did not pay attention to the wishes of their parents. However, most of them could not find the boldness to cause pain to their parents. There was also an additional problem. Neither America nor Eretz Yisrael was wide open for Jewish immigration. Nachum Uri also found himself in this terrible dilemma. On the one hand, he wanted to rescue himself from the stagnation that existed in the small towns in Eastern Europe, but on the other hand, because of his devotion to his parents and family, and because of his consideration of and respect for his parents, he did not take extreme steps, but rather gave in by not leaving home, and by waiting for an opportunity that might come. Unfortunately, he did not escape the tragedy of annihilation. If not for the Shoah, one could have expected a gradual process of Jewish youth leaving the small Shtetl on a mass scale.

Sadly, Nachum Uri's lot was similar to the lot of Chaim Leib. He was also conscripted by the Hungarians to a Munko Tabor forced labor battalion, and shipped to the Russian front. As the Hungarians and the German Armies advanced deep into Russia, Nachum Uri's battalion also marched with them to prepare fortifications at the front lines. They reached as far as the great river, Don. At first we received censored letters from him, but after a while his voice became silent and we received no more signs of life from him or any indication of his whereabouts.

During the major Russian offensive against the Axis (the Hungarians, Italians and Germans), in January of 1943, they crossed the River Don and the Fascist armies fled in disarray. Among them were also thousands of Jewish slave laborers from Ruthenia and Hungary who provided slave labor for the Germans. Among them was Nachum Uri's battalion. During the offensive, the Russians captured thousands upon thousands of Germans, Hungarians, Italians and other nationalities who helped the Germans in the war against the Russians. During this advance, the Russians captured some of the Jewish forced labor battalions, among them Nachum Uri's battalion. The Russians treated them as the enemy and established a huge P.O.W. camp in underground bunkers near Marshansk, about 400 miles south of Moscow. The camp held 8,000 prisoners, mostly Jews. The cold was unbearable, the hunger was terrible, and there was no medical care, or help whatsoever. In each bunker there were 200 prisoners. Thousands of Jews died there from hunger, the elements, sickness, and suffering. After six weeks, only about 1,300 Jewish prisoners remained alive. By chance, Shlomo Davidowitz, from Bilke, was also imprisoned in the camp. He heard that Nachum Uri Doft, the son of the Shochet, was lying sick with dysentery in one of the bunkers. His last words to Shlomo Davidowitz

Brothers Chaim Leib Doft and Nachum Uri Doft were conscripted as slave laborers for the Germans and Hungarians along the River Don in the Ukraine.

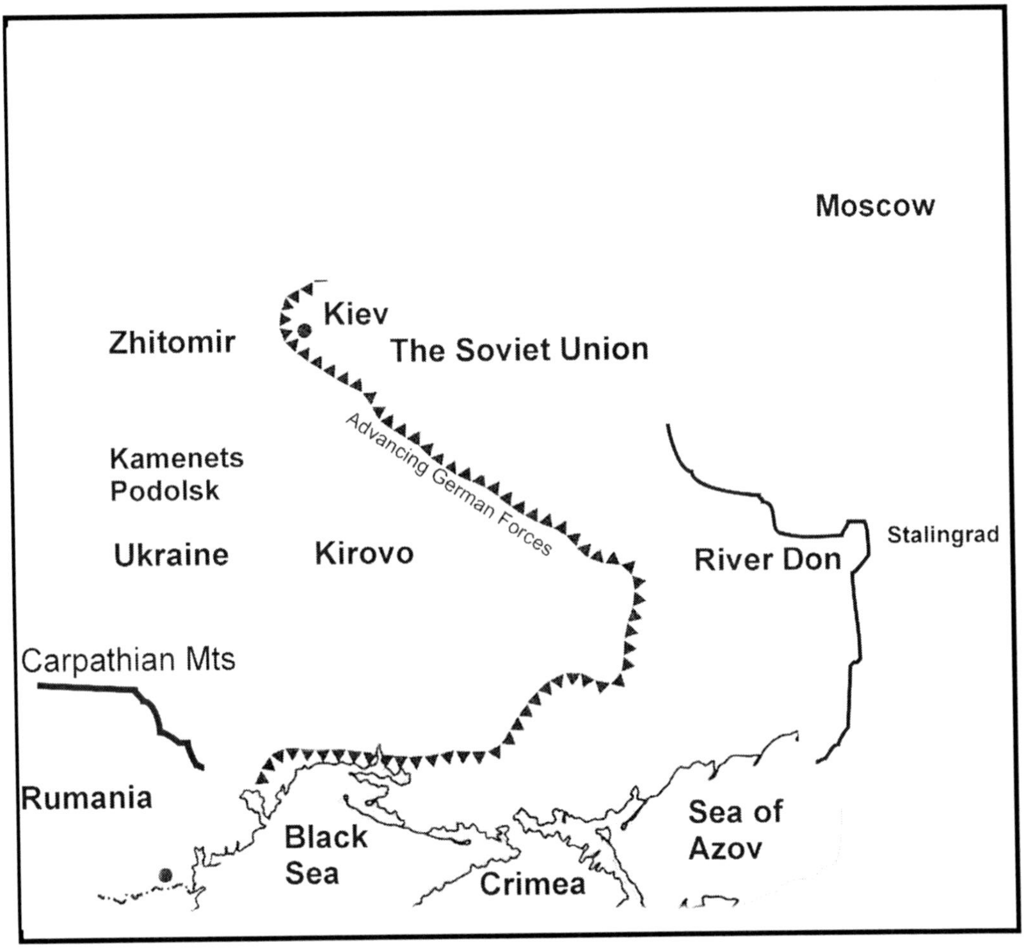

Reprinted from *McMillan Atlas Of The Holocaust*, © 1982, by Martin Gilbert, published by The Jewish Publication Society, with the permission of the publisher, The Jewish Publication Society.

Joseph (Yosef) Doft-Lipschitz

Joseph was murdered by the Germans in Plaszow. He perished in December 1944. He was 18 years old.

were: "What will happen to us? What will happen to European Jewry? I have one consolation, that my brother Shmuel Tzvi is in Eretz Yisrael."

He asked for water. Shlomo Davidowitz told him that with dysentery one should not drink water. Nachum Uri was extremely thirsty and begged for water. He said, "Please give me some water, and whatever happens to me will happen."

The next day Shlomo Davidowitz returned to Nachum Uri's bunker to find out how he was, but he was no longer alive. On the seventh day of the Hebrew month *Adar*, 5703-1943, in the faraway plains of Russia, his pure soul returned to his maker. Far from his home, without any close family members, only one landsman from Bilke still had a chance to hear his last words. He was only 26 years old. His lot was sealed with suffering and pain, when his last thoughts were about his family and the Jewish people. I should point out that many European nations had a share in the suffering and the bitter end of the Jews in these forced labor battalions, including the Soviet Union.

The tenth child in the Doft family was Joseph, born in Bilke in 1925. He was two and a half years older than I. Joseph received a traditional Jewish education from age three and a half in Cheder and in the Yeshivah, and accomplished a great deal. He also studied secular subjects in the Czech elementary and high school and there too, he excelled. He was a fine lad, beloved by his family and friends, and greatly sought after by his peers in Bilke.

Since he was still very young while at home in Bilke, he was an introvert and bashful. He did not reveal what was in his heart or what he was thinking. However, certain characteristics were already evident, which over time became a part of his nature. Everything he did was done with perfection and splendor. All the things he did, he did with all his heart and soul. No matter what happened to him, he accepted it with understanding, without bitterness or protest. To him, as to all of us, the centrality of the family was

(R-L) Yosef - 13; Shlomo - 16; Moshe - 11. Standing in front is Abraham, the oldest son of the author's sister, Leah. Abraham perished in Auschwitz together with his mother and three other little brothers and a sister in May 1944. This picture was taken in 1939 in Bilke.

supreme. His devotion to our parents, brothers, and sisters was his main goal, and in this he was most outstanding. He was always ready to help another person.

He dressed with a unique taste. He always left the house clean and polished, and he had a special sense for beauty and fashion. He was in the habit of standing every Shabbat afternoon at the gate of the Great Synagogue, which was located on the main street in Bilke, at the time when the Bilker Jews went for a stroll and dressed in their best. After he observed the clothing, and the dresses of the women especially, he would come home and give our sisters a detailed description of what he saw and what each one was wearing. Since my sister, Feige, was a dressmaker, this was very interesting and valuable to her. Our sisters loved and admired him very much. My brother, Joseph, in his spare time, learned from my sister, Feige, how to sew on a sewing machine and also about fashion. This knowledge came in handy later when his destiny brought him to the concentration camp, Plaszow.

When the rest of our family was deported to Ghetto Berehovo, he was with us. After six weeks in the ghetto, Joseph, with the rest of our family, was put on a train in boxcars and shipped to an unknown destination. The train arrived in the notorious slaughterhouse Auschwitz, where he and I were separated from our family. The two of us remained together for a while. At that time, neither he nor I knew what happened to our dear family who arrived with us in Auschwitz, or to our brothers who were conscripted to the forced labor battalions.

After two weeks of hell in Auschwitz, Joseph and I, with some 1,000 Jews from Carpathia, were transferred to the Plaszow Concentration Camp near Cracow, Poland. About 50,000 Polish Jews had already been interred in Plaszow long before we arrived. Most of these prisoners were utilized to make uniforms for the German armed forces. Many of these tailors were not real tailors before the war. They learned how to sew from each other. People were struggling to get into these factories, to get a job as a tailor because they assumed that by being a tailor, their lives were not as much at risk as doing other work. To a certain extent this was true, because it was easier to cope inside a factory than to perform hard labor outdoors and suffer from the elements.

My brother Joseph was such a tailor. I, however, had to work hard physical labor. Joseph had pity on me because I had to perform such tiring work. While we were together in Plaszow we watched over one another and shared everything. We slept in the same barrack one near the other on the wooden planks. We always made sure that during *apell*, roll call, we lined up in the same row of fives, so that we would not be separated. We had seen what had happened with other families. For four months in Plaszow, we strictly enforced this habit. One day at the end of September 1944, early in the morning, we were awakened by whistles, shouts and screaming, *"Heraus, Lous!"* which meant "Out, out, quickly, quickly!" The Kapos and the S.S. men drove us out of the barracks to line up. During the confusion, for the first time, Joseph and I ended up at the apell not in the same row of five. An S.S. officer walked in front of us and started to count the rows, *Eins, Tzwei*, one, two, and so on including my row. He gave an order, about face, and we were marched away to the rail station. My brother Joseph remained in the group standing on the apell platz, the roll call plaza. This was the last time I saw my brother Joseph. I was crying and thinking that we had suffered so much to be together, that this was not the time to be separated. Now, fate separated us. I lost all trace of him. After the liberation, I met a landsman, Mendi Mechlowitz, from Bilke, who was with us in Plaszow and remained there with my brother after I was taken away. He told me that Joseph entered the *revier*, the infirmary, in Plaszow at the end of December 1944 due to a grave illness. After that, Joseph was not seen again. Unfortunately, it was known that whoever was admitted to the *revier* did not come out alive. Joseph was murdered by the Germans in Plaszow. He was only 18 years old.

In this chapter, I have tried to describe my four brothers who all died at very young ages, three of them by the evil forces in Europe who rose up against the Jewish people to annihilate them. I have exhausted all my literary talent to give a full picture of their personalities, their deeds and their lives. When I think about them, and what they went through, and how they died, very strong feelings comes over me, but my meager and limited language is not adequate to really describe them.

Until this day, 59 years after our tragedies, I cannot remove the thoughts from my mind about my brothers who were beloved and pleasant in their lifetimes, and in their deaths were not parted from us. I don't think I will ever be able to find peace after what happened to them. Sometimes I dream that the tragedy that befell us was no more than a bad dream and that a miracle happened and our dear ones were alive again. I wish that such a miracle would happen in my lifetime.

Part 2

Bilke – My Hometown

From a beautiful folk song about a shtetl

"My little hometown where I spent my childhood years..."

That sentimental song of the past has turned into a lament in my thoughts and my heart. To me, it is just like a remote dream... as I remember Bilke.

Bilke's Jewish Community

My childhood in Bilke was a happy one and I was carefree. Little did I know, for I was only a boy of 10, that when the political upheaval began in Europe, these events would directly involve my family and me. One cannot begin to comprehend the magnitude of the loss to our people during the Holocaust without the knowledge of Jewish creativity and Jewish culture that existed before the second world war in Bilke.

Bilke *was* a beautiful little town, set in a valley, deep in the Carpathian Mountains in the region known as Sub Carpathian Ruthenia in the Bereg County, on the main road between Mukachevo and Chust. No fewer than six streams and rivers rushed down from the heavily forested hills to the big river at the bottom. There was a legend that centuries ago, a local nobleman's daughter drowned while bathing in the river, and the grieving father gave her name, Bilke, to both the river and the town.

Until World War I, this area had been the eastern territory of the Austro-Hungarian Empire. Upon the dissolution of the empire in 1918, the region was accorded to the newly created nation, Czechoslovakia. The new government, ruling from Prague, was progressive.

Bilke was not a homogeneous populace. With a population of about 10,000, the Jews of Bilke then numbered over 200 families. Since they were blessed with 10 to 12 children in a family, the total Jewish population came to about 2,000.

The Jewish population of Bilke lived an idyllic community life in their own tradition. They were like one big family living in clusters around the main street. Their simple homes of brick or clay bricks were spread along or near the main road, well mixed among non-Jews. Most Jews lived on trade or had small home businesses. They were storekeepers, tailors, cobblers, and farmers. There were a number of professionals such as civil servants, bankers, and teachers. Some families acquired large estates where they employed non-Jewish workers. Above all, Bilker Jews tried to observe all the commandments, and

Bilke's business center before the Holocaust.

were careful not to violate the Shabbat, even when they had difficulty in making a living.

Among the 10,000 residents of Bilke and the surrounding area, there were Ukrainians, Jews, Ruthenians, Hungarians, and Czechs. As a result, the people spoke a multitude of languages. In our home, we spoke Yiddish. In *Cheder* and *Yeshivah*, our religious schools, the Rabbi spoke Hebrew with Yiddish translation. In the Czech public school, we spoke Czech and with the non-Jewish populace, we spoke Ruthenian, the ancient dialect of the peasants.

Everyone in the community knew everyone else from their daily contact. While the market place and the surrounding business section was the center of the town, the Great Synagogue was the soul of the Jewish community. It was the center of many activities and several other places of worship including the *Beit Hamidrash.*

At dawn, one could find there *anshei maamad*, men reciting the daily selections of Psalms, or learning Talmud. The shelves and closets were full of many holy books – Bibles, Mishnayoth, sets of Talmud, Midrashim, and other scholarly books. Services were held morning and evening every weekday of the year and on Shabbat and the holidays year round.

The beauty of the town helped neither Jew nor non-Jew escape the general poverty that prevailed. Even the poorest families had at least a small garden in which an array of flowers, vegetables, grapes, and assorted fruits grew. But no Jewish family in Bilke was considered to be poor as long as they could manage to set a proper *Shabbat* table.

My mother, Pearl, may G-d avenge her death, was up at three o'clock in the morning each Friday or on the eve of a holiday, to bake the traditional *challot*, cakes, and bread for the week. From then on, the cooking and cleaning proceeded throughout the afternoon. One hour before sunset, the younger children brought the Shabbat main meal, *chulent*, in a pot to the communal oven in the Great Synagogue courtyard. When all pots were accounted for, the *shamash*, the sexton, *Reb* David Aaron Reisman closed up the front of the oven with an iron plank and sealed it with wet clay, so the oven would retain the heat until the next morning.

A moment before sunset, everyone in the family assembled at the Shabbat table to watch mother light the candles, and with her hands covering her eyes, she recited the blessing that welcomed the Shabbat as the Queen of days. In our home, it was traditional to light a candle for each member of the family. When Grandmother Rachel Yitte, of blessed memory, died, my mother took over the number of candles she used to light. At that time, my mother, may she rest in peace, lit a total of 22 candles every Friday night. This meant that the house was splendidly illuminated.

A row of Jewish stores in Bilke, prior to the Holocaust.

After the candle lighting, all the men of Bilke gathered in the various houses of worship. In the Great Synagogue, my father, Reb Yehoshua Doft, was the Cantor. He sang the prayers, assisted by a choir of his six sons. He was known as a strong tenor who could break suddenly into a falsetto, and his sons, for the sweet interplay of their voices. These prayers were sent up to heaven from a Synagogue with high ceilings and very airy with an array of Biblical scenes painted overhead. Graceful candelabras provided light from above. For the holiday of *Shavuot*, the Synagogue was filled with fresh cuttings of green branches.

After the conclusion of the services, the men of Bilke hurried home. At our Shabbat table, the entire family raised their voices in singing the traditional *zemirot,* welcoming the Shabbat and the angels of peace into our home. My father recited the *Kiddush* over the wine and after him all the sons did the same. (Bilke and the region was famous for their wines.)

The braided *challah* that had been covered with a white challah cloth, so as not to be embarrassed that the wine had been blessed first, was cut and the blessing, *Hamotzi,* was recited. Then we dined on the traditional foods of fish, chicken soup, noodle pudding, stewed fruits, and cakes or fruits. Eating, singing zemirot, and discussing scriptures were combined into an art, both subtle and regulated.

On Shabbat morning, the men were back in the houses of worship as were the women who prayed in the upper section of the Synagogue called *ezrat nashim,* court of women. After an inspiring holy service, which lasted for three hours, everyone went home to eat the second meal of the Shabbat. The younger children hurried to the communal oven where Reb David Aaron Reisman broke open the seal of the oven. With a long-handled spatula, Reb David Aaron drew out each family's pot for the noonday meal. Even in winter snows, it was too hot to touch, and the children carried the pots home with mittens. The afternoons were spent napping, studying, or visiting friends.

In those days, Jewish women in Bilke did not have much entertainment. They found ways of socializing in very original and productive ways. During the long winter nights, Jewish women in Bilke gathered in the evening hours at a neighbor's house, each time at a different neighbor, to help each other pluck feathers for bedding, peel corn from the cob, or sort out wheat grain for *matzah shmurah*, specially watched and carefully supervised from time of harvesting, before it was ground into flour. During these social evenings the women would sing Yiddish and Hebrew songs, as well as songs in other languages, tell stories about their families and discuss events of the times.

In Bilke, there were a few musicians and a Klezmer band. Two musicians conducted the band that entertained the Bilker Jews at the various affairs, such as weddings, Bar Mitzvahs, and other happy occasions. These musicians played an important role in the cultural life of Bilker Jewry. They had a tradition of hundreds of years that was passed on from generation to generation. Their melodies entered the heart through the ears and became embedded in the heart. They had a great repertoire of Yiddish, Chassidic, and Biblical melodies, including melodies of the local Ruthenian population, which the Jews of

Bilke knew. One of these musicians, Moshe, the son of Zion, was also a *badchan,* a comedian jester. His comedy included Jewish topics and world events. On Purim, he and his band went from house to house during the festive Purim meal, performed a skit, sang rhyming songs in Yiddish which they composed, and played their musical instruments for which they received tips and food. When Moshe, the son of Zion, was asked why he was a jester, he used to say, "The comedians will be entitled to a share in the world to come because by their acting, they minimize the pain of people by making them happy."

Most of the Bilker Jews traced their roots back to Galicia or the Ukraine, from which they had fled a succession of pogroms, commencing with those of Bogdan Chmelnitsky in the 17th century.

In Bilke, relations between Jews and non-Jews were decent and civil, although there were sporadic anti-Semitic manifestations. We experienced some anti-Semitic trouble from the Ruthenian youths as our paths crossed on the way to and from school. Sometimes they threw stones at us and taunted us by saying *Zhidi Do Palestina*, Jews go to Palestine. In reality, things were only civil on the surface, because they could never forgive the Jews for the killing of their Lord.

There was generally no intermarriage between Jew and non-Jew, however, it was known to have happened once in the 300-year-old Jewish community. A Jewish farm girl from an outlying part of town insisted on marrying the Christian boy from the farm across the road. All the tears and threats in Bilke could not dissuade her. With her marriage to the non-Jew, she was banished from the Jewish community, as well as from her family. The parents *sat shivah,* mourning for seven days, as if the young daughter had died.

Even though Bilke was not a city, or a great Jewish center, one can say that the spiritual activities of the Jews were on a high level. When one looks back on those years and reflects upon the Jewish community and all the spiritual activities that took place, one can be very proud that there were five houses of worship that were open day and night for prayer and study. Almost all the time, one could find Jews learning *Torah*, *Mishnayoth*, and *Talmud*, a commentary on the Bible and Oral Law, in these *batei midrashim*, houses of worship and learning.

In Bilke, there were eight *chadarim*, Hebrew schools for young boys ages three and a half to thirteen years, Bar Mitzvah age. These schools were graded to a certain extent. Children from age three and a half to age six studied in the same Cheder with the same Rabbi. They were sub-divided into groups by age and the Rabbi taught a small group while the others studied by themselves or were playing outside.

Those who studied the *Alef-Beth,* the Hebrew alphabet, and reading, were a separate group, and those who learned *Chumash* and *Rashi,* Bible and commentary, were a separate group. In a more advanced group for the older children, they studied Talmud and commentaries, the weekly Bible portion, prayers and laws and customs. In these various Chadarim, there were over 200 students. The Rabbis of the Chadarim lived in Bilke or came from the surrounding communities. They returned to their homes to celebrate Shabbat with their families.

Every Thursday was a day of judgment, because Thursday was the day when the Rabbi tested the students to see how much knowledge they retained. If a student showed lack of knowledge, he was usually punished. The students were petrified and dreaded Thursdays. Although we feared our teachers, we had great respect for them and their scholarship. Prior to the various holidays, the Rabbi used to tell us great and meaningful stories about the Jewish people. Before the holiday of Shavuot, my Rabbi explained to us the beautiful liturgical poem of *Akdamut* and chanted it with its unique melody. He told us this poem was a mystical description of G-d's creation of the world, the greatness of the Jewish people and the bright future that was in store for our people. These stories became deeply engraved in my heart. Many times his words strengthened my spirit and my resolve, which helped me overcome difficulties I confronted during the Holocaust.

The Cheder became virtually a second home to the Jewish children. Our daily routine was centered around religious observance, learning, and attending the house of worship so that the ancient tradition of Torah study would be passed on in Bilke from generation to generation. The Bilker Jews saved every penny in order to provide a Jewish education for their children.

I had many friends from Cheder and public school with whom I played for hours. We played football in the spring and summer, and in wintertime, we went sledding and skating on the ice. Even though it was quite a long day, the rigorous schedule of my secular and religious education did not mar the happiness of my childhood.

I rose at 5 a.m. to attend Cheder, the religious school where I studied Prayers, Torah, Bible, Mishnah, Talmud, Jewish laws and customs, the cantillations, the holidays, etc. We translated the Hebrew texts into Yiddish. Much of it was taught by rote. We memorized many passages, verse by verse, repeating them in a special chant fashion. We studied until 8 a.m. and from the

Cheder we walked over to the public school. Most of the students of the Czech public school were Jews and children of the Czech civil servants. The Ruthenian children attended a Ruthenian public school. We learned the Czech language, reading, writing, arithmetic, geography, history, music, and literature. The boys also had a workshop where we learned carpentry and other useful skills. The girls learned sewing, crocheting, and all kinds of needlework. We studied until 3:30 p.m.

From public school, we passed by our home and grabbed something to eat and rushed back to Cheder where we continued our studies until 8 p.m. Upon returning home, I ate supper and did my homework for public school. The Czech school was on a very high level and the teachers were true professionals. Our Jewish teachers, the Rabbis, were steeped in Jewish learning, but some of them were not great pedagogues. Discipline in both schools was quite strict. We had no problems with crime or misbehavior.

There was a beautiful custom in Bilke. When a Jewish woman gave birth to a baby boy, the Rabbi of the Cheder took the youngest children in his class, the day before the *brith*, the circumcision, took place to the home of the newborn baby. This was a welcome to the Jewish child and also to bless the baby boy so that no harm would come to him.

On the walls of the room where the mother and baby were, there would be Hebrew posters with chapters of Psalms *Shir Hamaaloth*, "A Song of Ascents: The Lord is thy keeper, behold, He that keepeth Israel doth neither slumber nor sleep... The Lord shall guard thy going out and thy coming in from this time forth and forever." (Psalm 121) This was done as a good omen so that no harm could come to the baby. Then the Rabbi sang *kriath shema*, Hear O Israel, and the passage from the Bible, *hamalach hagoel,* with us. "The angel who hath redeemed me from all evil, bless the lads; and let my name be named in them, and the name of my fathers, Abraham and Isaac, and let them grow into a multitude in the midst of the earth." (Genesis 48:16)

As a reward for our visit to the baby and our renditions, each one of us received a fresh small challah roll. Such a visit turned into a sort of holiday for us. First of all, we went for a nice stroll in the fresh air and were not cooped up in a crowded room. The challah was very tasty and above all, it was a great spiritual experience for us youngsters.

The Bilker Rabbi was Rabbi Naftali Tzvi Weiss, the son of the famous Grand Rabbi of Sapinka, a great Talmudic scholar, who was known for his scholarship. He established a Yeshivah, an academy, a school of higher learning in

Bilke, for boys ages 15 to 20, who came from near and far to study with him. The Rabbi of the town was the guiding spiritual force of the Jews. In the late 1930s, the Yeshivah had more than 100 *bachurim*, young men who studied day and night.

The Jewish inhabitants of Bilke welcomed the Yeshivah into their midst. Each family was canvassed to secure the daily meals for the bachurim. Many hard working families considered it a *mitzvah*, a duty and privilege, to share meals with these worthy Yeshivah students. These meals were provided free. This program was called in Yiddish, *essen teg*, meaning eating certain days at certain families. This was not always the best arrangement, but it did help a great deal to allow Yeshivah students to leave their homes and go to study in famous academies. Bilke became an important center of learning, which attracted many Yeshivah students who were seeking the fulfillment of learning Torah.

The young people who traveled to the larger cities to study at the universities acquired a liberal education, and tasted a different culture, but when they returned home, out of respect, they still observed the Jewish traditions. No one rebelled openly against the old way of life. When the boys became Bar Mitzvah at 13, and intended to continue their Jewish studies, they either studied at the Yeshivah in Bilke or traveled to other Jewish centers of learning, to great Yeshivoth in Carpathia or Slovakia.

Between the two world wars, the Zionist movement made great strides among the Jewish youth in Bilke. *Shlichim*, emissaries from the Land of Israel, and from the larger cities in Czechoslovakia, visited Bilke to inspire our youth. They told about the pioneers, the rebuilding of the land, and about the Jewish community in Palestine which was gaining strength. The youth established Zionist groups of every ideological persuasion in the Zionist Movement. The Jewish youth in Bilke got their nationalistic fervor from their homes, Jewish schools, and the traditional environment in our town.

Zionism planted pride in the hearts of the Jewish youth that helped a great deal against assimilation. The Bilker Jews had great feelings and sentiments for the land of our fathers. They learned about the Holy Places, the Temple Mount, The Western Wall – *The Kotel*, The Cave of *Machpella* in Hebron, The Tomb of Our Mother Rachel near *Beth Lechem* and many others. Many of them donated charity to the Jewish National Fund and the Rabbi Meir Baal Hanes Fund. They dreamed of liberation and redemption. They waited for the Messiah to come.

The youth were also inspired by the Yiddish Press such as the *Heint*, and *Moment*, which were published in Poland to which some of our youth subscribed including my brothers, and the *Yiddishe Shtimeh*, a paper published in Mukachevo, Czechoslovakia. The youth learned from the newspapers important information about what was happening in the world, especially in the Jewish world and in the land of Israel. These papers were passed from hand to hand and thus reached many of the Jewish youth. From time to time, Hebrew newspapers from Poland and the land of Israel arrived in Bilke, which some of the more knowledgeable in Hebrew tried to understand and increase their Hebrew vocabulary. When these newspapers arrived, there was a spiritual uplift among the youth.

The Zionist idea brought to Bilke an awakening to our youth and gave them a new meaning to be Jewish. They formed Zionist clubs where the youth gathered during the holidays of the Jewish calendar. These celebrations took on a deeper meaning. They observed these holidays by singing Hebrew songs and dancing pioneer dances. They studied the Hebrew language, told stories about the land being redeemed, and about Jewish heroic personalities including those of the Jewish underground in Palestine. These Zionist activities varied according to the ideology of the group. The religious Zionists of *Bnai Akiva*, the *Mizrachi*, *Poaley Agudat Yisrael*, also conducted services in these clubs on Shabbat, and holidays, sang religious songs, and discussed religious heroic personalities.

At first, these club meetings were held in secret because Rabbi Naftali Tzvi Weiss, the Rabbi of Bilke and other anti-Zionists, were against these activities. There was a misconception in that they believed all Zionists were against religion and tradition. The Rabbi forbade the youth to take part in the Zionist activities. A fierce struggle began between the youth, their parents and the Rabbinical leadership. In most cases the *Issur*, the prohibition, did not help. Zionism even affected the Yeshivah bachurim, the students of the academies, because the Zionist idea was in the air. Joining the Zionist movement by a Yeshivah student usually was accompanied by great spiritual agony. The soul searching was done by the individual, in secret, because this was the kind of struggle one did not reveal until he made a commitment of no return.

The anti-Zionists had their own reasons for opposing the youth joining the Zionists ranks. They feared their sons and daughters would make *aliyah* to Palestine. They said it was a land that devoured its inhabitants and the Arabs who lived there were wild people. They felt the Zionists discarded traditions and therefore they could not bring redemption... Only our true Messiah would bring the redemption. They argued that G-d made the Jewish people take an oath that they would not force the time of the redemption and therefore this was against G-d's will.

Even though many of the Bilker youth were involved in Zionist activity, only a handful succeeded in escaping the tragedy of the Holocaust, due to the difficulties acquiring a certificate of immigration, a permit from the British to enter Palestine. One dozen youths from Bilke succeeded in settling in Palestine in the 1930s, some illegally. Among them was my brother Shmuel Tzvi.

This kind of community life, which existed for 300 years, was destroyed in just a few years. In the 1930s, there was uneasiness among the Jewish youth of Bilke regarding their future. Some of them did not see much of a future in the small town. The well-educated, in particular, were striving for careers which were difficult for Jews to reach, since there was an anti-Semitic undercurrent. There were a number of young people who graduated from the Gymnasium and even from the Universities. Some made their way to America. A few who became ardent Zionists turned to *Eretz Yisrael*, the Land of Israel.

One of my brothers Shmuel Tzvi, decided to immigrate to Palestine. He was only 18 years old when he received a certificate from the British, after he was accepted to the Hebrew University in Jerusalem. Most parents were unhappy with their sons and daughters leaving home and emigrating to far away countries about which they knew very little. It seemed those who did leave Bilke had vision, and in hindsight, they did the right thing because they saved themselves, thus perpetuating their families.

In March 1944, Adolf Eichmann, the Nazi Evil, who was the prototype of the German Technocrat in the German killing machine, was dispatched with his S.S. units to force the ghettoization of Hungarian Jewry and the deportation from the ghettos to Auschwitz.

In October 1944, just a few months after the deportation of the last Jews of Bilke, the Red Army conquered Carpathia and our town, Bilke. As the Russian soldiers entered the Great Synagogue of Bilke, they poured out their anger at this holy place of the Jews. They robbed whatever they could. They destroyed the *Aron Kodesh,* the Holy Ark, and the *bimah*, the pulpit. They took away the seat of Elijah the Prophet, which stood in the center of the Synagogue. They threw all the holy Torah scrolls and other holy books into the *mikveh*, the ritual bath, which was located in the yard of the Great Synagogue. They took apart the pews and turned this holy place into a central storehouse for the occupying Red Army. Thus, a vulgar and crude hand desecrated the Holy of Holies of Bilker Jewry. Even the Red oppressor had no pity on a holy place, which had been a great creative center for many generations.

With this desecration, the *Shechinah,* the divine presence, the holy crown and beauty which was an inspiration to 15 generations, disappeared. The Russians destroyed whatever the Hungarians, the Germans and other Fascists did not finish.

After liberation from the concentration and labor camps, a few survivors from Bilke returned to the town to see if any members of their families had survived. Some were thinking of rebuilding their lives in their hometown. When they arrived in Bilke, they discovered that no one had survived. Then they realized how great their tragedy really was. There they discovered how bereaved and alone they really were. Only then, the few survivors who returned to Bilke came to the realization of how devastating the Holocaust was to their families and to the Jewish community of Bilke as a whole.

Some of the Jewish houses were empty and unoccupied. The doors and windows were broken and everything was plundered. Among the returnees were a few young men who were liberated in Auschwitz by the Russians in January 1945. Another few escaped from the forced labor battalions. They did not arrive in Bilke at the same time. They came in stages. Some arrived and others left because no one survived, and nothing was left of their properties or belongings. There was also a dangerous situation in Bilke under Russian occupation, and the hostile attitude they encountered by the Bilker Gentiles. One could feel the resentment and the open hatred with which the Ruthenian Bilker population greeted the Jewish survivors. They said to the Jewish survivors, "How is it that they did not also burn you in the concentration camps?"

The Ruthenians went so far in their hostility as to accuse the few survivors of planning to poison the water wells in Bilke, since one Gentile became very ill and they found out that he drank water from a certain well, which was polluted, causing his death. This incident gave the Ruthenians a good excuse to accuse the Jewish survivors who returned to Bilke of poisoning the wells. The Russian authorities arrested the Jewish survivors, and jailed them in the nearby town of Irshava. One of the survivors was severely tortured. They were trying to extract a false confession from him. Joshua Eckstein, a Jew from Bilke who was a high-ranking official in the communist party, bribed the official in Irshava who was in charge of the case. Only then were the Jewish survivors of Bilke released from prison. The Bilker Ruthenians threw stones at the survivors in Bilke. Those four or five survivors stayed in the house of the Heisler family. One night, shots were fired at the house. All these hostile incidents were a clear indication to the few survivors that Bilke was not a place for Jews anymore. They came to the conclusion that if they attempted to stay, the Gentiles in Bilke would make their lives an open hell. They realized that nothing had changed, that actually those were the same people who, at the town meeting in the beginning of 1944, voted unanimously to deport the rest of the Jews. The Hungarians and the Germans wanted the backing of the local population in their policies against the Jews.

The survivors decided to leave Bilke forever. But now they had another problem. The Russians were against anyone leaving their occupied territories. They had to cross the border into Czechoslovakia, illegally, by bribing smugglers to help them cross the border. In October 1945, they left for Czechoslovakia. The Czechs were very friendly to them. They settled them in the German houses in the Sudetenland from which the Czechs evicted the Germans, because of the destruction of their country by Nazi Germany. After a short period of time, they left the Sudetenland for Israel and America. Thus, our hometown of Bilke became Judenrein, without any Jews, after 300 years.

More than 50 years has passed since the Jewish communities of Bilke, Kulbasavo, Ulitkes, Mistichev, Rakovetz, Osy, Yilnitze, and Likiveh were eradicated. Two thousand of our dear ones, our parents, brothers, sisters, and other family members died in the Holocaust by the hands of the evil forces in Europe, with great suffering and torture.

All of the Jewish institutions, the Synagogues, the houses of learning, the Chadarim, Hebrew schools, the Yeshivah, the mikveh, hundreds of Jewish homes, businesses, the Jewish youth clubs, and many others were either destroyed or taken by the non-Jewish population. Bilke and its vicinity was emptied of Jews, *Judenrein*. Hitler accomplished his goal, which was the destruction of everything that was dear to us.

Passover – As It Was Celebrated In Bilke

In our town of Bilke, deep in the Carpathian Mountains, preparations for Passover began during the height of the winter. The women had the first task. On market day, which took place on Tuesday, the women searched for the best quality ducks and geese. They were brought home and for the next few weeks, these birds were relentlessly fattened. They were actually forced to eat grains far beyond what they would have eaten naturally.

In truth, this was not a practice in keeping with the Jewish law, which forbids causing any living creature to suffer. In Jewish law it is called, *tzaar baalai chaim*. My mother never practiced this stuffing, called *shtopen* in Yiddish. She was a very kind person and very observant, however, the majority of families in Bilke did it.

When the birds were good and fat, the women took them down to one of the six streams that crossed our town. There they broke through the ice of the frozen stream and washed the feathers of the birds so that they would be completely clean. Then they took the birds to Rabbi Yehoshua to be slaughtered according to Jewish law. Taking the esophagus of the bird, he would blow it up like a balloon. If there was any scar or any other evidence of sickness on the tissue, the bird would have to be discarded because it was *treifa*, non-kosher. If the duck or goose was kosher, Rabbi Yehoshua would cut off one leg and keep it separately. This custom was practiced only during the months of *Tevet* and *Shevat*, corresponding to December and January in the general calendar, depending on the Jewish calendar. This custom was passed down from generation to generation, that one leg belonged to the Shochet during those months.

When Rabbi Yehoshua accumulated a number of these legs, he would distribute them to the poor people of Bilke. This gift kept many of the poor alive. An especially delicious and nourishing dish they made was called *Pecheh*. This was a kind of gelatin, made from the feet in which the meat was bathed and also preserved.

The ample fat from these birds was most important. It was taken off and sealed in glass jars, not to be used until Passover. As the winters in the Carpathian Mountains were very cold, there was no spoilage problem. As for the feathers, these were used for pillows and quilts. The meat itself, of course, was eaten right away.

About the same time, the first steps were taken to prepare wheat for grinding into flour of the matzoth. On a winter's night, neighbors would gather in one home or another around a long, absolutely clean table, covered with a tablecloth. There could be no question of even a single particle of *chametz*, or leavened bread, hidden on the surface. Wheat would be spilled over the table. With care, the neighbors would pick through the kernels of the wheat removing any impurities, for example; chaff, stones, or a bug. Even a split kernel was cast aside. In this way, they ended up with the very best wheat available. There were some families in Bilke who bought regular wheat for Passover, but the more observant bought only special wheat that had been literally watched over from the moment it was cut in the field until the time it came out of the oven. Above all, this wheat had to stay dry so that it would not accidentally start to rise or leaven. The matzah baked from this special wheat is known as *Matzah Shmurah*, which means, guarded matzah. Among those who bought only this kind of wheat were my family and, of course, the family of the Rabbi Naftali Tzvi Weiss and a few others.

Before the matzoth could be produced for the Jewish community of Bilke, it had to be decided who would get the concession to produce the matzoth. This was a decision, which was put to a vote by the elders of the community. They gathered for that purpose at least two months before Passover in the side chapel of the Great Synagogue. The advantage of this chapel was that a wood-burning stove heated it unlike the Synagogue itself. This chapel served in wintertime for worship, study, and also for community meetings and affairs.

In Bilke, there were about six different families who competed for the concession to bake the matzoth for the community. In Hebrew they are called *baalay bateem*, or members. Among them were Reb Meshulam Friedman, Reb David Aharon Reisman, and Reb Noach Mechlovitch. These men would submit by sealed bids, the price per kilo at which they would deliver the matzoth to the community. A low price was essential because so many of the people were poor. The eating of matzah, which symbolized the bread of affliction and the journey from Egypt, was a *mitzvah*, a good deed, that had to be made affordable to the poorest of the poor.

The sealed envelopes were opened by the *Rosh HaKahal*, the president of the community, Chaim Isaac Rosenbaum. All the bids were read aloud. That year Reb Meshulam Friedman had submitted the lowest bid. In addition to the low price, this was a man who had other good qualities and points in his favor. He was a *melamed*, a teacher, in one of the better Chadarim, Hebrew schools. He also was a religious man, a *yareh shamayim*, one who feared heaven.

With six streams flowing down from the mountains and through Bilke, there was no lack of water-powered mills. Each year the Jews of our town negotiated the rent of these mills a month or two before Passover so the holiday wheat could be ground into flour. Since most of these mills belonged to Gentiles, the negotiating could be delicate. Some of the owners did not want to give up their mills for such a short period of time as was required to grind the flour. Others, although they never explicitly said it, didn't want to rent to Jews.

That year the community did rent a mill. It was in the outlying suburb of Kolbasovo. Early one morning, a small group of Bilker Jews set out in a wagon to go to *kasher*, make the mill fit for Passover use. There was Reb David Aharon Reisman, the *shamash,* sexton, Reb Meshulam Friedman, the *melamed*, the teacher, who had the concession to bake the matzoth, and the sons of the Shochet, Chaim Leib and Shlomo Yeshayah and also after crying and begging, I, the youngest son, Moshe'leh, was finally allowed to join. For me, it was an occasion, which I will never forgot.

All the machinery of the mill and especially the grinding stone wheel itself, was thoroughly scrubbed, so as to be utterly free of any taint of *chametz*, leavened bread. This meant not only sweeping and scrubbing every surface but also burning the surface of the grinding stones with hot coal. That is how thoroughly it had to be done. This process of preparing the mill took all day and all night.

When the process of kashering was complete, the Rabbi of our community, Rabbi Naftali Tzvi Weiss, was called to inspect the premises to see if everything was according to *halacha*, Jewish law. Once he gave his okay, the grinding of the Passover flour commenced. The first wheat to be ground was the wheat for Matzah Shmurah. The reason for this was because if the regular wheat had been ground first, it would obviously bring Matzah Shmurah down to the level of the regular matzah through contact and contamination. Therefore the purest was first ground.

It was very late when our wagon finally returned home. I, little Moshe'leh, bragged to the other boys of Bilke how I, alone, had been allowed to take part in the important mitzvah of the day.

The Great Synagogue of Bilke

Drawn from memory by Yitzhock Reisman

One of the nice things about Reb Meshulam Friedman's winning the concession to bake the matzoth was that he had to dismiss his school a few days earlier than usual so he could commence the preparations for the baking of the matzoth. We students were full of joy that the Cheder was ending early. I was in the habit of wandering around the building where the community oven was located. In the community building three activities were going on – the *Beit HaSchita*, the slaughter house; the community oven; and the Cheder. I liked to watch how the matzoth were baked. All was of interest to me; who was bringing the flour, how many matzoth were baked, and so on. Sometimes I was given a little piece of matzah to nibble and also allowed, from time to time, to pierce the holes in the rolled out dough, which kept the matzah from rising.

The oven, which served year round for cooking the Chulent, was kashered as thoroughly as the mill had been. Besides being swept clean all over and around the rooms, the oven was fired up a full 24 hours to make sure all the chametz, leavened bread, was burned out.

After a while, I got up my courage and went up to Reb Meshulam, *my* teacher, who had the concession to bake the matzoth, and said, "Rabbi, I have a request. Maybe you could hire me to make the holes in the matzoth; you can see I did it a few times already." To my surprise, he said yes.

The process of producing the matzoth started immediately after Purim. Only pious women were chosen to roll out the dough. Any young woman who was not perfect, from a moral point of view, was passed over. This was a decision which Rabbi Naftali Tzvi Weiss himself made about each woman who applied for work. The kneading of the dough was hard work and it was done by the men. No juice, no salt, nor any other ingredient was added to the flour. This was to fulfill the commandment in the Bible, "Seven days shalt thou eat unleavened bread, the bread of affliction; for thou camest out of the land of Egypt in haste." (Deuteronomy 16:3)

The water for the making of the matzah dough had to be drawn from spring water the night before because of the possibility that the water might become chametz. It says in the Talmud (Tractate *Pesachim* 94), "In daytime wells are cold and warm at night." This water, which was drawn before evening, is called *Mayim Shelanu*, water that stayed warm overnight and, therefore, one is supposed to knead the flour only with water that has stayed in a cistern for the night. As a double precaution, when this water was poured into the barrel, it was strained to be sure that no chametz got into the water.

There was a *mashgiach*, a supervisor, who watched over the women as they rolled out the dough. He hurried them because after eighteen minutes from the moment the dough was ready to roll and put into the oven, the dough becomes chametz. It happens very fast. Once the dough was brought to the table where it was pierced, it was folded over a very long stick and brought to the oven.

The man actually in charge of the oven was Reb David Aharon Reisman. It was the job of a young lad to bring Reb David Aharon the unbaked matzah on a paddle at the end of a very long narrow rolling pin. The matzoth would be laid across the paddle, side by side. Reb David Aharon would then thrust this paddle deep into the hot oven wiggling and rolling it so that the individual matzoth would come off and lie in an orderly row. This took quite some skill. But he had done it for years and he knew what he was doing.

The baking lasted no more than two minutes; maybe even less. The oven was very hot and the matzoth very thin, so that was all the time it took. Then Reb David Aharon used a wooden spatula, also with a long handle, to slide out the baked matzoth. Each family brought its own flour, which they ground in the kashered mill, to the community oven and paid Reb Meshulum Friedman for the baking. The family to whom a certain batch belonged would hold out a large basket and in it the hot baked matzoth would be placed and then taken home. This was the procedure by which the Jews of Bilke prepared the matzoth for Passover.

In the house of the Doft family, there was a big commotion before Passover. The entire house was painted. All the furniture was removed from each room and the house was cleaned thoroughly. The entire house was renewed in every way. From the 13th day of Nissan, one day before Passover began, nobody would go into the house without first removing their shoes. That's how strictly things were done. It was Miriam, one of the five daughters who was in charge of preparing the house for Pesach. She devoted herself to this task, not only putting the house in order before Passover, but also before each Shabbat and other holidays. She did it, not only with attention to tiny details, but also with enthusiasm.

Two days before Pesach, the Doft family took down from the attic the special *Pesachdikeh* dishes for Passover. These were well covered and locked in a trunk so that G-d forbid, no chametz could sneak in. From the oldest to the youngest, the whole family stood in a line beneath the ladder leading to the attic door as, item by item, the Passover plates, pots, and other utensils were passed down. Each member of the family had a favorite dish. For me, it was the saltwater dish made from crystal. Each year, when this bowl was handed down from the attic, I was so happy with it. It was as if I had found a treasure all over again.

The Passover dishes were washed and dried and put on the table, as if on exhibition, so that everyone could see them.

In our house, there were two ovens, one for cooking meat and one for dairy. My mother allowed no crossovers. G-d forbid if a dairy dish was put on the meat oven, or vice versa. Before Pesach, my mother kept the ovens going for 24 hours, just like the matzah oven in the communal building, in order to make it absolutely kosher for Passover. Nobody saw such cleaning in any house in Bilke. If even one granule of chametz had been left after cleaning of the ovens, it was surely burned away by this long period of firing.

The tables were also washed and scrubbed. In order to protect them, a thin tin cover was put over them, which was stored in the attic from year to year. Although the home of the Shochet was very clean year round, at Pesach time, there was a special brightness, a special whiteness.

On Passover eve, my father came home from the Synagogue and performed *Bedikat Chametz*, the search for the leavened bread. This meant that he went around the house checking to see if any chametz had accidentally been left. In order not to pronounce a blessing in vain, someone in the family placed small crumbs here and there. With a candle, a feather, and wooden spoon in hand, he collected the crumbs, and placed them in the wooden spoon. He recited the blessing, *Al Biur Chametz*, meaning we were commanded to clear out the chametz from the house.

All the chametz that had been collected was wrapped in a cloth and put away until morning. Then before 10 a.m., (there was a very strict limit of time) my father and brothers went out in the yard and made a fire. Into the flames we tossed the wooden spoon, the feather and the cloth with the crumbs. As it burned, we recited the formula of *Kol Chamira.* It is a vow that any chametz still in the house which somehow had escaped notice should now be declared not to exist. It is a kind of legal declaration similar to selling the chametz to a non-Jew.

In the afternoon before Pesach began, Passover eve, a group of men, the elite of the community, gathered at the communal oven. They included the Rabbi of Bilke, Rabbi Naftali Tzvi Weiss; Reb Yehoshua and his six sons; Reb Laybush the *Dayan* and his sons; Reb Yaacov Weingarten, who was also a Shochet, but was not practicing, with his sons; Reb David Aharon Reisman and his sons; Reb Meshulum Friedman and his sons; Reb Naftali Schwimmer and his sons; and other important members of the community. They were there to bake the *Mitzvah Matzoth*. At this time, only men did the entire work, the rolling of the dough, the perforation of it so that it would not rise, and the cutting. As they worked, they sang *Hallel*, the songs of praise to G-d from the Passover service. In this way, the men themselves had the experience of baking the Passover matzoth, which is a great mitzvah. Of course, my father and brothers, who had lovely voices, were singing most of the time, and the whole atmosphere was very beautiful and very uplifting. When the baking was done, each family rushed home with their Mitzvah Matzoth they had baked.

My father did not forget to send some of these Mitzvah Matzoth to some of the baaley bateem. With my older brother Yose'leh, who was two and a half years older, we brought the packages of Mitzvah Matzoth to the baalay bateem. We liked to make these deliveries because we would get a tip from the recipients of these packages.

In the meantime, the women of the Doft family were at home preparing the Passover table. All the fine dishes were there and polished candlesticks with special large candles so they would last throughout the Seder, the red sweet wine for the *arba kosoth*, four cups, the *kaarah*, the Seder plate, and *kos Eliyahu*, the cup of Elijah the Prophet. There was also a cup for each member of the family, as well as salt water and Mitzvah Matzoth. At the head of the table, a couch was placed with pillows. This was for the leader of the Seder to enact, the mitzvah of *hasavah*, reclining. It was to symbolize that we were free people.

When the sun set into the trees, my mother lit the candles. She wore a beautiful white dress with a kerchief on her head that matched her dress. She looked like a Queen. She did not cover her eyes with her hands before she made the blessings, for on a holiday you are not required to cover your eyes, only on Friday nights. Her lips moved in a silent prayer. When she completed reciting, *Lehadlik ner shel yom tom,* and *Shehecheyanu,* she said, “Good Yom Tov,” a happy holiday.

My father put on his silk garment always made new for Pesach by Naftali Schwimmer, the tailor. He put on his *shtraimel*, his fur hat, also special for the holiday. All of my brothers were also specially dressed, though only some had new clothes. Then the men went to the Great Synagogue, which was rapidly filling. Meanwhile, the children of Bilke were roaming around, comparing their new holiday clothes. I was proud of my new shoes for Pesach.

At the moment of sunset, the congregation prayed *Mincha*, the afternoon prayer. Then my father, Reb Yehoshua, who was the Cantor as well as the Shochet of the community, approached the pulpit with his six sons. There in his loud, yet sweet voice, he sang first the *Borchu*, using a special moving melody, which is designated for the three festivals in the Jewish calendar. Reb Yehoshua and his six sons were a choir known not only in Bilke, but in the surrounding towns. This was *Lail Shimurim*, the night when the guardian of Israel watches over the Jewish people, as well as the night when a Seder which had yet to take place, would last into the wee hours of the night. Reb Yehoshua actually finished the service with a bit of extra speed. As soon as the *Maariv*, the evening service, was over, the Synagogue quickly emptied as each one rushed to his home to start the Seder. Burning candles were seen from all the Jewish homes, which created a spiritual atmosphere.

As the men entered the house, they said *Chag Sameach*, a joyous holiday, and the women answered with the same greeting. My father put on a white robe, which symbolized freedom, and sat down on the couch at the head of the table. My mother sat on his right, dressed in white. They looked like a king and queen. In fact, on Passover night, they are called *Melech* and *Malkah*. Their faces were shining as they looked with joy at their clean house, their beautiful table, and their special family.

Reb Yehoshua now turned to those seated around the table. "Pesach is a holiday," he said, "that unites our people wherever they may be, now and throughout the generations. The cup of Elijah symbolizes the announcer of the redemption and the hope of our people. The melodies we sing have likewise been passed on to us from previous generations. The symbols of the Passover table and the stories told in the Haggadah, emphasize this continuity of our people. The suffering we have undergone throughout the generations has strengthened our resolve so that even as enemies rise up against us anew, G-d saves us from them." Then he said to me, "Moshe'leh, since you are the youngest in the family, you may now begin with *Kadesh*." This is a listing of the ten parts of the Seder, a sort of index of the Seder ritual. I sang Kadesh, then he explained the meaning, that one fills the first cup of wine and a blessing is recited over it. Chaim Leib, the oldest son in the family, then filled all the cups. Reb Yehoshua stood and the family also rose. He sang the Kiddush over the wine according to the Passover melody. "G-d chose us over all other peoples," he said, "to celebrate this holiday with joy – a holiday of the matzoth, a holiday of freedom." After Reb Yehoshua had recited the Kiddush, each son also recited the Kiddush, one after the other.

Then it was my turn to announce the next part of the Seder, *Urchatz*, washing of the hands. All the men went to a bowl and washed their hands while I went on saying the order of the Seder. *Yachatz*, Reb Yehoshua took the middle matzah, symbolizing the tribe of Levi, and broke it in half. The larger half, he put into a cloth and hid it away for the *Afikoman*. Until it is found at the end of the Seder, the service cannot be concluded. It is the children who search for the Afikoman, the hidden matzah, and a prize is awarded to the one who finds it. From this Afikoman matzah, a piece is given to each person at the table.

Then we recited together the *Motzi* as well as the blessing, *Al Achilat Matzah*, meaning we were commanded to eat the matzah. *Magid*, Reb Yehoshua lifted up the matzoth and he said, "This is the poor bread of affliction..." And he continued reading in the Haggadah, as the entire family began singing a sad melody. It was a melody that hovered all over Bilke in the night air from all Jewish homes, as the Gentiles of the town slept their peaceful sleep.

My father now turned to me, his youngest son, Moshe'leh, with great love and said, "My son asks the four questions." With a sweet voice and a twisting melody, in the Yiddish language, "My dear father," I began, "I want to ask you four questions. The first one is, why is it, that on all other nights, we eat either chametz or matzah, but tonight we eat only matzah?" Then I asked the second question, and so on, through the fourth question. Then I said, "I have asked the questions. Please father, give us the answers."

My father answered, "*Avadim Hayinu Lefaroh B'Mitzrayim*, we were slaves to Pharaoh in Egypt..." And he continued to read the paragraph that explains why we were celebrating Passover. Each one at the Seder table read to themselves silently. From time to time, Reb Yehoshua explained interesting passages, which sweetened the entire evening. He also mixed in stories and sayings, which told of wonderful things that happened to the Jewish people. He emphasized the important points by standing, which added special feelings. The melodies and stories, which were heard at the Passover *Seder*, had all been passed down from one generation to the next. That's how Reb Yehoshua learned from his father, and how his father learned it from his father. Perhaps these melodies go back to the *Beit Hamikdash*, the Holy Temple in Jerusalem.

Each one of the men at the table sang certain sections as a solo. They embroidered the melody especially when they wanted to emphasize a particular passage. Chaim Leib, the oldest son of the family, liked to emphasize this passage, "If G-d would have given us the Torah, and not brought us into the land of Israel, *Dayenu*, it would have been enough for us!"

And Shmuel Tzvi, the second son in line called out, "And in each generation each person has to see himself as if he was the one who came out from Egypt."

"*Marror,*" I announced, and we passed around two different types of marror or bitter herbs. One type was large pieces and the other was ground. The women and youngsters only ate that which was ground and a little bit milder. The men ate both. After quite a long time, I finally announced, "*Shulchan Orech,*" meaning set the table for the meal.

When the women heard the signal, they began to serve all the courses. At this moment, a very relaxed atmosphere existed in the house. With great satisfaction, the women listened to the praises and compliments they received from the men with each new dish they presented. When the meal was at last finished, I announced, "*Tzafun,*" meaning that the Afikoman, the hidden matzah, should be presented, and each person should eat a piece from it, a *kzayit*, at least the size of an olive. Then my father turned around to look for the Afikoman that he had hidden. He suspected that I, who was sitting on his left, probably took it and said, "Okay, what should I give you to get back the Afikoman!" I thought about this for a moment and then said, "For Passover you bought me new shoes. For Shavuot, which is coming in seven weeks, I want you to buy me a new suit."

"Let it be so," said Reb Yehoshua. So I brought forth the Afikoman from the place where it was hidden. Only then was the family able to continue with the Seder ritual.

When the Doft family reached the paragraph *Shfoch Chamatcha*, meaning pour out thy wrath at those who have been persecuting the Jewish people, Yose'leh was asked to go to the front door and open it for *Eliyahu Hanavi*, Elijah the Prophet. It is believed by the Jewish people that at this moment at the Seder, Elijah comes into Jewish homes and takes a sip of wine from the cup designated for him. The entire family rose to their feet and with great feeling, recited this passage in the Haggadah, which tells of the tremendous injustices that have been brought upon the Jewish people throughout the generations. The children looked to see, during the recitation, if Elijah had really been drinking from the cup. The door was closed and we continued to recite and sing the rest of the Haggadah. When it came to the sentence, *Leshanah Habaah Beyerushalayim*, next year in Jerusalem, the entire family joined in the singing with special feeling.

From all the Jewish houses in Bilke, such passages could be heard as, "G-d build Your house soon!" "The Mighty One will soon build His house!" "Soon You will lead the afflicted ones to Zion in joy and in song!" It was after midnight when the Doft family completed the Seder in high spirits.

During Passover, the elders of the community recounted events that happened in Bilke many years before; events which left a tremendous impression. Here is one example. It happened on the Passover holiday, some years back, when the Christian Easter holiday coincided with Pesach. This always caused tension in the Jewish community. The Jews tried, during this period, to keep a low profile so as not to arouse the Gentile population. All the Jewish celebrations were a little restrained so there would be no pretext for trouble. This was something that happened more than once in Jewish history.

The Christians in Bilke had a legend that during Easter week, the bells of their church flew away to Rome. Obviously, during the entire Easter period, no bells rang in Bilke.

There was a certain Jewish family in Bilke that had been there for many generations and had grown prosperous. One branch of the family owned a store, another a bank, still another handled big real estate transactions involving fields and vineyards. In short, they were well to do. The name of the family was Friedman. They lived close to the Great Synagogue. One of the sons of the family was Yitzchak. One could describe him as a *meshugener*, someone mentally unstable. He had to be kept on a chain so that he could not run away and perhaps hurt people. By nature, he was so violent that not even his closest family members could control him. Only Reb Shmuel Mayer Klein, who had been a teacher of small children, could handle him at all. Being old, the Rabbi had retired. But he found a way of handling this young Yitzchak. Yitzchak actually liked the old man.

Reb Shmuel Mayer would help him get dressed, feed him, and in general, attend to his needs. He handled him very gently. Although Reb Shmuel Mayer was not a doctor or psychologist, he knew how to deal with the disturbed young man. He was easy going and a jokester. If you asked him how old he was, he would tell you in terms of Bar Mitzvahs. "I was a Bar Mitzvah six times already."

On the first day of Pesach of that year, which was also the first day of Easter week, Reb Shmuel Mayer came as usual to Yitzchak, the insane one. When he came into the room, he saw at once, or rather sensed, that there was some change that had come over Yitzchak. What this change was, however, he was not able to say. "Take off the chain from my leg," Yitzchak said suddenly. "Only for a few minutes." Reb Shmuel Mayer was afraid to oblige him, fearing he would run away. But Yitzchak suddenly hit the old man on the head, and then grabbed one of his payot, sidecurls, and tore it out. "If you don't unchain me, I'll rip out your other payah," the insane man said.

The old man saw he had no choice. He unlocked the chain that bound

Yitzchak. The insane man began running like a wild animal. By the time Reb Shmuel Mayer had fetched the other members of the family to search the grounds, it was as if the ground had swallowed him up.

On this first day of Pesach of that year, the Jews of Bilke gathered in the Great Synagogue to give thanks to the Almighty for their freedom. It was spring, of course, and the weather was already beautiful. The leader of *Pesukai Dezimrah*, of the preliminary service, had just finished when Reb Yehoshua began the Shacharit, the morning service, according to the special festival melodies. The entire congregation had been waiting for this and each word, each melody, elicited great joy in them.

Reb Yehoshua was also a composer of melodies. For each holiday he would try out new tunes. The members of the community listened carefully and afterwards each one gave his opinion. Reb Meyer Berger who was also a bit melodic said *L'eyla Ul'eyla*, meaning, superb, superb. During the Shacharit service, Reb Yehoshua especially showed his strength in the prayers called *Yotzrot*, and in the *Piyut*, a poem, called *Brach Dodi*. When he reached the Hallel, he poured out his heart to G-d. Each line had a special rhythm, a certain musical meter. When he reached the passage *Yisrael B'Tach Bashem*, Israel trust in G-d, he would twist it and enhance it with the manipulation of his voice, with various innuendos and shadings. In some of these passages, Reb Yehoshua and his sons sang in harmony. Chaim Leib and Shmuel Tzvi sang the bass, Nachum Uri and Shlomo Yeshayah were the baritones and the two youngest, Yose'leh and I sang the high notes. Above them, however, was our father, Reb Yehoshua.

After the Torah reading, Reb Yehoshua sang a special melody for the paragraph called *Ya eyli*, You are my G-d. It was in the form of a march as if we were marching toward G-d. Before the Musaf, the additional service, Reb Yehoshua put on a white gown for the singing of *Tefilat Tal*, the prayer for dew. He introduced this prayer by saying, "I am trying to express the secret existence of our people." And by this he actually prayed for dew for the land of Israel rather than in the Carpathian Mountains, which did not count on this source of water for the crops. In Israel, this was the date that the dry season usually began.

Reb Yehoshua continued with the passage that asks for a year of blessing and not curse, of life and not death, of bounty and not hunger. His voice echoed through the Synagogue and it was heard all over. Twice a year, Reb Yehoshua would sing this special melody – on Pesach, the prayer of Tal, for dew, and on *Shmini Atzeret*, for *Geshem*, the rain. At the end of the service, each person came up to Reb Yehoshua to shake his hand and tell him their delight in

The Jewish cemetery in Bilke - 1996

his singing of the prayers.

It was noon. The Jews were just leaving the Synagogue. The Gentiles were going about their holiday business. Suddenly, the bells of the church began to ring. The town was filled with the echo of the bells. Everyone was stunned. People looked up to the church tower and asked, "What is happening?" Because everyone, Jew as well as Gentile, knew that according to the legend, the bells were supposed to be in Rome. Not for three more days, at the end of Easter week, were they supposed to return to Bilke.

The people of the town ran towards the church where the bells continued to ring wildly. The ringing was not gentle and melodious, but rather a wild urgent cacophony, as if the devil himself was in the bell tower. The young, the elderly, everyone crowded around the front of the church. There was a sense of fright, and also anger among the Gentiles.

Abruptly, the ringing stopped. The sexton of the church, accompanied by several of the Gentiles, climbed up into the tower. There they found Yitzchak Friedman, the insane one. They brought him down roughly. When the crowd saw who it was, hate welled up in them. They were ready, on the spot to lynch the offender. The *Goyim*, the Gentiles, were expressing the hatred of generations, which had accumulated in their hearts. They began to beat Yitzchak.

Suddenly, shouts of the police were heard: "Keep away! Keep away!" They broke through the mob and rescued Yitzchak, who by now was nearly beaten to death. But he still had the strength to shout in a clear voice, "I am a Jew! You see the bells of the church did not fly to Rome!" Having shouted this with his last bit of strength, he fell to the ground.

This incident shook up all the inhabitants of Bilke. The Gentiles were totally confused. The Jews feared that this incident would cause even more hatred for them than had been felt before. Who knew what the next day would bring upon them!

The holidays ended with no further incident. Everyone continued about their usual business as if the whole bizarre event had never happened. But the Jews of Bilke saw in Yitzchak the insane, something of a wonder. Who could evaluate a Jewish soul! Some asked and wondered. Those who pondered the happening a little deeper also asked, "Who knows?" Perhaps this Yitzchak is a *Gilgul Neshamah*, the reincarnation of a soul from a previous life, who had sinned and who had to do this act of Kiddush Hashem, the sanctification of the name of G-d, in order to redeem himself. This story was told to the young of Bilke year after year during the holiday of Passover.

Street scenes from Bilke in 1996

From Tranquility To Persecution

The Jewish community of Bilke was a mother city, a metropolis among Jews. Bilke was blessed with Torah, Jewish scholarship and enlightenment, fellowship and support of the fellow Jew. The Jews of Bilke conducted an orderly and organized community until the very end, until their deportation. It was a democratic Jewish society, which the non-Jews envied. Although there were differences of opinion and controversies for the sake of Heaven (and also not for the sake of Heaven), Jewish Bilke consisted of almost 2,000 souls with religious and social institutions which existed for almost 300 years. For many generations in our town, Jews were a vital spirit, while the voice of Torah, learning, and *tefilah*, prayer, echoed throughout the town.

The Great Synagogue was built at the beginning of the 20th century. As was customary in many communities in the Diaspora, so in Bilke too, the shul was built with massive thick walls, big and strong doors. It was almost a fortress. The purpose being, that G-d forbid, if trouble came, the Synagogue would serve as a temporary *miklat*, a refuge, until help came from the outside.

The inside of the beautiful and majestic Synagogue was painted in a multi-color facet, with Biblical decorations. The ceiling was quite high and was adorned with large copper chandeliers. The entire interior of the Synagogue created an aura of holiness and reverence. Everyone related to it as if it were a miniature replica of the Holy Temple in Jerusalem, facing east. An overflowing spirituality emanated to all those who took refuge in its shadow. Anyone who entered the *Mikdash M'at*, miniature Holy Temple, would tread in it with reverence and love. Even the local Gentiles were seized by fear and reverence as they walked near the Great Synagogue.

The shul also served the entire community of Bilke as a center for family and holiday celebrations year round, according to the Hebrew calendar. It was bustling with activity during happy occasions and during sadness. It represented the Jewish spiritual emotional identity and the continuous Jewish existence by instinct of the will to continuity. Hundreds of years of cultural, social, and religious creativity was encompassed in this holy structure, which enriched the Jewish soul. The building was the spiritual fortress from which the Jews of Bilke drew their strength of life. The heart and mind of the Jew beat there. This institution guarded the uniqueness of the Jewish community, deepened and enriched its roots and its tradition, which served as a guardian of our people. It was a very constructive tool bringing the Jews of Bilke closer to their Creator and to their people. It equipped them with healthy, rich, spiritual sustenance, which strengthened them against foreign influences and against despair in times of stress. It was where the Jewish community of Bilke was formulated and united, as we knew it prior to the Holocaust.

Our community was blessed over the generations with positive personalities who lived their lives according to our ancient Jewish tradition. Not only the Rabbi, the Shochet, the Cantor, and other scholars who excelled in the love of the Jewish people and Torah, but the merchants, the ordinary folks, the laborers, the artisans, the poor people, the ordinary multitude, did not stray from the golden path. The very holiness that surrounded the Jews of our community added to their strength and immunity so they were able to overcome the constant struggle of existence. The holiness was especially felt during holidays, festivals, and special days in the Jewish calendar.

Soon after the Hungarian conquest, harsh ordinances were decreed against the Jewish inhabitants. Under the reign of Admiral Miklos Horty, the Hungarians instituted racial laws against the Jews. Every Jew was required to wear a yellow badge, the Jewish Star of David on their outer garments. The branding of Jews with a special sign in Nazi occupied Europe was designed to distinguish them from the general population, and consequently isolate them and degrade them in the eyes of the non-Jews. The Jews were required to prepare the Star of David at their own expense.

On May 3, 1939, the Hungarian government legislated decrees, so-called *Jewish Laws*, patterned after the anti-Jewish *Nuremberg Laws*. Their aim was to curtail normal activities of the Jews, requiring them to get permission to travel from town to town, engage in trade, or practice a profession. Jews were no longer allowed to own properties. Many businesses were closed or transferred to non-Jews. Loss of livelihood, property, and civil rights marked the beginning of the harassment of Jews by the Hungarian authorities. Their radios were confiscated. The Jews were ordered to register at the town hall and present documents to prove their citizenship. Such laws encouraged open anti-Semitism, which led to violence against the Jews.

Reb Chaim Isaac Rosenbaum, the last president of the Bilker Jewish community, was ordered to present to the authorities a list of all Jews living in Bilke. This list served as a guide for the Hungarians in the subsequent treatment of the Jews of Bilke. They used it for deportations to the Ukraine, for the mobilization of males into forced labor units, and for all kinds of work the Bilker Jews had to perform for the town. Jewish teenagers were forced to serve in the *Levente*, the youth battalions, and finally, the list served to confirm the final expulsion of the remnant of Bilker Jews, which left Bilke *Judenrein*, purged of Jews.

The second great blow fell upon the Jews of Bilke in May 1940, when the Hungarians mobilized all Jewish males, ages 18 to 50, into *Munko Tabor*, the forced labor battalions. Hundreds of men; husbands, fathers, sons, brothers, cousins, and brothers-in-law were taken away to do forced labor under the command of the Hungarian Army. They were sent to the front lines in the Ukraine, Russia, Germany, Italy, and Hungary. They built fortifications and rail lines and dug tunnels and trenches.

Tens of thousands of Jews in the forced labor battalions died from hard labor, starvation, sickness, and frostbite. They were also victim to enemy actions, at the hands of the fanatically anti-Semitic Hungarian Fascist Cross Arrow units, as well as being murdered by German and Ukrainian anti-Semites. Many sons of Bilke perished. Among them were my two brothers – Chaim Leib and Nachum Uri. May G-d avenge their deaths. Some of the units remained in Hungary where they performed similar work. They too suffered from the brutality of the Hungarian officers and many times were in mortal danger. Their food was poor and meager. Many were sick and suffered from malnutrition. Most of these men died in faraway places because of the harsh conditions that existed there. Many families were left without livelihoods and struggled to make ends meet. Only a handful of the Jews in forced labor survived the war.

During the Hungarian occupation of Bilke, there were three young men who could not stand the Hungarian discrimination and persecution anymore. They decided to cross the border, to the other side of the Carpathian Mountains where the Russians were positioned in Galicia, which belonged to Poland previously. Poland was dismembered according to the infamous Molotov-Ribentrop Agreement. Russia occupied certain parts of Poland and the Germans occupied the rest.

Even though it was a very dangerous and risky undertaking, these three young men decided they had had enough of Hungarian anti-Semitism and Fascism and wanted to start a new life. They believed the Russian communist

УКРАЇНА

БІЛКІВСЬКА СІЛЬСЬКА РАДА НАРОДНИХ ДЕПУТАТІВ

295210 с. Білки Телефони: 4-12-86, 4-15-71

06.II.1996р. № 2200

На №

Д О В І Д К А

видана виконкомом Б!лк!вськоо! с!льсько! Ради в т!м, що на територ!! села до 1945 року/ встановлення Радянсько! влади/ проживало 1068 /одна тисяча ш!стдесят в!с!м / евре!в.

/Дан! Укра!нсько! Радянсько! енциклопед!!, 1969 р!к./

Голова Б!лк!всько!
с!льсько! Ради: Ю.Сенина

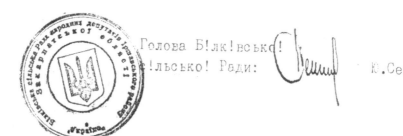

A translation of the above document from Ukraine: Dated November 6, 1996, Document No. 2200. Confirmation: The local municipality of the village of Bilke wishes to inform that prior to the year 1945, 1068 Jews resided in Bilke. These facts were taken from the 1969 Encyclopedia. Signed by Y. Cehnha, The Bilke Municipality chairman. (Author's note: This document does not count all the men who were sent to forced labor camps.)

regime stood for equal rights for all nations and people. They thought that they would be welcomed as heroes. We later found out the great suffering these Bilker boys went through. As they crossed the Russian lines they were caught, put on trial as spies of the enemy, and were sentenced to hard labor in the Russian Labor Camps. Even though the war was over in May 1945, the Russians kept the Bilker boys in their labor camps. Only in May 1947, when a new commander of Camp 222 was appointed, did their situation change. It seemed that this Jewish officer was observing the *yahrzeit*, a memorial day, for his brother. He was looking for Jewish prisoners to make a *minyan*, a quorum for a religious service. He found out about the Bilker boys. They participated in the minyan. Because of this, the officer helped them escape and cross the border into Rumania. From there, one of them made aliyah to Israel. The others settled in Canada. This experience of the Bilker young men proved again that there was a conspiracy of the European nations against the Jews during World War II.

The non-Jews of Bilke, who for generations had maintained outwardly cordial relations, showed their true faces when they realized that shedding Jewish blood was cheap. Overnight they changed their attitudes. All along they had coveted the property of the Jews, their way of life, and all that the Jews stood for. Many Gentiles helped the Hungarians enforce the anti-Jewish decrees. The leaders of the Jewish community learned of a special meeting of Bilke's non-Jewish representatives at which they approved the deportation of all Jews in Bilke because they knew that their reward would be great. The old hatred of Jews came to the forefront in all its ugliness.

The next blow came in August 1941, when an order was issued to deport all Jewish persons who could not certify their area citizenship. There were some families that could not prove their citizenship even though they lived in Bilke or in the area for generations, because in those days people did not keep documents and some got lost.

The Doft family was among those who could not prove their citizenship. My father, who was born in Poland, came to live in Ruthenia with his family in 1885. In 1918, when Ruthenia became a part of the Czech Republic, my father never applied for Czech citizenship, so when Hungary demanded proof, my father had none. In order to save ourselves from definite deportation, my mother and her 11 children, who where all born in Bilke, changed the family name to her maiden name, Lipschitz. My father went into hiding. Later on, the Hungarians deported all the Jews, whether they were citizens or not.

Jewish holy days were violated with special roundups and increased violence. In August 1941, two dozen families of Bilke were deported on Tisha B'Av, a fast day, on which both Temples in Jerusalem were destroyed. Approximately 50,000 stateless Jews from the Carpathians were deported across Polish borders where they fell into the hands of the Germans and the Ukrainian helpers. Among them were the families of Reb Meshulam Friedman, the scholarly teacher; Yeshayah and Mendel Kalech, the sons of Reb Leibush Kalech the Dayan and their families; Reb Itzik Yoel Bohm and family; Moshe Elazar and his family from Kolbasovo, and others.

The deportation of Jews from the Carpathian Mountains served as an experiment for handling the rest of Hungarian Jewry. In order to prevent panic and alarm throughout the rest of Hungary, a rumor was spread among the Jews that they were being repatriated to safe zones, due to the closeness of the Russian front as the Russians were just across the border.

The Hungarians knew what was in store for the Jews in the Ukrainian wilderness. The Hungarian support units, the Ukraine Volunteers and the German *Einsatzgruppen* (S.S. mobile killing units) perpetrated a terrible slaughter of the Carpathian Jews, among them about 100 Jews from Bilke, on August 27 - 28, 1941. The murderers lined up the Jewish families in Kamenets-Podolsk and machine gunned them with brutality, and buried them in mass graves. My father's brother, Yitzchak Doft and his entire family of eight, were among the deportees. Only two teenage boys, Avraham and Yaakov Hersh, escaped during the confusion of the massacre.

On March 18, 1944, the Germans took direct power over Hungary with the help of the Hungarian Fascists, who with great zeal, gave permission to Adolf Eichmann and his hangmen to organize the deportation of the Jews from the Carpathian Mountains and other areas. They were deported into ghettos first, then a few weeks later to the Valley of Weeping, to the largest slaughterhouse, to Auschwitz.

The Germans lured Admiral Horty, the Hungarian crown prince, to a meeting at Schloss Klessheim and arrested him. He was taken to the concentration camp, Buchenwald, where all the V.I.P.'s were kept. Eichmann, with his team, arrived in Budapest and organized the deportation.

In spite of the frightening news which reached the Jews of Bilke, the remnant of Bilker Jews and their families tried to observe the last holiday of Passover according to tradition. On the seventh day of Pesach 1944, the Hungarian authorities informed the Jews of Bilke that on the day after Passover, they must gather their elders, women, and children in the yard of the Great Synagogue. They were told to bring their allotted baggage, 50 kilograms for

This map shows Kamenets-Podolsk in the Ukraine, where the first deportees from Bilke and other towns in Ruthenia were massacred by the Germans, Hungarians, and Ukrainians. The numbers below the names represent the number of Jews murdered between July 17 and August 31, 1941.

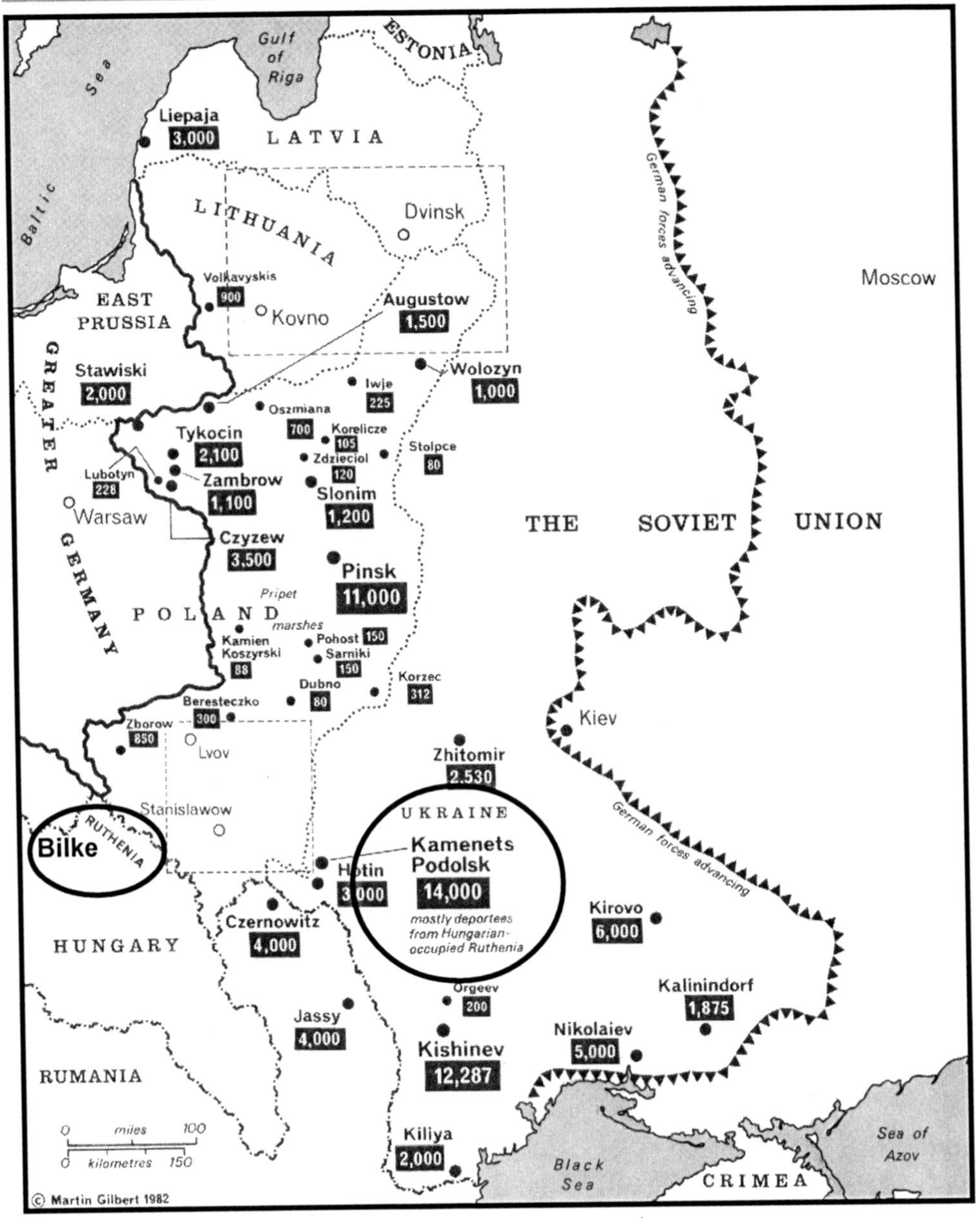

Reprinted from *McMillan Atlas Of The Holocaust*, © 1982, by Martin Gilbert, published by The Jewish Publication Society, with the permission of the publisher, The Jewish Publication Society.

> The entire holy Jewish community of Bilke, which had existed for 300 years, was erased completely in just a single day.

each person. All other property they were to leave behind – all that they had gained over the generations.

The bad news spread quickly among the Jews. Preparations were made to abandon Bilke. Feverish packing of a lifetime of precious items such as family pictures, prayer books, Bibles, and other valuables began. The Jews packed clothing, bedding, foods such as sugar, coffee, hard-boiled eggs, and wine for Kiddush. The leftover matzah from Passover was broken into small pieces and packed, too. All of these possessions were packed into backpacks, valises, and bags. All life's needs were capsuled into compact bundles. In addition, everything had to be reduced into small parcels to be carried to the cattle boxcars. The Hungarian police searched from house to house to make sure that all Jews had left before they sealed them.

The day after Passover, on April 15, 1944, about 1,500 Bilker Jews assembled with their baggage and families in the courtyard of the revered Great Synagogue. The Hungarian police stood there and called out the names of Jews from their lists, family after family. Then, with their guns outstretched, the police marched the Jews to the train station. Since most of the males ages 18 to 50 were already in labor camps, this march was difficult and took a long time with many elderly women and children. Each carried his or her own packages and one tried to help another in this march.

The Gentiles stood at the sides of the road leading to the train station and showed their great satisfaction with the expulsion of the Jews. They were waiting for the moment when they would be able to pillage our homes. We Jews became the victims of both the conquering Hungarians and the subjugated Ruthenians.

My sister Feige had acquired beautiful and expensive linens as a dowry for herself and also had two very expensive and stunning fur coats. There was a Gentile neighbor who came to my sister Feige to tailor all her dresses. Feige always thought she was a nice person. Before we were deported, Feige took her linens and fur coats to this Gentile woman for safe keeping with the understanding that when we returned, she would give back the items. She was so comforting and promised to keep them safe. Little did we know what would really happen. (After my sisters, Feige and Reise lived through the hell, they returned to Bilke to see if any of the family survived. When she approached the Gentile neighbor to whom she entrusted her dowry and the fur coats, the neighbor refused to return the items.)

One could see the great sorrow and pain in the eyes of the marching Jews; their grave worry about the destination awaiting them on their way into the unknown, and leaving their birthplace which they loved. At that moment, it reminded me of the story in Exodus, chapter 12, where there is a description of the Israelites leaving Egypt, but that was in a happy mood. Going down the main street of Bilke for the last time, we glanced at the Jewish homes, the shopping center, the market place, the fields with the beautiful trees that had just started to bloom.

This memorial plaque to remember the destroyed communities in Carpathia, including Bilke, is posted in the "Valley Of The Jewish Communities Of Europe" at Yad Vashem in Jerusalem.

After a march of about two hours, they reached the train station where boxcars awaited them. They were loaded, some 80 to 100 souls to a boxcar, along with their belongings. The Hungarian police and their local helpers, the Ruthenians, pushed the Jews into boxcars and urged them to hurry because they wanted to get rid of this human cargo as fast as possible.

The entire holy Jewish community of Bilke, which had existed for 300 years, was erased completely in just a single day.

Since the Hungarians occupied my hometown, Bilke, and caused our community and my family so much grief, I hated them with a passion. Now that we were being uprooted and shipped to the ghetto, I hated them even more. Three transports of trains carried the Bilker Jews to the Berehovo Ghetto, about 40 miles away. In Carpathia, they established the first ghettos and from there the first transports were sent to Auschwitz.

Until this day, I hate the Hungarians and cannot stand anything Hungarian. These people were devout anti-Semites from their roots, an uncultured people with a strange and profane language. I think of them as a gypsy tribe who took power in the heart of Europe and made my people suffer.

The Dismemberment Of Czechoslovakia

In September of 1938, the Czechoslovak Army mobilized to be ready to defend the country against a German assault. President Edward Bennesh, the Czech government, and the rest of the country were waiting for support from Europe's super powers, France and England, against Germany's claim to the Sudetenland, where there was a German-speaking population.

The Czech Army was demobilized when Neville Chamberlain, the Prime Minister of England, announced the Munich Pact, which compelled Czechoslovakia to surrender the territory to Hitler.

This policy by the French and the British was a turning point and a shift of power on the European continent, in favor of Germany. The declaration by Chamberlain that he brought peace in our time, was a terrible deception by the Germans, who were great masters at this. It was a very sad time for the Czech people and others all over the world who were stunned by the turn of events. Many people were angry and worried.

At the time, the Czech Republic had the best military equipment. The armed forces were in good shape. They thought they had an alliance with France and England and that these super powers would not let Czechoslovakia down. Instead they forced the Czechs to yield the Sudetenland to the Germans. In October 1938, the Germans took control of the territory, a mountainous region with excellent military defenses. The Czech Army, well equipped and well trained, could have resisted quite well, however, now that they were left without the support of the big powers, the country was left defenseless.

Having taken the Sudetenland did not satisfy Hitler; his appetite just grew. On March 15, 1939, at five in the morning, the Germans marched into Czechoslovakia. This gave Hitler one of the largest and best arms factories in Europe, the Skoda Works. This boosted the German military strength tremendously. The French and the British did not come to the aid of the Czech people, even though they had promised that if they cede the Sudetenland to Germany, Hitler would have no more claims to Czechoslovakia. The Czech people were betrayed once again. This classic appeasement policy of the super powers of the time, England, France, and Russia set the stage for Germany's appetite to conquer the rest of Europe. When England, France, and Russia realized what they had done, it was too late. World War II broke out, when at last, Britain and France declared war on Germany as Hitler attacked Poland.

The Jews of Bilke understood that the rise of Hitler to power was a grave development for them too, but they hoped that the wicked hand would never reach them in Bilke.

As Hitler dismembered the Czechoslovak Republic, he threw scraps of territory to those nations whose help he might need. To Hungary, he offered Ruthenia, the Carpathian Mountains, which they quickly accepted. This did not sit well with the local Ukrainian Nationalists, who on March 13, 1939, declared an independent Ruthenian Republic with its capital, Ushorod. Under immediate Hungarian attack, this Republic lasted only one day. The Hungarians quickly subdued the uprising of the local Ruthenians.

Bilke, in particular, was a hotbed of this movement and many young Ruthenians were marching in the streets, singing nationalistic songs, and shouting slogans, which the local population applauded.

In the Synagogues that night, the Jews of Bilke finished their evening prayers, and hurried home in advance of the nine o'clock curfew the local municipality had imposed on the town. Among them was the cobbler Reb Moshe Benyamin Klein, an officer of the *Beit Hamidrash*, the small Synagogue and of the *Chevra Kadisha*, the burial society. His piety and charity were well known. Between the blows of his hammer in his shop he would sing words of scripture and sayings of the Sages. He welcomed destitute wanderers to stay at his home. It was said, in fact, that his house was situated at the edge of Bilke so that wanderers would see it first. That very evening, Reb Moshe Benyamin had collected some coins in the Synagogue for a poor man who was staying at his house. While on his way home from the evening services, Reb Moshe Benyamin Klein became the first Jewish victim to fall in Bilke. He was shot in the head in the crossfire of the local militia and the

The house in Bilke that was Moshe Benyamin Klein's home. Photographed in 1996.

Hungarian occupying forces. This tragic incident was an indication of what the Jews of Bilke could expect.

On March 14,1939, the Hungarians occupied Ruthenia. The land of the Ruthenians was located in the central Carpathian Mountains. At various times, it had been under the control of Poland, Austro-Hungary, Czechoslovakia, Russia and now the Ukraine. The Hungarians declared martial law and night curfew. Cut off from the outside world and at the mercy of the Hungarian Fascists, we could only hope for help from heaven, which was not forthcoming. We learned quickly, how good neighbors of yesterday could turn overnight into today's preying wolves. The local non-Jewish population now showed their true colors.

The Hungarian persecution of the Jews came in stages and each stage was a greater blow than the previous one.

Part 3

Imprisoning The Jews

How long G-d will You endlessly forget me?
How long will You hide Your countenance from me?
How long will my enemy triumph over me?
(Psalm 13)

"The Jews are the eternal enemy of the German people, their destiny is annihilation. We have to annihilate every Jew we can lay our hands on without exception. If we do not succeed to destroy the biological foundations of the Jews, then some day the Jews will annihilate the German people."

...Heinrich Himmler, the Commander of the S.S., in the name of Adolf Hitler, stating the goal of the Final Solution.

Ghetto Berehovo (Beregszasz)

The Hungarians concentrated Jews from the entire vicinity into Ghetto Berehovo. Approximately 15,000 Jews were pressed into a very small area, into a brick factory. The area was sealed off with barbed wire and Hungarian guards. This factory, which had many structures, had been used to store bricks, consisted of nothing more than a roof with poles at the corners, and a few supporting columns. It had no walls, no doors, and no windows. It was exposed to the cold, wind, and rain.

The Jews of Bilke were placed in such a structure. Each shed held many families; each family was allocated a small area according to the number of its members. People were lined up on both sides of the barracks.

The first thing each family did was to roam the ghetto and bring bricks to make a kind of wall around the sides of the shed to protect themselves from the elements. Inside, they divided their area from the neighbors by hanging blankets over ropes to provide as much privacy as possible. They spread their bedding on the floor before going to sleep. The members of each family slept close together because the space allotted to each was very limited. The ghetto was a convenient holding pen until a decision could be made as to what to do next with the Jews. With the Jews arriving by the hour from the surrounding villages, as well as from Berehovo itself, the fenced in and guarded population of the brick factory soon stood at 15,000.

In the ghetto, the Bilker Jews made efforts to organize themselves and to conduct their lives in this new situation. Services were held three times a day inside their structure at the area of Rabbi Naftali Tzvi Weiss and Reb Yehoshua Doft. Each family had to improvise their own meals. They tried to preserve and retain the food products they brought with them, not knowing how long this would last.

Outside the structures, in the field, the men put together a few stones and bricks and made a makeshift cooking place. They gathered branches and pieces of wood to make a fire for cooking. Each woman tried to improvise

This map shows the Jewish population in the ghettos and the deportation routes when the Jews were sent to Auschwitz. Moshe Avital's hometown, Bilke, is shown in Ruthenia. His family was transported from Ghetto Beregszasz to Auschwitz.

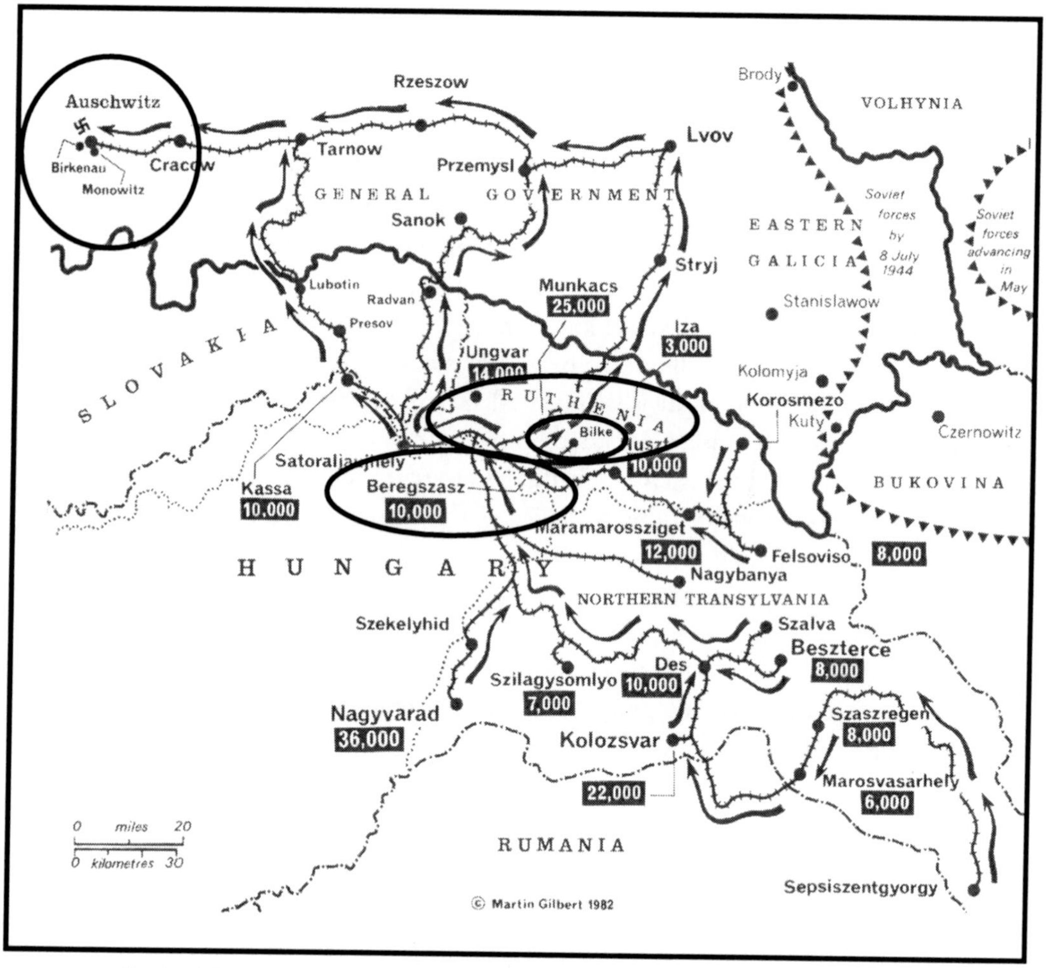

Reprinted from *McMillan Atlas Of The Holocaust*, © 1982, by Martin Gilbert, published by The Jewish Publication Society, with the permission of the publisher, The Jewish Publication Society.

and show her expertise in cooking. Once a day, the ghetto management provided soup, but many did not eat it since there was a question whether it was kosher, so only the small portions of bread which were provided was eaten. My mother, Pearl Doft, made all kinds of goodies from the matzah pieces we brought with us from home, which lasted a few weeks.

The men were ordered to shave their beards and payot. Only Rabbi Naftali Tzvi Weiss and my father, Reb Yehoshua Doft, of Bilke did not shave their beards. They wrapped their beards with kerchiefs in order to hide them from the enemy.

A handful of Jews from Bilke who lived in one of the suburbs near the forest made an attempt to hide in a cave. After a few weeks, they surrendered to the police and they were shipped to the ghetto. Also, a handful of elderly and critically ill, as well as one woman who was about to give birth, remained for a short while in Bilke. Even they were finally brought to the ghetto.

The last one to be shipped to Ghetto Berehovo was the pharmacist, who was not known to be Jewish, since he never had social or religious contact with the Jewish community. It seemed the Hungarians discovered his real identity, that he was also a Jew.

Also Miriam, the daughter of Isaac Hersh Teichman, the milkman, who years ago, had married a non-Jew, was shipped to the ghetto with her three boys. As she entered the ghetto, the Jews of Bilke did not believe their eyes when they saw them escorted by the Hungarian police. Being married to a Gentile did not help her. She told the Bilker Jews that her husband did not try to save them. It was said that her husband was actually very pleased to get rid of her since he had had enough of the Jews.

One Jewish woman from Bilke lost her mind. She was running around the ghetto yelling, "Save yourselves! Escape! Leave this place." Some people thought that perhaps she was not mad after all. Perhaps she saw what was going to happen. A number of very sick people were taken from the ghetto to the town's hospital. Among them was my sister Leah's small boy, Eliezer. Just a day before the deportation from Berehovo to Auschwitz, all the sick were returned to the ghetto.

Hygienic conditions in the ghetto were a big problem with thousands of people concentrated in a crowded area without shower facilities, without sewers. However, since the Jews always kept clean as part of their religion and culture, they made extraordinary efforts to keep clean and healthy. In order for someone to take a shower or a bath, one had to heat water on the makeshift stove outside in the field. From there, water was carried into the barracks in pails, inside the specific area where that family was placed, and the family members helped with this bath.

The Germans and Hungarians ordered the Jews to establish *Judenraete*, Jewish Councils of Elders, in each ghetto. The members of the Jewish Councils were held responsible for the execution of all instructions. From the Nazi point of view, these councils were to receive and implement their orders. They were created to serve the German and Hungarian purposes, helping them to carry out their diabolical plans. From the Jewish point of view, they assumed the leadership in the ghettos and struggled to ameliorate conditions.

Not all Jewish leaders cooperated. Because of their resistance, they lost their lives right from the beginning. Some of the Jewish elders displayed great courage and loyalty to the Jewish people. There were some who thought that perhaps they could serve as a shield for their people and tried to minimize the suffering. However, they found out very quickly that the Germans and Hungarians intended to exploit them and in time, they murdered most of them.

A half century later, we know more and understand the Judenraete, Jewish Councils of Elders phenomenon, thanks to the diary of Adam Chernikow, the head of the Judenraete in Ghetto Warsaw, and the reasoning for their participation. We learned after the Shoah that many of them committed suicide and almost none survived the Holocaust. Today, the one dimensional Judenraete stereotype, as collaborators with the Germans, or traitors to the Jewish people, is no longer condemned. This was an opinion that was widespread in the early years after the Holocaust. Unfortunately, at the time, they did not understand that the Germans and Hungarians used them as tools against their own people.

Some historians think the Judenraete helped the Germans and Hungarians in their devilish plans. There are other historians such as Jacob Rabinson, who think the opposite. In his book *Heakov Lemishor*, The Rugged Shall Be Made Level, he proves that in many of the areas in the Soviet Union where there was no Jewish organized leadership and no Jewish institutions because of the communist's policy before the war, that after the German occupation of these areas and the forming of ghettos, all the Jews were immediately annihilated because there was no official Jewish leadership. On the contrary, for instance in Lodz, the first large Jewish ghetto in Poland, whose head was Chaim Rumkovsky and who was a known German collaborator, more Jews survived proportionately.

It is my opinion that under any circumstances, turning over Jews by Jews to be annihilated, is a sin that has no forgiveness and no atonement.

Unfortunately, most of the Jewish leaders in the Judenraete miscalculated, because they thought that by cooperating with the Germans and their collaborators, they would be able to save Jews, or at least to contain the annihilation until outside help would arrive. We now know that the Germans used them cynically because in the long run, it helped them to accelerate the killings.

The ghetto management used certain people for various chores and work. They even sent some groups into the town of Berehovo, Beregszasz, to work for the municipality. This activity opened the way for smuggling food and other articles, such as money, silver, and gold.

One morning it was announced by the ghetto officials that all monies, jewelry, gold, etc., must be given to the authorities. The Hungarians designated Jews from the ghetto, who made their rounds in the barracks, and they demanded all valuables. They placed buckets in front of the barracks where one had to place his valuables such as money, watches, marriage rings, earrings, bracelets, necklaces, coins, gold and silver. It was announced that whoever disobeyed would be shot. The police threatened they would search.

Before we left Bilke, my family decided to hide our valuables by sewing them into our garments. When the decrees were made to give the Hungarians everything, my father, may G-d avenge his death, instructed all of us to take out the valuables and give them to the authorities. I, as a young boy, could not stand this injustice and yielding to the Gentiles, rebelled against my father, may he rest in peace. I ran away from the barrack and hid in the fields until the trouble passed. Actually, I did the right thing. With this money, we were able to buy food on the black market, which sustained us for another few weeks. I lost my childhood very quickly. I felt that overnight I became an adult, without any transition.

All the valuables that the Hungarians confiscated from the Jews in the ghetto are kept until this day in the basement treasury of the Hungarian National Bank. Some say that with the valuables the Hungarians robbed from the Jews, they paid off war reparations which were levied against them by the Allies, and that a good portion of the valuables serve now as the Hungarian gold reserve.

One day, Yitzchak Reisman, a Bilker, arrived for a visit in the ghetto. He was stationed with his labor unit in Budapest. The Hungarian Army allowed him to visit his family in the ghetto because he claimed that his mother, Rachel, was very sick. The townspeople welcomed him with great love and affection. He was looked upon as if he came from a different world. He was asked all kinds of questions as if he had the answers. Many wanted to know if he had seen any of their loved ones. Each bit of good news and good humor brought hope and life for the poor people in the ghetto.

The Jews of Bilke and the rest of the Jews in Ghetto Berehovo did not read the writing on the wall. Their moods swung from fear of death to the hope for life. They were in the midst of a desperate struggle under impossible conditions, on a personal and community level. They coped by trying to put out of their minds the worst that might happen. Under the circumstances, the Jewish individual was alone, abandoned, and exposed to the cruel enemy. This situation was one of the main reasons and causes that assisted the murderers of the Jews, the Hungarians, the Germans, and their collaborators in their work of destruction of the Jews. The Jews did everything in order to delay their end, except uprising and rebellion. In the brick factory, which the Hungarians converted into the ghetto, the Jews retained their humanity and dignity in an inhuman atmosphere. Black clouds were looming over the ghetto, which forebode disaster. We sensed that something, over which we had no control, was about to happen.

Like Job, the Jews of Bilke, as the rest of European Jewry, did not believe the tragic news which came from various sources. Whoever relayed the horrors was shouted down, that he was spreading fear and despair, that he saw only darkness because it was irrational. What human being would take thousands of innocent women, children, and men and kill them, make them disappear from this world? How could such a terrible thing happen in the 20th century? However, in spite of all the rumors, and all the terrible things they saw, there was no crying and no panic.

The ghettoization of the Carpathian Jews was the first step in an elaborate plan laid out by Adolf Eichmann and his team. In the ghetto, everyone hoped that Nazi defeat was imminent and that the remnant of European Jewry would be spared the Nazi hatchet and that the Nazi war machine would be crushed.

The frontline was collapsing in retreat. But to the Germans and Hungarians, the deportation of the last vestige of Jews in Central Europe became a top priority. No one could believe that in the last stages of the war, the last remnant of Jews would be in peril. The heinous plan of the Nazis challenged the race against time. As part of their last stand, the plan for deportation was intensified. The Germans pursued their enormous crimes to the bitter end. The unknown and unbelievable fate of tyranny and extermination ironically was just a few months away from liberation.

Mikor, honnan, hányan?

Íme a lista:

V. 14.	Nyíregyháza	3200
V. 14.	Munkács	3169
V. 16.	Kassa	[illegible]
V. 16.	Beregszász	3818
[illegible]	Máramarossziget	3007
V. 16.	Munkács	3629
V. 16.	Kassa	3629
V. 17.	Kassa	3352
V. 17.	Ungvár	3455
V. 17.	Ökörmező	3052
V. 17.	Munkács	3306
V. 18.	Máramarossziget	[illegible]
V. 18.	Beregszász	3569
[illegible]	Sátoraljaújhely	[illegible]
V. 18.	Munkács	3025
V. 19.	Felsővisó	3032
V. 19.	Mátészalka	3299
V. 19.	Szatmárnémeti	3060
V. 19.	Munkács	3222
V. 20.	Máramarossziget	3104
[illegible]	Nagyszőllős	3458
V. 20.	Munkács	3026
V. 21.	Felsővisó	3013
V. 21.	Nyíregyháza	3274
V. 21.	Sátoraljaújhely	3290
V. 21.	Munkács	2861
V. 22.	Máramarossziget	3490
V. 22.	Ungvár	3335
V. 22.	Szatmárnémeti	3300
V. 22.	Mátészalka	3298
V. 23.	Felsővisó	3023
V. 23.	Nyíregyháza	3272
V. 23.	Munkács	3269
V. 23.	Nagyvárad	[illegible]
V. 24.	Beregszász	2602
V. 24.	Kassa	[illegible]
V. 24.	Huszt	3328
V. 24.	Munkács	3080
V. 25.	Ungvár	3334
V. 25.	Nagyvárad	3148
V. 25.	Kolozsvár	3130
V. 25.	Aknaszlatina	3317
V. 25.	Felsővisó	3006
V. 26.	Huszt	3249
V. 26.	Szatmárnémeti	3336
V. 27.	Sátoraljaújhely	3325
V. 27.	Nagyszőllős	3415
V. 27.	Nyíregyháza	2708
V. 27.	Ungvár	2988
V. 27.	Marosvásárhely	3183
V. 28.	Técső	2208
V. 28.	Dés	3150
V. 28.	Nagyvárad	[illegible]
V. 29.	Beregszász	860
[illegible]	[illegible]	[illegible]
V. 29.	Kolozsvár	3417
[illegible]	Szatmárnémeti	[illegible]
[illegible]	[illegible]	[illegible]
[illegible]	Kisvárda	3475
V. 30.	Marosvásárhely	3203
V. 30.	Nagyvárad	3187
V. 30.	Szatmárnémeti	3300
V. 31.	Ungvár	3036
V. 31.	Kolozsvár	3270
V. 31.	Nagybánya	3073
V. 31.	Szilágysomlyó	3106
VI. 1.	Mátészalka	3299

VI. 1.	Kisvárda	3421
VI. 1.	Nagyvárad	3059
VI. 1.	Szatmárnémeti	2615
VI. 2.	Huszt	2396
VI. 2.	Beszterce	3106
VI. 2.	Kolozsvár	3100
VI. 3.	Nagyszőllős	2967
VI. 3.	Kassa	2499
VI. 3.	Nagyvárad	2972
VI. 3.	Szilágysomlyó	3161
VI. 4.	Szászrégen	3149
VI. 4.	Sátoraljaújhely	2567
VI. 5.	Nagyvárad	2527
VI. 5.	Mátészalka	3100
VI. 5.	Nyíregyháza	2253
VI. 5.	Nagybánya	2844
VI. 6.	Huszt	1852
VI. 6.	Dés	3160
VI. 6.	Beszterce	2875
VI. 6.	Szilágysomlyó	1584
VI. 8.	Dés	1364
VI. 8.	Kolozsvár	[illegible]
[illegible] 8.	Marosvásárhely	1163
VI. 9.	Kolozsvár	1447
VI. 11	Maklár	2794
VI. 12.	Diósgyőr	2675
VI. 12.	Balassagyarmat	2810
VI. 12.	Diósgyőr	2941
VI. 12.	Érsekújvár	2899
VI. 12.	Diósgyőr	3051
VI. 13.	Hatvan	2961
VI. 13.	Komárom	2790
VI. 13.	Salgótarján	2310
VI. 13.	Miskolc-Diósgyőr	3968
VI. 13.	Balassagyarmat	1867
VI. 15.	Léva	2678
VI. 15.	Miskolc	2829
VI. 15	Érsekújvár	1980
VI. 16.	Győr	2985
VI. 16.	Komárom	2673
VI. 16.	Dunaszerdahely	2969
VI. 25.	Debrecen	2286
VI. 26.	Szeged	3199
VI. 27.	Debrecen	3842
VI. 27.	Kecskemét	2642
VI. 27.	Nagyvárad	2819
VI. 27.	Békéscsaba	3118
VI. 28.	Bácsalmás	2737
VI. 29.	Kecskemét	790
VI. 29.	Szolnok	2038
VI. 29.	Debrecen	3026
VII. 5.	Sárvár	3105
VII. 5.	Szombathely	3103
VII. 6.	Kaposvár	3050
VII. 6.	Pécs	3100
VII. 6.	Kaposvár	2066
VII. 7.	Sopron	3077
VII. 7.	Pápa	2793
VII. 7	Paks	[illegible]
[illegible]	Monor	[illegible]
[illegible]	[illegible]	[illegible]
VII 7.	Sárvár	[illegible]
VII. 8.	Pécs	2523
VII. 8.	Óbuda	2997
VII. 9.	Monor	[illegible]
VII. 9.	Óbuda	3072
VII. 9.	Budakalász	3072
VII. 9.	Monor	3079
VII. 9.	Békásmegyer	1924
VII. 20.	Rákoscsaba	[illegible]

Összesen: 137 vonat, 401 439 ember!

A Hungarian document listing the various deportation transports from Carpathia to Auschwitz, the dates, how many people, and from which ghetto. The four brackets show the transports from Ghetto Berehovo, Beregszasz, the ghetto in which the Jews of Bilke were incarcerated.

These men are Jews from Bilke, upon arrival at Auschwitz. They are dressed in their best Shabbat clothing with the yellow Star of David on their left chest. Front right is Meyer Berger. Next to him is Samuel Heisler, both distinguished Jewish men from Bilke. Below is Zoltan Friedman and Jacob Berger, Meyer's brother.

A special transportation conference was held in Vienna by the Germans and Hungarians on May 4-6, 1944. A decision was made to begin the deportation of the Carpathian Jews on May 15, 1944, and to carry it out by means of four trainloads daily via Carpatho-Ruthenia, Kassa (in Slovakia), Muzyna (on the Polish border), Tarnaw (Galicia), and Cracow, Poland. Each train had 45 boxcars. Between 80 to 100 human beings were crammed into each boxcar. In Auschwitz, there was a daily arrival of 14,000 Jewish victims.

A few weeks later, Ghetto Berehovo was emptied in a few transports of about 2,500 people each. By the end of May 1944, all the Carpathian Jews were on their way to the slaughterhouse, Auschwitz, in Poland.

On The Way To Auschwitz

At the beginning of the Hebrew month of *Sivan* 5704, (May 1944), on the eve of the holiday of Shavuot, a rumor was spread in the ghetto that the Jews of Bilke, and then the rest of the ghetto Jews, would be moved to a more secure place because the Soviet Army was advancing and was very near the area. Some Jews believed this story and thought redemption was very near. However, there were others who knew that the fate of the Jews had been tragically decided. The next day, the Hungarians began to load the Bilker Jews into boxcars for their trip to the unknown... on their way to Auschwitz.

On May 15, 1944, a freight train consisting of 45 boxcars, crowded with approximately 3,000 Jewish souls, left the brick factory compound in Berehovo. The entire holy community of the Bilker Jews who were still alive was in this transport. In each boxcar, the Hungarians loaded 80 to 100 souls with their few belongings, to which they still clung. Hungarian police and military guarded the important train and accompanied it to the railroad station at Kosice, *Kassa* in Hungarian. This was a very important rail juncture on the Czechoslovak frontier where the train was transferred to the S.S. henchmen, the Nazi units who were known for their cruelty. The door was opened. A German officer, accompanied by a Hungarian, announced that from this moment on they were under the authority of the Germany Army. The doors were closed again and hermetically sealed.

After days on our hellish journey, the train stopped again. The train stopped at a number of stations and after a few days it stopped at the huge railroad station at Cracow, Poland. It was terribly crowded in the boxcar and it was impossible to lie down. We took turns sitting down,

As the Hungarian Jews disembarked in Auschwitz from the cattle cars, they were ordered to line up on the ramp, men on one side, and women and children on the other side for final selection. The officer standing on the right side appears to be Dr. Josef Mengele. He decided who would die immediately and who would live in the meantime. The concentration camp is in the background.

a few at a time. The air was very stuffy and it was hard to breathe. The water in the container was gone and we felt a terrible thirst. The receptacle was now overflowing with human excrement. During the day, the heat was unbearable and during the night, it was quite chilly. Whatever food we took with us was eaten up on the first day of the journey. People were very hungry. The elderly and the children suffered the most from the inhuman conditions. We continued our journey.

In the boxcar where my family and I were located, there were a few other families from Bilke. Many of them were thinking aloud, expressing their fears of what one could expect outside the boxcars.

My father, may G-d avenge his death, confessed before our family and before our townspeople by saying the following, "I had 11 children. One of them was smart or wise, who foresaw what would happen." He was referring to our brother, Shmuel Tzvi, of blessed memory, who was a pioneer of Jewish youth in Bilke. He made aliyah to the Land of Israel in 1937, when most people in Bilke looked at him as if he were mad. Even though my parents and family were against him making aliyah, in retrospect, they were proud of him.

From Cracow, the train continued to what would become our hell. I don't know how we managed to survive the hellish journey nor do I remember exactly how many days passed since we left Ghetto Berehovo, maybe five or six. The train had barely stopped when the gates of hell opened up for us. Someone next to the little window in the boxcar said that the sign at the station said Auschwitz. No one had ever heard that name.

The doors of the boxcars suddenly opened with screams, beatings, pushing and shoving by the S.S., who spoke a strange language which most of us could not understand. All of us were forced to disembark. We were bewildered. We did not know where we would end up. We suddenly realized that we arrived in a very strange place. We saw some odd-looking people dressed in striped clothing like a coat of many colors. We were now in Auschwitz, the largest and most sophisticated slaughterhouse of the Germans in all of Europe.

German S.S. men with hunting dogs shouted, "*Schnell, Schnell*, everybody out, get out. Everyone out of the wagon." We hurriedly jumped off the wagon; we tried to take our little bundles that we took with us from the ghetto, but we were ordered to leave everything in the boxcar. Until this day I can hear the shouts of our arrival in Auschwitz. Every few steps S.S. men were stationed with ferocious dogs barking wildly and with submachine guns trained on us.

An S.S. officer came and gave an order: "Men to the left! Women and children to the right!" This was the moment when I parted from my dear mother, my five sisters, and their children. I saw them disappearing into the crowd. My father, my brother Joseph, and I remained together for a few moments before an order was given to form rows of fives.

Rudolf Hoess, the Commandant of Auschwitz, received orders from Heinrich Himmler, the Commander of the S.S., in the name of Adolf Hitler, to execute the Final Solution.

S.S. guards and officers directing Jews to their destiny.

Arrival and Selection in Auschwitz

Hoess added the following statement: "The Jews are the eternal enemy of the German people, their destiny is annihilation. We have to annihilate every Jew we can lay our hands on without exception. If we do not succeed to destroy the biological foundations of the Jews, then some day the Jews will annihilate the German people."

On May 10, 1933, in the Opera Square of Berlin, the Germans burned books by Jewish authors. Heinrich Heine said, "Where one burns books, one will, in the end, burn people."

Tired, broken up, weak, and frightened, we arrived at a ramp where the demon Mengele stood and conducted the selection. He was the top S.S. medical officer at Auschwitz. He forcefully separated the dear and loved ones. The women, children, elderly, the martyrs, he sent directly into the gas chambers, into the kingdom of death. Those who appeared to Mengele as young and able-bodied to work were directed to the other side, into the camp. The movement or signal of the oppressor Mengele's hand decided the fate of the Jews of Bilke, who would live or who would die. Those who were not annihilated immediately were destined to a long tortured process, which most of the time ended in death or murder.

The day had 12 hours, the night had 700 minutes. Each minute had 60 seconds. Each second was filled with suffering and sickness. The minutes looked like eternity. It was a tangle of life and death, of fear and hope, of despair and will to live. One could not know what a new day or another moment would bring. From the first moment of encounter with the camps, with the movement of a finger, a free, normal human being lost everything – his identification, his name, his social position, his profession, his habits, his home, his property, and his family. In one moment, his whole world turned upside down.

When I stood before him, I saw that he hesitated for a moment where to send me. Suddenly, he gave a signal for me to go to the right, together with my dear brother, Joseph, may G-d avenge his death. This was the last time I saw my father, my mother, my sister Leah and her five small children, and my sister Sarah, with her small daughter, and the other Jews of Bilke with whom I had lived all my life. At that time, I did not know that my three other sisters, Feige, Mani (Miriam) and Reise went to forced labor. We had no time even to say good-bye. At that time, we did not know which side was which or what it meant. Which was for slave labor and which was a death sentence.

In the great confusion, as we disembarked from the boxcars, we saw the military men in grey S.S. uniforms. There were guards in black uniforms, made up of the units of various European nationalities that volunteered to take part in the annihilation effort against European Jewry, their sole enemies. Also, Jewish prisoners from Auschwitz and non-Jews in a peculiar uniform, like a shirt of many colors, were also there. Their job was to gather the valises and all the items the Jews abandoned in the boxcars and on the ramps by the order of the S.S., and load them on wagons and trucks for assortment. Little did we know that a few hours later, we too would be turned into the same kind of queer creatures with shaved heads.

Those of us who were chosen for forced labor and slavery were directed into a huge barrack for disinfection. We were ordered to strip our clothes and throw them on a pile. There was already a great heap of suits, coats, shoes, jackets, shirts, underwear, etc. The S.S. men were in this barrack to see to it that everything was done to the last detail. We followed orders like robots, our senses blunted. We felt as though we were on a strange planet. We were ordered into the next large room where there were a number of barbers; first they shaved the hair off our entire body from head to toe. When the head was shaved, they left in the middle a dividing stripe down the middle of the head. That was the mark of a concentration camp prisoner. There we were forced to immerse ourselves in some kind of disinfectant, which had a horrible odor. We were led into another large room that was a shower house. As we entered, we were not sure what would come out of the shower heads, water or gas. As the

The person standing in the striped uniform in the lower left corner was a veteran prisoner from the "Canada Brigade." His job was to collect the belongings and baggage that the Jews were forced to leave. The baggage was later sorted and shipped to Germany.

Rabbi Naftali Tzvi Weiss (left), the Bilker Rabbi, was photographed by the S.S. upon his arrival to Auschwitz. One can see the deep sadness in his eyes. The S.S. picked out great personalities to photograph.

water came down on us, we were greatly relieved. They provided us with striped prisoner clothes, and wooden shoes, something like wooden slippers, but these wooden shoes caused a lot of pain and constant problems. The size of the clothing was determined by the distributor's whim. The size I was given was too big for me. Later I exchanged it with a taller person who was given clothing that was too small for him.

Each one of us received a number. My number was A-13740. We were from then on identified by our number, no longer by name. My name was eradicated. Here we lost our names for the first time in our lives. The name which accompanied us all our lives was no longer a means of identification. You became a number among many numbers. You became only a part of many, only like a crumb. The entire group lost its quality and character. After we got dressed in the prisoner's clothes, my brother Joseph and I looked at each other and cried. We did not recognize one another. We had lost our Jewish looks and appearance. Each nationality had to carry a triangle of cloth on the chest of his camp uniform indicating that he was a political prisoner. We Jews had a yellow triangle. The green triangle indicated a common criminal.

We, a few hundred people, were then pushed into a barrack that had, inside on both sides, compartments built of wood. These shelves were a few stories high. These were the so-called beds on which eight people had to lie. Each compartment was so narrow that if someone wanted to turn, the entire group had to get up, otherwise it was impossible. This problem, of course, caused much friction. These beds gave the prisoners a bit of rest, but not any relaxation. It was as if whoever survived the day, was only to be stored for the night in these compartments.

In the barrack where my brother Joseph, may G-d avenge his death, and I were placed, there were only a handful of Jews from Bilke. In the great confusion, those of the Bilker Jews who were directed to go to slave labor were dispersed into various barracks.

A typical routine for the day was as follows. We were awakened at 5:00 a.m. with screams and whistles and beatings. We had to run to the so-called latrines, washrooms. Each morning this huge crowd ran at once into the washrooms and it was impossible for anyone to get near a faucet of water. The latrine was a giant-sized long building that served as a public outhouse for the inmates. On one side was a row of faucets of cold water for washing. On the other side were the so-called bathrooms, which were actually just holes in the ground.

A half-hour later, we had the morning *apell,* roll call. Each barrack lined up five people across in front of the barrack in long lines. We were told the tall people should stand in the back row, and the short people in front of them. This lineup made it easier for the Germans to see each face. These lineups were mostly a time of torture for us. Not only did we have to stand in the rain, cold, snow, and wind, but also it served for all kinds of cruel punishments.

The *Blockaeltste*, the barracks commander, (usually a German criminal who was also a prisoner), and the *Kapos*, (mostly non-Jews, or Jewish prisoners who turned against their own), stood in front of the units. They counted and recounted the prisoners to be sure that all were present. These prisoners ran the barracks with an iron fist. It was like when a slave becomes a king. When the S.S. entourage arrived with the camp commander, the *Lageraeltse*, the prisoner commander, jumped to attention and roared the command, "Attention!" All the units jumped to attention. Nobody dared move because we knew what would happen to us if we did. The camp commander, who himself was a prisoner, reported to the S.S. officer a detailed report of how many prisoners were present, how many were in the infirmaries, how many at work, and how many died during the night. Then the S.S. officer walked around the rows and checked and counted. At these roll calls, we suffered a great deal. The Kapos and Blockaeltste utilized the time for all kinds of drills. They shouted *achtung*, attention, *rue*, at ease or *mutzen ab*, caps down or caps up. We were hungry and tired and weak and they tortured us.

After roll call, breakfast, which consisted of one small bowl with black coffee for every five people, was served. There were always frictions and fights.

The concentration camps were surrounded by a double barbed wire fence – one was electrified.

The one who drank first was always asked not to drink too much so that something would be left for the others. The last of the five was sometimes left with nothing because his other four inmates finished it all.

Then all the units marched to their designated jobs. Each prisoner had to work. If a prisoner was ill, his fate was sealed and he was selected to die. At noon, we stopped working for about half an hour. They brought the food, which consisted of soup, to the place where we worked. Each person lined up in front of a huge kettle and was given a small bowl of soup. This soup consisted mostly of colored water. If you were lucky, you would find in your soup a piece of carrot or cauliflower, which was like a treasure. There were no spoons, so we had to drink and eat the soup or the coffee, directly from the bowls. The struggle for survival was fierce and our morale low. My brother Joseph and I gave each other moral support. We helped each other every step of the way. We made sure that at the roll call, we always stood in the same row of five.

We were in Auschwitz only two weeks, but it seemed an eternity. So much happened in those two weeks. We became completely different creatures. We thought about our parents, our sisters, and their small children. We had no idea what happened to them. We heard all kinds of rumors, but we did not want to believe them. Our Jewish moral way, our upbringing, could not allow us to think of such horrible things.

After this break, we returned to our slavery. At night, we returned to the camp. The guards were German, Ukrainian, Latvian, Croat, Muslims from Yugoslavia, and other nationalities who volunteered for this work. They marched along side us with their guns drawn. If anyone took just one step out of line, he was shot on the spot. At the camp entrance we had the evening roll call, the same as in the morning. We were counted and the S.S. officer came, checked it out and a report was given to him of the status of the unit.

Lineups: On the upper left chest of each prisoner, a piece of cloth was sewn on with the prisoner's number and a colored triangle. Each nationality or category of the prisoner – criminal, communist, Jew, Pole, Czech, and others had a different color. Jews wore a yellow triangle.

Then we were released into the barracks where we received a slice of bread, jam, margarine, and coffee. After a day's or night's work (because we worked in 12-hour shifts, one week days, one week nights) of slave labor and after great stress and tension, we fell on our cramped triple-deckers. At 10:00 p.m., the sirens were sounded to signal for everyone to be in his barrack. Twenty minutes later the lights went out. Anyone who stepped out after curfew was machine-gunned by the tower guards, without any warning.

One day an S.S. officer came and gave us a speech. He said: "You are in the Concentration Camp Auschwitz. Remember this, remember it forever. It is not a recuperating center. It is a concentration camp. Here you have to work. *Arbeit Macht Frei*, work makes a person free. If not, you will go straight to the furnace, to the crematory. Work or crematory. The choice is yours."

In this brutal and corrupt German system, devoid of G-d and human conduct, the women and men were persecuted on different levels, with unique experiences for women.

The Jewish women and children became strategic targets to accomplish the Nazi goal of Jewish annihilation. They suffered even more than the men because there was an additional dimension to their torment. First of all, they were physically the weaker ones so the German brutality was even harsher to them.

The Germans knew that by annihilating the children, they were annihilating the coming generation. Since the Nazi ideology categorized the human race according to race and sex, they saw in the Jewish woman a special target for annihilation.

The Germans exploited the sexuality of the Jewish women and their sensitivity and motherly obligations toward their children. As a result, the experiences of women in suffering during the Holocaust had a special emotional component. They were the victims of sexual exploitation, sexual manipulation, and rape. Abortions were forced upon them, which was, in a way, an unwilling participation in destroying their own flesh and blood. In many ways the Germans violated the woman's body. Many times they demanded sexual favors in return for survival.

The S.S. became slave traders. They filled orders for cheap slave labor from the various German industries, which operated day and night to help the war effort. Nobody was cheaper than the Jewish slave laborers. The S.S. command received good pay from the manufacturers for guarding the prisoners and providing them with room and board, while performing 12 hours of hard physical labor. Room was the barracks in the concentration camp, and board was the meager diet of 700 calories a day. It was a system of systematic starvation. By the time we were liberated, we had lost almost 50 percent of our body weight.

In Auschwitz, my brother Joseph and I did not do much work during the two weeks we were there. We were assigned to a cleaning unit in the camp and also carried all kinds of things from one place to another. However, the regimentation was the worst part of it – the apell, the Kapos – the entire regime was monstrous.

The camp administration constantly looked for skilled laborers. My brother Joseph and I had no skills at all. We were just teenagers out of school. We were students since the age of three and a half.

One morning at the roll call, the S.S. officer who took the count of the prisoners ordered our barrack to step forward. S.S. men with submachine guns surrounded us and marched us to the rail station at the edge of the camp where boxcars were waiting for us. We were ordered to board the train. My brother Joseph and I gave thanks to G-d that we were lined up together and so we remained together for the moment. We were given a portion of bread for the journey. Under heavy guard, the train moved slowly and stopped many times. After one day on the train, we arrived in the concentration camp, Plaszow, near Cracow, not far from Auschwitz. Joseph and I, and for that matter, the other 1,000 prisoners, had never heard of this place called Plaszow. Auschwitz, the inferno, the incarnation of hell on earth, was behind us. We were wondering what we could expect from this new place where we had just arrived.

In The Plaszow Concentration Camp

To the shouts of the S.S., "*raus, raus,* (get out, get out) and *schnell, schnell,* (quick, quick)," we got off the boxcars, lined up in rows of fives, and marched into the concentration camp, Plaszow. At the *apell platz,* the place where the roll calls took place, a number of tables were lined up. Behind them sat S.S. men. Each one of us was interviewed and asked our number, how old we were and what, if any, skills we possessed. My brother Joseph claimed he was a tailor. We heard that there were clothing workshops in Plaszow. Joseph was familiar with how to use a sewing machine. He learned it from our sister Feige who was a seamstress. I could not claim any profession since I was 15 years old. They marked me down for manual labor. We arrived in Plaszow in the middle of June 1944.

Gravestones in the Bilke Jewish Cemetery (1996) "survived" the kind of destruction that was implemented by the Germans in the Cracow Jewish Cemetery.

We were placed in barracks, which were similar to the barracks in Auschwitz. The camp was situated on the edge of the Jewish cemetery of Cracow. The Germans ordered us to uproot many of the *matzevot,* the gravestones, from the Jewish cemetery of Cracow, to be used for paving roads to the S.S. quarters and the commandant's villa.

Cracow was a very important city in Jewish history and always had a large Jewish population. The *Ramah*, Rabbi Moses Eserlish, the author of the *Kitzur Shulchan Aruch*, the abbreviated code of Jewish law, lived in Cracow. His Synagogue survived the Nazi onslaught and exists there until this day. The Jews of Cracow were first assembled by the Germans in a ghetto in Cracow itself. Many were sent to death camps. A few thousand who survived the selections were sent to the Plaszow Concentration Camp, which was built as an industrial camp where the Jews worked in sewing shops making uniforms for the German military. (Oscar Schindler, the German industrialist, saved over 1,000 Jewish prisoners by employing them in his factories near the Plaszow Concentration Camp.)

The Polish Jews in Plaszow still wore their civilian clothes and their leather boots. Only we, the Jews from Czechoslovakia and Hungary, wore the striped prisoner clothes. We looked at them with envy because they still looked human and comfortable.

Amon Goeth, the notorious S.S. Commandant of Plaszow, used to ride inside the camp on a white horse. When we saw him from a distance, we used to hide because whoever encountered him was in trouble. He was a brutal Nazi despot. He had built himself a large beautiful villa on top of the mountain from where he could see every move in camp. If he saw a prisoner standing inside the camp not working, he would shoot and kill him from the villa. In Plaszow, there was also a separate camp for women. There were Jewish women from Hungary who were transported to Plaszow via Auschwitz.

The Germans rounded up the Polish *intelegentzia*, the elite, the educated, and the well to do and brought them in trucks to Plaszow to the Jewish cemetery where they were executed. They were buried there in mass graves.

The Polish Jews in Plaszow were very cold to us. We asked them why they behaved like that to us, to their own brothers? They answered: "Where were you up until now? You enjoyed life in your homes in Czechoslovakia and in Hungary while we suffered here for years." They resented the fact that we were latecomers.

The work I did was very hard physical labor. Every morning, after apell, we marched from Plaszow to the Cracow railroad station. This was a very important juncture. All the military trains with personnel and supplies on the way to the Russian front passed through Cracow. Our job was to load and unload military equipment and supplies. We were always carefully watched by the S.S. guards. Fellow prisoners, who were not used to hard labor and primitive conditions, were the first ones to collapse. As soon as prisoners lost hope of being free one day, they lost their reason for struggling, and so, one by one, they began to die. We were exposed to various kinds of degradation. We were victims of recurrent selections for death. Most of us experienced partial or total loss of family. It was a dehumanizing atmosphere in Plaszow. I encountered the *Wachman*, the guards who were Ukrainians, Latvians, Lithuanians, and

Muslims from the Balkans under German command. These were Jew haters who volunteered to help the Germans in the Final Solution. They were murderers who took professional pride in their work.

The Kapos were also a constant threat to us. Some of them were veteran criminal prisoners, and rumor had it that they had been brought to the concentration camps to maintain discipline. They could make our life either easier or harder. They treated most of us cruelly, according to their whim, especially the Jews.

From time to time in each of the camps, the Germans surprised us and made a *selectzia*, a selection. They used to weed out the weak and sick prisoners. During this ordeal, we had to get completely undressed and were paraded, one by one, before an S.S. doctor. If a prisoner wanted to save himself from certain death, not to be branded a *Musselman*, a Nazi slang word for a prisoner on the brink of death, he had to gather all the strength he had in himself. Prisoners had to actually run to prove their usefulness. The S.S. doctor examined each prisoner, from top to bottom and wrote down his findings. If a prisoner passed the test, he was very happy for that meant his life had been extended. I experienced this kind of selection in Plaszow. I was one of the lucky ones together with my brother Joseph.

We managed to survive from day to day on the hope that our lot would eventually improve and that all we had to do was to somehow hold out.

Joseph worked in the tailor shop, which was not too hard. He had great pity on me since I had to work so hard. In the evenings we would talk about our day and how it went. We would talk about the family and home and about our brother Shmuel Tzvi who was in Palestine. We used to say that he must have been going out of his mind, knowing from news reports that our family, together with all the Carpathian Jews, were deported to Poland. Joseph used to tell me Shmuel Tzvi's address so that I would remember in case we were separated, because this was always a danger that it might happen.

After four months in Plaszow, one morning we were awakened by whistles, shouts, and screaming *Heraus Lous*, out quickly. The Kapos and the S.S. men drove us out of the barracks to line up. In the confusion, for the first time, Joseph and I ended up at the apell not in the same rows of five. An S.S. officer walked in front of us and started to count the rows. He stopped in front of my row, gave an order, about face, and we were marched away to the rail station. My brother Joseph was in the group that remained in Plaszow. This was the last time I saw my dear brother. It was very painful for me. We had already suffered so much, borne so much together. This was not the time to be separated. For four months we stuck together, always near each other and now fate had separated us. Now I was completely alone, a young boy in a hellish system. I tried to calm my anxiety by remembering that, according to Jewish tradition, a person must never lose faith, even when the sword hangs over his head.

We were loaded into the boxcars, but we did not know our destination, except that we were now on our way from one harsh camp to another. By now I was already a veteran in traveling in boxcars; this was my fourth one. From Bilke to Ghetto Berehovo, from Berehovo to Auschwitz, from Auschwitz to Plaszow. This time I was alone, without family or landsleit, without anyone to share my thoughts and feelings.

I wanted to believe that my brother was okay and that some day he would also come in my direction. I thought a great deal about the abnormal existence of the Jewish people. In Cheder, I learned that we, the Jews, are the Chosen People by G-d, that we are a unique people. Why then were we always singled out for persecution and such cruelty? And why were we the scapegoats and victims whenever there was a war between nations?

In the concentration camps, we wondered about G-d. How could a merciful, beneficent G-d allow millions of innocent men, women, and children to perish in such a brutal way? How can one understand the idea of the Jews being a Chosen People? It seems we had been chosen for suffering.

The old question of good and evil could not have been answered by any one of us prisoners. The traditional answer was then, and still is, that G-d in His great wisdom knows what He is doing and it is not for us humans to question His actions. Very few of us could accept this kind of an answer. A human being may be a believer in G-d, but he can only take so much. In the situation we were in, a living hell, we had the right to question the existence of a merciful G-d.

The Jews in most European countries were forced out of their homes and made to live like animals – even worse than animals. Free people were turned into slaves.

Before the war, I had been a young boy who had never tasted the personal struggle for existence. The experiences I had accumulated since we were driven from our home, consumed me with suspicion, fear, caution, and determination.

In Gross-Rosen And Bolkenheim Concentration Camps

After two days on our journey, the train suddenly stopped. During the trip we heard explosions. We heard rumors that our train was supposed to go to Czechoslovakia and from the shouting of the guards, we understood that we were supposed to work there in a factory. However, the rails that our train was on were severely damaged by the Partisans, Jews who were living in the forests and able to fight back against the Nazis. The train had to turn back and take another route. After another day on this train we entered a concentration camp, which we found out later was Gross-Rosen, located in Silesia.

A number of prisoners died in the boxcar from the inhuman condition on the train. We were ordered out of the train with the usual shouts, *Heraus, heraus; Lous, Lous.* Those of us who had no strength to move fast were beaten and kicked by the S.S. and Wachman guards. The Germans hired Ukrainians, Latvians, Estonians, Lithuanians, and other East Europeans who wore black uniforms. They helped murder hundreds of thousands of our people. They were working everywhere in a number of the concentration camps in which I was incarcerated.

Silesia was an industrial region largely of the upper Oder River. It was once a province of Prussia and Germany. It changed hands a number of times. During the second world war it was in German hands. Now it forms the Southern part of Poland. The main city was Breslau and now it is called Worclaw in Polish.

In Gross-Rosen, everything had to be done on the double. There were Kapos all over with clubs in their hands. You were not allowed to walk. One had to run. If you didn't run, you were clubbed by the Kapos. It was a huge camp composed of various nationalities; Jews, Poles, Russian prisoners of war, German criminals, and many others. A double barbed wire fence surrounded the camp. One of them was electrified. On the fences there were large captions: "Halt, stop, Achtung, warning, Achtung, warning, danger of death." Every

This document, issued by the International Red Cross, states the facts related to Moshe Avital's imprisonment in the concentration camps.

COMITE INTERNATIONAL GENEVE

SERVICE INTERNATIONAL DE RECHERCHES
INTERNATIONAL TRACING SERVICE
INTERNATIONALER SUCHDIENST

Notre Ref / Our Ref / Unser Az T/D - 476 590 | Votre Ref / Your Ref / Ihr Az - - - | Arolsen 18th February 1993

EXTRAIT DE DOCUMENTS	EXCERPT FROM DOCUMENTS	DOKUMENTEN-AUSZUG
Il est certifié par la présente que les indications suivantes sont conformes à celles des documents originaux en possession du Service International de Recherches et ne peuvent en aucun cas être modifiées par celui-ci	It is hereby certified that the following indications are cited exactly as they are found in the documents in the possession of the International Tracing Service. It is not permitted for the International Tracing Service to change original entries.	Es wird hiermit bestätigt, daß die folgenden Angaben den Unterlagen des Internationalen Suchdienstes originalgetreu entnommen sind. Der Internationale Suchdienst ist nicht berechtigt, Originaleintragungen zu ändern.

Nom / Name / Name: LIPSCHÜTZ/LIPSITZ -/-
Prénoms / First names / Vornamen: Moricz/Mozes -/-
Nationalité / Nationality / Staatsangehörigkeit: Hungarian, Czechoslovakian -/-

Date de naissance / Date of birth / Geburtsdatum: 18.7.1928 -/-
Lieu de naissance / Place of birth / Geburtsort: Bilke -/-
Religion / Religion / Religion: Jewish -/-

Noms des parents / Parents' names / Namen der Eltern: not indicated -/-
Profession / Profession / Beruf: turner -/-

Dernière adresse connue / Last known residence / Zuletzt bekannter Wohnsitz: Bilke 222, district Irsava -/-
Etat civil / Marital status / Familienstand: not indicated -/-

Arrêté le / Arrested on / Verhaftet am: not indicated -/-
à / in / in: not indicated -/-
par / by / durch: not indicated -/-

Emprisonné / Confined / Eingeliefert: in Concentration Camp Buchenwald -/-
No de détenu / Prisoner's No / Häftlingsnummer: 133713 -/-

Le / On / Am: 7th March 1945 -/-
venant de / coming from / von: Concentration Camp Gross Rosen -/-
par / by / durch: not indicated -/-

Catégorie / Category / Kategorie: "Polit." (* Politisch), "Jude" -/-

Transféré / Transferred / Überstellt: not indicated; liberated in Concentration Camp Buchenwald by the American Army on 11th April 1945. -/-

Indications complémentaires / Further indications / Weitere Angaben: In the records is remarked: Auschwitz-prisoner's number A 13740. -/-

Remarques du SIR / Remarks of the ITS / Bemerkungen des ITS: According to the information which we could ascertain, the prisoner's number A-13740 of Concentration Camp Auschwitz was issued on 7th June 1944 (transport from Hungary, by order of the "Reichssicherheitshauptamt"). -/-

G. Birke
for the Archives

L. Jäger
for the Archives

A 1431

* Explication du SIR * Explanation of the ITS * Erklärung des ITS

D - 3548 AROLSEN, Grosse Allee 5 - 9, Tel. (0 56 91) 60 37, Telegr. ITS Arolsen

few hundred meters there were watchtowers, mounted with machine guns.

Our group, which came from Plaszow, stayed in Gross-Rosen only a few days because Gross-Rosen was actually a transit camp. In the vicinity of Gross-Rosen there were a few dozen satellite camps which provided slave laborers for the heavy industry in Silesia. We were loaded onto military trucks, escorted by heavy S.S. guards. The convoy was also escorted by regular German troops. We went through some towns but we could not see much because the trucks were covered with canvas. After many hours, we arrived in a camp called Bolkenheim. It was located on a hill approximately six kilometers outside the city of Breslau. It was not a large camp. It had about 10,000 prisoners.

Each concentration camp had an entry gate with a sarcastic provocative sign. On the gate of Auschwitz it said *Arbeit Macht Frei*, work makes one free. Rudolf Hoess, the Commandant of Auschwitz, said that the inscription was supposed to resemble *Dante's Inferno* which said, "All who enter here give up hope." In this inscription one finds the hidden essence of denying the Holocaust. The deceit behind this inscription was a mockery to the victims who were incarcerated in the camps without a time limit for no wrong doing. Each Jew who entered Auschwitz had his or her lot sealed either for immediate murder or a slow tortured death. In some of the barracks, there were sayings such as *Reden is silber – schweigen is gold*, speaking is compared to silver, but silence is compared to gold. *Sauberkeit ist deine gesundheit*, cleanliness is your health, *Eine laus dein tod*, one louse will bring your death.

In Bolkenheim, there were observation posts and towers with mounted machine guns and double rows of barbed wire fences. One row was electrified. There were gallows and torture chambers and mass graves. Each group was assigned to a barrack. In the barrack, the prisoners administration was waiting for us, which consisted of the Blockaelteste, the German criminal prisoner who was the top man in the barrack, a few Kapos among them, some low life Jews, and *Stubenaelteste*. They were in charge of a certain section in the barrack since each barrack was divided into separate areas. As we were standing in front of the barrack, the Blockaelteste delivered a speech telling us what we could and could not do. He said that we were *heftlings*, prisoners.

We settled in the barrack. The barracks in Bolkenheim were identical to the barracks in the other camps. The beds, the food, the latrines, washroom, all were the same as in Gross-Rosen and Plaszow.

Very early in the morning we were awakened when the Kapos burst into the barrack shouting, "Heraus, heraus!" We rushed down from the wooden planks and made our way to the latrine, the washroom, to wash ourselves. The

Arbeit Macht Frei – This misleading sign (work makes you free) was at the entrance to Auschwitz and other concentration camps.

same problems existed in Bolkenheim as in the other camps. Everybody rushed to the latrine at the same time. The stronger ones pushed their way to the faucets, the weaker ones and the sick never got to them because we had only 15 to 20 minutes to wash and go back to the barrack.

We lined up for roll call. The prisoners administration hurried us to line up according to height, in rows of five. The people who died during the night were piled up outside the barrack. The Blockaelteste, the Kapos and the Stubenaelteste stood in front and in the back of our unit.

The S.S. commander of the camp, who was a young major, and his entourage arrived. The *Lageraeltes*, the prisoner in charge of the administration inside the camp roared, "Camp Bolkenheim, Attention." Everyone jumped to attention. "*Mutzen ab.*" Remove hats. He now gave a report of the status of the prisoners. How many heftlings, prisoners, were present. How many were in the revier, the infirmary, and how many died during the night. The number had to be exact otherwise the counting started all over again.

The S.S. Major and other S.S. officers went from unit to unit and counted. This Major shouted all the time. He was a ferocious beast. They did not trust the prisoners administration officials. At the same time they looked at us as if we were a bunch of horses to be examined. He made all kinds of derogatory remarks, a barrage of discordant commands that cut deep into the body and soul, such as, "You Jude Swine, why haven't you washed today," or "*Es is mir sheis egal.*" I do not care what happens to you. "*Juden ir sind kaput.*"

Jews, you are finished. "*Do blode Judenbande.*" You stupid, dirty band of Jews. "*Verfluchte bande.*" You cursed bunch and so on.

The S.S. officers wore white gloves. Many times they would slap a prisoner's face at the apell and then wipe their glove on the prisoner's clothes. The roll calls were always great torture for us. After the S.S. officers left the apell platz area, we were given our breakfast, a bowl of black coffee.

After that, we were lined up by the Kapos, marched to the gate of the camp where S.S. guards and Wachman, East European volunteers, lined up alongside each unit with guns aimed at us. We marched six kilometers to an airplane factory that made planes for the German Air Force, the *Luftwaffe.* Anyone who just as much as stepped out of line was shot on the spot. It was a very heavy guard, every few meters there was a guard. The Kapos accompanied us to work. They did not work. They got better food and bigger rations, cigarettes, regular beds, and other privileges.

The Kapos wanted to show off to the civilian population on the outskirts of Breslau how high our morale was. While marching to and from work, they forced us to sing German marching songs which were against the Jews and which they taught us whenever we had a moment free from work. These were some of the words:

> "Far away is the road back to the homeland, so far, so far, there, where the stars shine over the forest, dawns a new era. The Jews are pulled like a magnet to the Red Sea; the waves drown them and the world is at peace."

These marches to and from work were great torture and weakened us slowly, but surely.

We worked in this factory on a 12-hour shift, one weekday shift, and the next weeknight shift. When we worked at night, we slept during the day and vice versa. But many times when we were supposed to sleep or rest during the day, the Kapos bothered us with extra work, to clean the barrack or if they needed help in the kitchen to peel potatoes or other chores. Those who were taken on a kitchen detail sometimes sneaked out a few potatoes, which became a feast among us. The Kapos also used the daytime, which was supposed to be for sleep, to teach us the marching songs.

This airplane factory was hidden underground in a forest and it was well camouflaged. It was a huge complex subdivided into separate areas. Thousands of Jewish slave laborers and non-Jewish forced laborers from the surrounding camps near Breslau worked in this factory. The forced laborers were

Frenchmen, Italians, Poles, Czechs, and many other nationalities from occupied Nazi Europe. These laborers were taken from their countries and forced by the Germans to do work for the war effort. They had separate camps. These were detention camps, not concentration camps like for the Jews. They could leave the camp, but were restricted to the area. They received pay from the Germans and could receive packages from home. Their situation was far better than ours. However, they had to stay in the area and show up for work. They were not allowed any contact with us and they worked in separate workshops. They were not in danger of annihilation as long as they did their work, but the Jewish prisoners were always in danger of death when their last drop of strength was squeezed out of them. It was annihilation through slave labor.

The first time I entered this factory I met the *meister*, the foreman of our unit who was supervising the work. He was a civilian German in his forties who limped. I was directed to a huge machine, which was cutting steel. In German, it was called *Drey Bank*. The foreman's name was Hans. He taught me how to operate the machine. I had to cut from large planks of steel very delicate parts for the fighter airplanes. It had to be very accurate – to the minutest millimeter. He worked with our shift day or night. He asked me all kinds of questions about my family, how old I was, from where I came, etc. He seemed to be a liberal person. After a while, he took a liking to me. He would try to encourage me by telling me that the war would soon be over and that he wanted to adopt me as his son. I thought it was very nice of him, but if I survived the war, I didn't want any part of the Germans, even the liberal ones. I must admit though, that his encouragement and his help probably extended my life. It was an extraordinary thing. I had a tool cabinet near the machine. From time to time when I arrived at work and opened the cabinet to take out my tools, I found a sandwich of bread and jam or bread and margarine. I was sure that Hans put it there. He did not say anything about it and I didn't ask him. Unless it was Elijah the Prophet who helped me, but who knows. Many times I thought that perhaps Hans was not a German but an agent of the Allies. After we were evacuated from Bolkenheim, I never saw Hans again. I often wondered who he was and what happened to him.

From time to time inspectors came and measured the parts we produced to make sure that we weren't sabotaging the delicate parts. We had a terrible feeling that we were actually helping the enemy by producing these fighter planes, which were destroying the Allies' warplanes and their pilots. We had no choice, either work or die.

Many times there were air raids, mostly during the night shifts. It seemed that the Allies knew about this factory and tried to destroy it. However, no matter how many times they flew over us and bombed the area, they never hit the factory itself. It was too deep underground and in those days the bombs were not sophisticated enough to penetrate that deep. For us prisoners, these air raids were a double blessing. We were glad the Allies were attacking our tormentors and destroying parts of Germany. We were hoping they would hit the factory, even though we would have also been harmed. It gave us a little bit of rest. We stayed in the factory. The lights went out and we were able to rest or sleep. As soon as the raid was over we returned to our work.

While I was in Bolkenheim Concentration Camp, there was a Rabbi from Hungary who was a very gentle person. I had great pity on him. He must have been in his fifties. He also worked in the same factory with me. The Rabbis lips moved constantly. He used to recite pages of holy books by heart and pray a lot. From time to time, especially on Shabbat or holidays during our break for food, he would come over to me and say "Moshe'leh, you know what day is today?"

And I would say, "Yes, Rabbi, I know today is Shabbat." He would say, "Let's pray together." We used to recite the Shabbat prayers by heart. I remembered them all, since I was taught practically all the prayers by heart during my childhood.

One Saturday night when we worked the night shift, at midnight during our break for food, the Rabbi came over to me and said Moshe'leh, you know tonight we begin to say Selichot, the penitential prayers, "Let us pray together." I did not know the Selichot prayers then by heart since we recite them only for a few days before Rosh Hashana, the Jewish New Year. Only some prayers, which are also recited at other times, I did know.

The Rabbi, however, knew quite a few passages by heart. One of the passages which he recited with me with great *kavanah*, with great emotion and tears, was *Aich Niftach Peh*, "How shall we open our mouth before Thee." This prayer was engraved in my heart and mind because it had then, and still has now, a powerful expression about the lot of the Jewish people.

It says: "Ever since, we have been dispersed, slaughtered and butchered, only a few of us have survived amidst mean thorns... They rise up against Thee, scornfully asking Thy people; you who are broken, crushed in what do you trust? The oppressors of Thy people, why do they prosper morning and evening? O Thou who abidest forever, Holy One, look at the humiliation of the distressed who rely upon Thee and are united in Thee. May we forever be saved by Thy wondrous power for we trust in Thy abundant mercy." This

Moshe Avital was first imprisoned in Auschwitz and then incarcerated in five other camps, including Bolkenheim, Plaszow, Reichenow, Gross-Rosen, and Buchenwald.

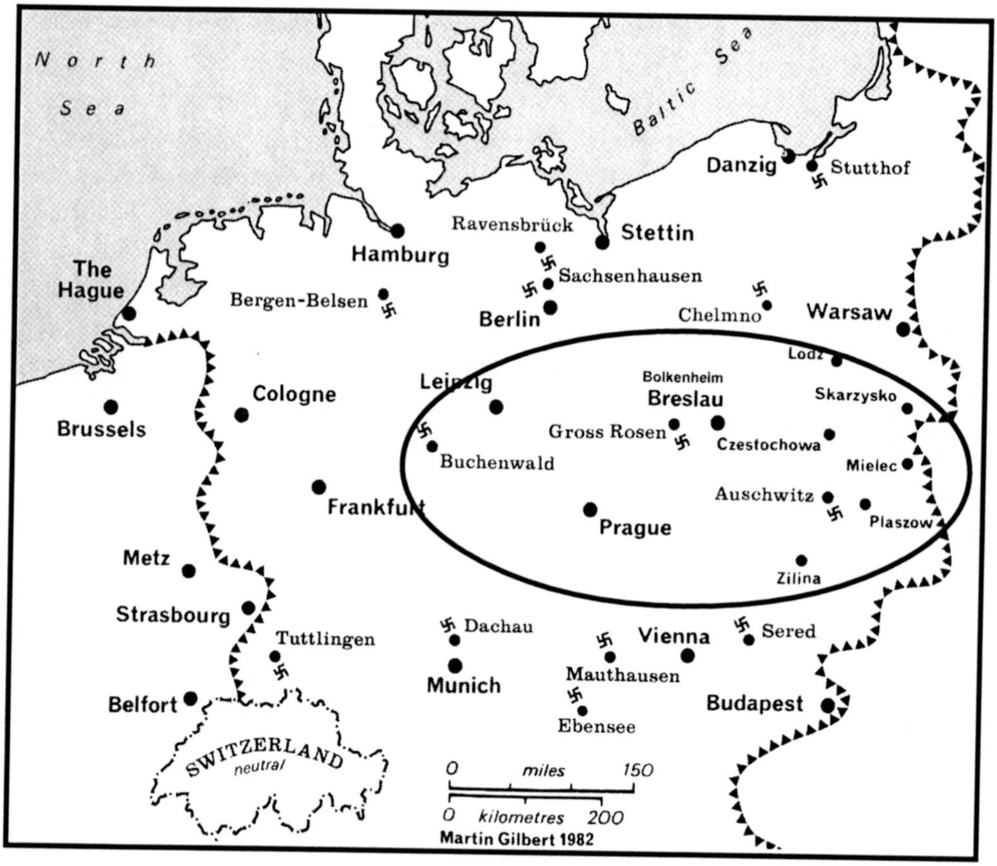

Reprinted from *McMillan Atlas Of The Holocaust*, © 1982, by Martin Gilbert, published by The Jewish Publication Society, with the permission of the publisher, The Jewish Publication Society.

Hungarian Rabbi had a bitter end. One day when we were standing on the apell platz, the S.S. commandant, the Major, was in one of his beastly moods. He was seized with one of his frenzies. As he was reviewing our unit, he saw the Rabbi standing in the front row. He said sarcastically to him, "*Herr Rabiner* Rabbi, Sir, where is your G-d?" And the Rabbi motioned to heaven. The Major broke out in laughter and screamed, "You know where He is? I am your G-d, I can do with you whatever I want." He leaped onto him like a wild animal. He threw the Rabbi on the ground. He kicked him in the stomach with his shiny boots many times. His blows were growing more violent until a tremendous kick in the pit of his stomach brought blood gushing out of his mouth. This beast continued kicking him in the face and head until he stopped moving. Such beatings were commonplace in Bolkenheim. But this time his fury was like a sudden hailstorm, lava-like and furious. It was something that triggered him, a rage which was there all the time. Nothing could be done until his rage had run its course, until the storm was over. After the commandant cooled down, he ordered that the Rabbi be taken away. A few hours later he died. He was a gentle man who always tried to comfort the prisoners around him. He had an unusual face which radiated an inner purity. He was asking us to hold on to a spark of Judaism, a spark of faith, even under hellish conditions. Many times he saw my confusion and tried to bolster my faith and restore my trust and faith in Divine Providence. He emphasized it was not for us to question the workings of Divine Providence. His conversations with me brought a certain spiritual calm and solace.

Winter was upon us, and in Eastern and Central Europe, 1944 - 1945, it was an especially severe winter. The snow presented us with special problems. Our clothing, which we received in the spring, remained the same for the winter season. Some of us tried to wrap ourselves under the clothing with empty cement paper bags. This was, however, strictly forbidden. If someone was caught, he was severely punished and was given 25 lashes.

Once I received 25 lashes. Before Christmas 1944, we were given small packages, which were sent by the International Red Cross. In it were some cigarettes, a bar of soap, and a bar of chocolate. I ate the chocolate immediately. The soap came in very handy because I hadn't had soap since I was driven from home. I tried to barter the cigarettes, for bread, which was strictly forbidden. I did succeed in getting food for my cigarettes. One of the Kapos learned about my exchange. He came to me and said, "I know what you did. If you do not give me some of the cigarettes, I will report you." I told him I had no more, that if I had any, I would give them to him. My reasoning and my begging did not help. He brought me before the Blockaelteste, the chief of the barrack. Then they also brought the prisoner to whom I bartered the cigarettes for the food. The barrack chief went into a rage. He took a chair and started to hit the other prisoner with it. He broke the chair on him, continued to beat him until he passed out. He calmed down a little. Then he turned to me and said, "You are lucky, because you are a young lad, you will only receive 25 lashes. The Kapo took me immediately to the torture room. There they had all kinds of torture devices. By then, two more Kapos arrived. They ordered me to lie down on the stretcher, "Lie down on it, on your stomach," they ordered me. I did as I was ordered. Then the strokes of the whip began. They told me that I should count. When I reached number six, I passed out from the severe pain. I don't know whether they continued lashing me. When I came to myself, I felt wet and terrible pain on my behind. They must have poured cold water on me to revive me. I could not move. Two prisoners from my barrack with whom I was friendly waited for me outside. They came in and carried me out, brought me to our barrack and put me on the wooden plank bed. They put cold wet rags on me to relieve the pain and the burning sensation I felt. Since the next day was New Years (1945), we did not have to go to work. I was able to gain back some of my composure and some strength. It took some weeks before the pain disappeared. The Jewish prisoners, especially those who were brought up in human environments, were unable to get used to the inhuman conditions. We were ill equipped to cope with the brutal realities in the camps. The physical abuse, the hunger, the arduous slave labor, the beatings, and the disease, undermined our mental balance. No one could get accustomed to the prevailing bestiality. Some of us managed to preserve our human dignity; others lost all hope and gave up. German brutality was unprecedented. They subjected us to a degrading regime of shame, humiliation, and loss of identity, even deprived us of control over our bodily functions before actually killing fellow prisoners.

In the concentration camps in which I was incarcerated, our constant problem was lice. They were a real plague. It reminded me of the plague inflicted upon the Egyptians. Nobody knew where they were coming from, but suddenly they appeared. This problem didn't go well with the Germans. The S.S., too, was anxious to see us get rid of this ugly creature. They were afraid of a typhoid epidemic and perhaps they might get it, too. From time to time, we had an *antlousung*, delousing. It was usually done after we came back from work. We were taken to a special barrack where they had tremendous disinfecting machines, something like huge dryers. All our clothing was thrown into this dryer-container which had a very high temperature. In the wintertime we would shiver because we had to stand naked for hours at a time. We had to shave all of our hair and shower; after that, our clothes were returned to us. The lice did not survive the high heat and the disinfectant material they put in those machines, but the eggs did. So they started to flourish all over again. That is why we had to do it every once in a while.

The daily small piece of bread which we received was a very valuable, cherished, and precious commodity that every concentration camp prisoner treasured. The prisoners developed many theories of how to get the most out of this bread of affliction. There were all kinds of approaches and systems of eating the bread in order to satisfy the nagging hunger. Some divided it into three or four portions, for morning, noon, evening, and before falling asleep. Some of us would nibble the bread, crumb by crumb. This was one of the methods which was supposed to help overcome sharp hunger pangs. Others would eat their portion of bread at once because it was dangerous to hold on to it, since there were prisoners who attacked you and grabbed your bread. If you ate it at once, it was secure in your stomach.

We were constantly hungry because of the starvation diet of 700 calories a day and the hard work we had to perform. We dreamed about food. We knew that our survival to a great extent depended on food. We knew that all we could expect was a slow and painful death by starvation. Fellow inmates were dying every day from weakness and malnutrition.

In Bolkenheim, they would punish an entire barrack collectively or the entire camp population if something happened, and they could not find the culprit. The Germans used all kinds of punishments such as standing outside in the cold or rain or sun for hours or standing outside naked in the winter. They also made us run around the barracks many times, special work, starvation, etc. The punishments for individuals were as follows: beating, lashes, cold showers for long periods, solitary confinement, and many other techniques. After those punishments, many people collapsed and died. Some died after a few months, and some after a while. Although I was weak physically, I had a strong mental resistance to the German psychological warfare they conducted against the concentration camps inmates, which helped me overcome these experiences. I did not lose the hope that the day would come, that they would lose the war and we would take revenge for their atrocities. The deep faith, which was planted in me in our home in G-d Almighty, in the eternity of the Jewish people and in the redemption that would come one day, helped me to overcome the hell on earth. Although I also sympathized with some of my inmates when we would discuss the whereabouts of G-d, his mysterious ways, the sins of the Jewish people and of their future deliverance, in my mind, I sympathized with Job, because, like him, I did not deny G-d's existence, but I did question His absolute justice.

In Bolkenheim, we witnessed some horrible things. One day we were lined up on the apell platz as usual according to the barracks. Suddenly a platoon of S.S. soldiers with officers arrived on the plaza. The S.S. aimed their loaded sub-machine guns at us. Word passed around among the inmates that some Russian P.O.W. prisoners from Bolkenheim attempted to escape. Now they were going to be executed in front of the entire camp population. On the side of the plaza stood gallows, which had been prepared for this occasion. An S.S. officer stood next to the Russian prisoners awaiting the order from the Major, the camp Commandant. The S.S. gleefully invited all their friends and wives to view this joyous, public spectacle. As the prisoners stood upon the gallows with the rope around their necks, a dead silence descended upon the multitudes of Jewish and non-Jewish onlookers. Suddenly the voices of the prisoners to be hung broke the silence with a resounding loud cry, "*Za Rodina, Za Stalina.* For our country, for our Stalin. Long live the Soviet Union." Their voices pierced the air and reverberated through the silence. Then they became silent. We saw them dangling in agony until they died. We all were terrified by the inhuman scene. We, the forced onlookers, stood not moving, and we cried within the innermost chambers of our hearts. This was the first time in my life that I had witnessed a hanging. These hangings were a further indication to us to what depth the Nazi beasts, the most degraded and bestial of men, can stoop. We saw death all around us. People died from hunger, disease, from beatings, by shooting, and from the terror of the hangings. Then the entire assembly, block after block, had to march past the hanging prisoners and look at them so that we would learn a lesson.

After four months of the hellish place of Bolkenheim, in the middle of January 1945, we heard that we were to be evacuated, due to the Russian breakthrough of the front lines. We could hear intense artillery barrages coming from the East. For several nights, we saw flames and smoke on the horizon. Clearly, the Soviet Army was getting closer to Bolkenheim Concentration Camp. We were hoping our dreams of liberation would soon come true. Hans, my foreman, told me himself that we would be leaving, but he did not know, or did not want to tell me where we were going. I learned that in the camps one had to rely on oneself. One needed a strong desire to live and had to constantly be on the alert.

The Death Marches Of Winter 1945

Even though the Russians were very close to our concentration camp and the Germans knew their end was near, they did not think for a moment to relent as far as the Jewish prisoners were concerned. We were happy to hear that the Russians were beating the Germans, but we were very worried about what the Germans had in store for us. The order was to empty Bolkenheim and march us deeper into Germany. We were told that on the next morning we would be leaving. We saw that the preparations were going on all over the camp for the journey. In the S.S. barracks and in the administration offices, they were packing and burning documents.

It is difficult to relay the extent of our torment. Every day there was a new calamity. Troubles came upon us in quick succession. The Germans realized that they faced defeat at the hands of both the western Allies and the Soviet Union. They diverted S.S. units from the front lines to speed up the process of the extermination of the Jews in the concentration camps and on the death marches. Their sole mission was the slaughter of the Jews before the Allies could liberate them. In the death marches that were ordered from concentration camps in Poland to go westward to Germany away from the advancing Russian forces, thousands of Jewish prisoners perished by the brutality of the German guards. These were men and women who were weakened by starvation, disease, and ill treatment during the marches. The S.S. soldiers cherished this assignment. It saved them from the fighting on the fronts and at the same time, they killed Jews. By the time the marches reached the destinations, 80 percent of the prisoners perished. Some were transported in open railway wagons, exposed to the full fury of winter. Some marches lasted six weeks.

The block chief gave orders to give each one of us a double portion of bread, margarine, and jam to take for the journey. We were wondering how much longer we were going to be dragged from one camp to another. We tried to find some additional garments to put on, one on top of the other, in order to keep us warm in the severe weather. In the morning, we lined up according to the barracks and marched to the gate of the camp with the Kapos. As we exited the camp, hundreds of S.S. men and Wachman lined up on both sides of our column with loaded sub-machine guns aimed at us, accompanied by vicious shepherd dogs.

Our march began in a relentless snowfall. It was bitterly cold. The guards made us increase the pace with curses such as: *Juden swine*, dirty Jews, faster, faster. They were in a hurry to distance themselves as fast as possible from the closing in of the Russian forces. We could hear at a distance the echoes of artillery fire. The guards had orders to shoot anyone who either stepped out of the line or could not keep up with the pace of the group. Some of us dreaded to be on the outside rows of the column, which was very dangerous.

I will never forget the inhuman scenes that I witnessed in these death marches. Many of the prisoners with whom I became acquainted were shot before my eyes without mercy. Many of us tried to help the weaker ones who struggled to keep up with the march. Sometimes two of us would support another prisoner in order to save him from certain execution. However, the guards were in a hurry and so they pushed us aside and shot the stragglers and ordered us to push the victims into the ditches on the roadside. The murderers were trained for this and were immune to human feelings and so they were able to kill in cold blood. It was hard to realize what human beings were capable of doing to totally innocent fellow human beings.

Most Germans looked away and others wanted to outdo one another in zeal because they wanted to get rid of the Jews. When the Madagascar Plan, (to deport all European Jews to that island in the Indian Ocean) turned out to be impractical, German police units, S.S. killers, local thugs, and soldiers of the *Wehrmacht*, the regular army, were unleashed to shoot, burn, or club the Jews to death. When it turned out to be too long of a process, the gas chambers were put into operation.

How was it possible that so many people turned towards barbarism? Various explanations have been offered. How could the Germans, who were a nation of poets, scientists, writers, and thinkers, turned into beasts overnight? Perhaps they already harbored genocidal feelings toward the Jews and all that Hitler, may his name be eradicated, had to do was tap that well of poison. Nazism appealed to the Germans because it promised not merely prosperity to them, but greatness and even salvation.

During these difficult moments I also wanted to die because I could not stomach these kinds of atrocities. The outcries of the victims reached up to the heavens. We were hoping these scenes would reach G-d Himself, and perhaps He would finally have mercy on his persecuted children who were being denigrated and slaughtered. Oceans of tears were shed, however, these tears did not fill the oceans and did not cause a flood on the sinful and defiled world. The Jewish people, who were put in the hands of the destructive satan, drank from the bitter cup of annihilation until the last drop. We had a brutal choice, either to give in to the S.S. murderers, to be shut up, or to try to overcome the grief and continue on and hope for the redemption, in order to avenge the blood of our dear brethren.

After awhile, we marched like robots. We were just dragging our bodies. Prisoners were constantly collapsing in the snow. The guards shot them and ordered the other prisoners to throw them into the ditch on the side of the road. We did not know where they were taking us. Whatever food we had, we finished. The hunger pangs became unbearable by the hour. At night, we were deposited in village barns and other structures guarded by the S.S. and Wachman guards. Hungry and freezing from the fierce cold, we could only huddle together to get some warmth. We could not sit down or lie down because we were crowded like sardines in a can. But this was to our advantage because the body warmth kept us alive; otherwise we would have frozen to death. The dead were left in the village without burial. They were abandoned like someone leaves an object that he has no use for anymore.

The death march continued in the snow and slush from first light to darkness. At dawn, the guards opened the doors of the barn and shouted *eintreten*, ranks form up. Whoever could not rise or could only stumble was shot on the whim of the guards. I felt that I could not go on. I thought it was all over for me. I could not keep up the struggle and I had no strength left in me. My hope to come out alive from this inferno grew weaker. I started to pray. I remembered some verses from the Psalms, "How long G-d will You endlessly forget me? How long will You hide Your countenance from me? How long will my enemy triumph over me?" (Psalm 13) But even the heavens were helpless on that day. A force so evil ruled on earth, that it altered human order on the continent of Europe, which devoured the Jewish people. The Jewish horizon was forever darkened by the unthinkable evil.

I was fluctuating between hope and despair. I remembered a verse in Ecclesiastes which says: "Wherefore I envied the dead that are already dead more than the living that are yet alive." (Ecclesiastes 4:2) The Talmud tells us that, "for two and a half years the school of *Shammai* and the school of *Hillel* were in dispute, the former asserting that it was better for man not to have been created than to have been created, and the latter maintaining that it was better for man to have been created. They finally took a vote and they decided that it was better for man not to have been created." (Babylonian Talmud Tractate *Eruvin* 13B) At that moment I thought that death was better than this kind of existence when brutal masters ruled over us. We said, "We are lost, we will never come out alive from this inferno?" As I assessed the situation, I thought that it was madness and folly to go on.

The guards ordered us to carry their backpacks and their belongings. One of the prisoners who carried a German's backpack, opened it up during the march and found precious food in it. He ate some of it and also distributed it to his fellow inmates and then threw away the backpack. This guard started to look for his backpack, but was not sure which prisoner he gave it to. Since we all were dressed alike and looked alike, it was hard to distinguish one from the other. We were all skeletons, with only our eyes sticking out. The march was stopped. The S.S. officer in charge demanded an immediate return of the backpack and ordered the prisoner to come forward. No one moved. It was a very tense moment. The S.S. officer shouted and cursed the Jews and warned that if the one who took the backpack did not come forward immediately, he would shoot every tenth prisoner. No one stepped forward. The S.S. started to count and every tenth prisoner was pulled out of the group. At the last moment, one Jewish prisoner stepped forward and confessed that he was the one who took the food because his hunger was unbearable. He was shot on the spot and his body thrown in the ditch.

In spite of the unbelievable suffering that we went through, most Jews did not lose the image of G-d and behaved according to Jewish morality. It was evident when this Jewish prisoner realized that because of what he did, many Jews would lose their lives, he surrendered to the S.S. murderers.

When the guards became tired, others replaced them. But we had to go on without any relief. At this point in the march, elderly guards guarded us. These were from the regular army. It seemed the younger soldiers were sent to the front to help stop the Russian offensive or they were already a rare commodity since so many of them were killed on the front lines.

The fact that we now had older guards brought us some relief since these guards were not able to march as fast as the younger S.S.. They had their orders and the shooting of prisoners continued. I saw a number of prisoners lying in the ditches. The snow around them turned red from their blood. Nazi atrocities were committed both by the Wehrmacht and especially by the S.S.

and other fanatical death squads.

The cold, the hunger, the fatigue, and the long imprisonment, hit us all at once. Death was haunting us every step of the way, even without being shot by the German guards. People constantly collapsed, thus their suffering came to an end. Some purposely stepped out of the line to be shot since they could not endure anymore. After a few weeks on the death march, we arrived in Reichenau. More than half of the Jewish prisoners died from exhaustion and exposure in the freezing weather. The roads inside Germany were littered with the bodies of Jews who fell or who were shot by the German guards because they could not keep up with the pace of the death marches.

One evening, we marched into the town of Reichenau. The German civilians filled up the sidewalks in order to gaze at these odd creatures. I don't know if this was the first time they saw Jewish concentration camp prisoners being led through the streets. Suddenly I felt my feet were stepping on bundles of prisoner's clothing. Not only did I feel it, but many of us bumped into them. After we passed the town, the guards stopped the prisoner's column. They counted us and realized that a number of prisoners were missing. It seems that during the time we marched through the town, some prisoners removed their striped uniforms and threw them on the ground. They must have had on civilian clothes under the striped clothing, and during the crush of the crowds on the streets they took a chance and disappeared into the crowd. The officers and guards were furious, they shouted *Juden Swine*, dirty Jews, and wanted to know who escaped. On the one hand, we were very happy that some escaped, but on the other hand, we worried about their fate if they were apprehended. We were also very concerned about the punishment we would suffer. They marched us to a concentration camp, which was located on the outskirts of the town of Reichenau. There we were placed in barracks. Those of us who had survived so far, tried to grab a place on the wooden planks to get some rest. We fell into a deep sleep, even though it was very dangerous to fall asleep because one might not wake up. But in the condition we were in, one did not care to think too much about it. We stayed in the Reichenau camp for two days. We were given a ration of bread and black coffee. We devoured it instantly. We were not allowed to leave the barracks. The German guards were watching outside the door. The two days rest and the little food we received prolonged our lives again. Within me, there was a fierce determination to survive which became a driving force behind the everlasting battle against hunger. This was a form of resistance in the face of the Germans' death wish for all the prisoners. But under these horrible conditions, how did a person maintain his will to survive? What happened was that each individual prisoner developed his own unique method of endurance.

We were lined up again. Shouts were heard again, *"Sofort antreten,"* line up immediately, but this time we marched to the train station. We were very thirsty, so we ate the snow. The guards looked at us and had a good time watching this unusual spectacle. We were loaded into cattle wagons without any roofs. The guards were sitting on the walls of the wagons with their sub-machine guns aimed at us. The wind, the snow, and the icy rain became almost unbearable. The icy wind was going through us. Our bodies were practically frozen. The striped prisoner's clothes we wore were very light and thin. We tried to huddle up one against another. We prisoners were warming each other. We were covered with layers of snow and frost. After a while the train stopped. We were ordered to remove the dead overboard. These poor human beings were thrown overboard like sacks of flour. At least 15 to 20 bodies were removed from our wagon. The train resumed the journey, leaving the dead somewhere on the border between Poland and Germany. All this time we lived on snow.

Since the Allied planes were bombing all over, our train proceeded very slowly and made many stops. We stopped counting the days we were on this death march. As we passed through German towns and villages, curious crowds of spectators came to see the Jewish prisoners they heard so much about. They stared at the skeletons, the likes of which they had never seen before. After weeks, we finally reached our destination. It was late at night. We did not know where we were. The S.S. guards in the camp opened the doors of these wagons and shouted, "Heraus! Heraus!" Out! Out! Only about 20 prisoners of the 80 who were shoved into the wagon of this cattle train at Reichenau were still alive. I was among them. The others all died on the train ride. The same occurred in many of the other wagons.

The camp we arrived at was Buchenwald, near the city of Weimar. Thus ended the death march, which began in Bolkenheim and ended in Buchenwald, a distance of some 500 kilometers. Of some 5,000 prisoners that started out from Bolkenheim Concentration Camp, only 400 reached Buchenwald.

In The Notorious Concentration Camp Of Buchenwald

From the 1930s to 1945, hundreds of concentration camps were built to hold potential and real enemies of the Third Reich. The first camps were built in Germany, but as the war progressed, the Germans built them in all the countries they occupied. Some were slave labor camps, others were labor camps, concentration camps, and death camps, with most of them in Poland, expressly for the purpose of killing Jews, with Auschwitz-Birkenau as the primary factory of destruction. One of the early concentration camps was Buchenwald.

Buchenwald was built as a concentration camp in July 1937, on the fringe of a forest north of Weimar, Germany. It was built on a mountain called Ettersberg, where the famous tree was planted where Goethe wrote his most famous poems. At first, the concentration camp was named, Concentration Camp Ettersberg, however, 10 days later it was changed to Buchenwald, a supposedly innocent name that meant boxwood forest. It was changed so as to not blacken Goethe's name. Its first prisoners were German political prisoners, anti-Nazis, communists, socialists, and some 1,000 Jews. Over the eight years that Buchenwald existed, a quarter of a million prisoners passed through the camp – most of them Jews. It was a reservoir of slave labor for the German ammunition factories. There were torture rooms and a crematorium for the burning of the bodies, but there were no gas chambers in Buchenwald. Iron-fisted S.S. discipline and very harsh conditions existed in the camp. It was a policy of *vernichtung durch arbeit*, extermination through work and slave labor.

The S.S. organization, the highly trained criminal elite of Germany, supplied slave labor from the various concentration camps to the big German industries such as AEG, Ig-Farben, Krupp, Messerschmidt, Volksvagen, Rheinmetal, Siemens, and many others according to the request and needs. The S.S. head office for economy and administration (WVHA) calculated that the life expectancy of a slave prisoner was to be nine months. They determined how to maximize the profits of the slave labor prisoners by working them to death. The S.S. treasury received six marks per day from the industrial companies for every slave laborer. Accordingly, the S.S. income from every slave laborer amounted to 1,631 marks for the 270 days of his service to the German war machine. They also had additional income of a few hundred marks for valuables, which were found on the bodies of the prisoners and for gold teeth. Also the ashes and the bones of the disposed bodies were sold by the S.S. for fertilizer. The annihilation of the Jews by the German Reich had a double purpose: to get rid of the Jews and at the same time to get rich from their properties and their labor. Until this day, people are puzzled how perfectly ordinary fathers and family men could have been persuaded by a Fascist system of repression that negated humanity. How could they murder millions of human beings with such deliberation, and in such a premeditated way?

One of the first laws the Germans enacted against the Jews of Germany and Austria was forbidding Jewish *schechitah*, animal slaughter according to religious law. They used the excuse that it is *tzaar baalai chaim*, cruelty to animals. Isn't it an irony that the Germans supposedly had pity on animals, but behaved brutally to Jews and other human beings. As the Prophet Hosea stated with bitter scorn: "They that sacrifice men, kiss calves." (Hosea 13:2)

Karl Koch was the commandant of Buchenwald. Ilse Koch was his notorious wife. One of her famous hobbies was to look for healthy attractive men. Those that she liked, she tattooed a picture on their chest. Then she would order them executed by injection. Then she had the tattooed skin removed, to be used for a lampshade. When the Americans liberated Buchenwald we heard that they found a storage room with a collection of these lampshades. It is also known that the Germans produced soaps out of human fat and brooms made out of human hair. When we think about what they did, it is revolting to think that any human being would come up with such criminal ideas. It is sickening. It is just not human at all.

I was searching in the history annals to see whether women performed this kind of cruelty. I came across the story of the *Asarah Harugey Malchut*, the 10 Jewish Martyrs, whom the Romans put to death with many cruel and brutal tortures. It was to satisfy the anti-Semitic Roman rulers. A Roman Princess, who was greatly impressed with Rabbi Yishmael's handsomeness and who refused her overtures, ordered his flesh to be flayed so that she could then stuff the skin to preserve his handsome features for her to gaze upon. I wonder whether the beast, Ilse Koch, learned her cruelty from the Romans, or if it was her own sick imagination.

We arrived in Buchenwald in the middle of February 1945 in the middle

The entrance to Buchenwald

of the night. The train rails reached the edge of the camp. From there the S.S. marched us to the main entrance of the camp. On the top of the Iron Gate, there was a large clock. The gate was facing the apell platz, the roll call plaza which was quite large. S.S. officers were waiting for us. They counted us and looked at us. We were ordered to form columns of five in a row, 100 prisoners in each group. They took us to the showers, we undressed and showered. This was the first shower since we left Bolkenheim. All this was done under the watchful eyes of the S.S.. I and a few other prisoners were picked to stand separately. At first I was worried. I was wondering why I was selected to stand aside. That usually meant trouble. Then I noticed the others in my group were also young boys my age. Soon afterwards they gave us clothes, the same kind we had worn since we arrived at Auschwitz. Then, we the young boys, were taken to the children's barrack. In this barrack were some 600 Jewish teenagers from the various countries of occupied Europe. We were the remnants of the various death marches that reached Buchenwald. Among them were Elie Wiesel from Sighet, Rumania; Naftali and Lulek Lau from Piotrkow, Poland; and Menashe Klein from Ungwar, Hungary.

The Blockaelteste chief of the barrack was a Czech political prisoner. In Czechoslovakia, he was a principal of a school, but was an anti-Nazi. Therefore he was sent to Buchenwald.

This barrack was unique in many ways. It had only children and the leader was an educator. He was a wonderful human being who looked out for the children. He was a type like the Polish Jewish educator Janusz Korczak. He was a real *Chasid Umoth Ha-Olam*, Righteous Among The Nations. Many times he endangered himself in order to protect the children under his care. Of course he could do only so much. But it surely made a big difference to have such a person as the Blockaelteste. He arranged with the Germans for the children to not leave the camp to do hard work in quarries around Buchenwald or on *baustele*, construction sites. We did all kinds of work inside the camp. I was assigned to clean and sweep the rooms of the camp staff and the S.S. quarters.

Buchenwald was a large camp subdivided into smaller sections separated by barbed wire. Once I was taken on a cleaning detail into a camp, which was different from all others. It was a more luxurious camp. It was the camp of the V.I.P., the privileged. These were leaders of countries, whom the Germans held as bargaining chips. Among them was Leon Blum, a former Prime Minister of France who refused to cooperate with the Germans, the Crown Prince of Hungary, Admiral Miklos Horty and others. He was lured by the Germans to a meeting at Schloss Klessheim in Germany where they arrested him. He was taken to Buchenwald where he remained until the end of the war. Although they were prisoners, they had everything they needed; food, clothing, rest, good quarters.

Buchenwald was like a large city spread out over a vast area. Before the liberation, there were some 80,000 prisoners in the camp. Beyond the barbed wires and watch towers was a huge forest. In the camp there were various installations such as latrines, infirmary, kitchens, workshops, crematoria, shower houses, torture rooms, and others. All this was activated by the prisoners administration, which was appointed by the Germans for their reasons. They needed these people in order to enforce order and discipline in the camp. The old timers, those who had been there for a long time, knew the camp thoroughly. They even established a secret resistance underground, which was going to act in case the Germans tried to annihilate the camp.

At the end of March 1945, as spring was in the air, I was in bad shape. My legs were swollen, as was my face from malnutrition. My upper body was skin and bones. My health was rapidly deteriorating. We heard all

Buchenwald Scrip: Used by privileged prisoners to buy items in the camp canteen. Valued at half a German Reich mark.

An unimaginable horror met the American liberators in April 1945.

kinds of rumors that the Americans were nearby. Practically every day new arrivals came to Buchenwald who were also evacuated from other camps. One day, by chance, I met Dr. Avigdor Engel who was the doctor in Bilke for many years. He was a very fine gentlemen and a great doctor who took care of hundreds of patients. He came to Buchenwald with his brother who was a dentist. He was a personal friend of our family in Bilke. He remembered me as a child and was astonished that I was still alive. Unfortunately, he died a few days before the liberation.

Pesach (Passover) that year began on March 29. We were hoping that just as the liberation of the Jews from Egypt took place on Pesach, that this time history would repeat itself. I was reminiscing about the beautiful time of Pesach in our home, of all the preparations and the festivities during the holiday. Maybe G-d would show his mighty hand once more and finally destroy the evil Germans who caused my people so much destruction.

Now it was a race with time. Many people were dying every day. The Germans were preparing to annihilate the prisoners of Buchenwald so as not to leave any witnesses to their crimes. It was a question of who would arrive first – the Americans or death. Thousands of men lay dying of typhoid, dysentery, diarrhea, pneumonia, and all kinds of sickness. There was no food. The camp stopped providing food the last few days before the liberation. Even the meager portions which we were given before, were stopped.

Rumors had it that the Western Allies broke through the German defenses in our area. Our spirits rose and fell according to the news we heard. We hoped the news was true which would put an end to our suffering.

After the liberation, we found out a few things that directly involved our lives during those crucial last days. On April 7, 1945, an order was given by the Nazi hierarchy to eliminate all the prisoners in Buchenwald. The Buchenwald command systematically began to empty out the camp, barrack by barrack. This time they did not use the usual practice of selecting the sick and the weak first. At each barrack appeared a company of S.S. with sub-machine guns. The officers with pistols and clubs in their hands and with fierce shepherd dogs forced the prisoners to line up in between the cordon which the S.S. formed. The prisoners were driven to the main gate of the camp. They were marched into the forest where the S.S. had hidden heavy machine guns in covered trucks. As the prisoners arrived deep into the forest the canvas covers

The liberated prisoners of Buchenwald.

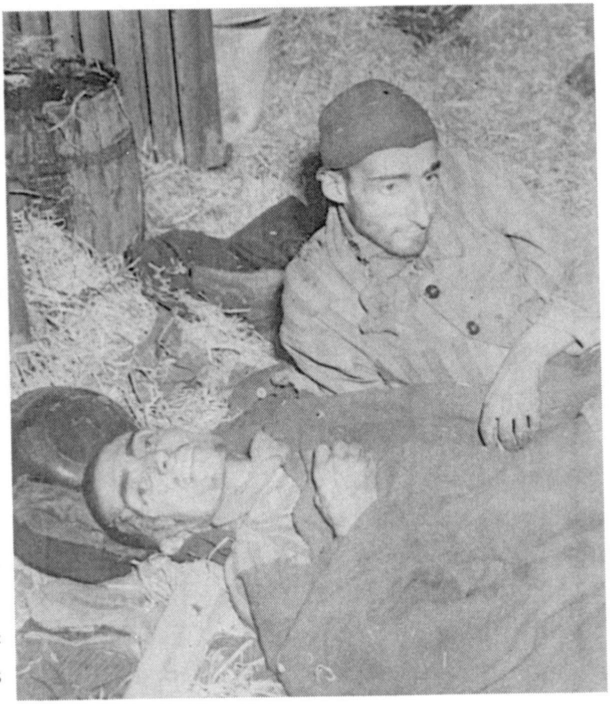

were removed and the shooting commenced. This massacre continued for four days, barrack by barrack, until our turn came, the children's barrack. On April 10, 1945, only 20,000 prisoners were left from the 80,000 that were there just a few days ago. They were all massacred in the forest. The camp commandant received an order to eliminate all prisoners at once and blow up the camp installations so that there would be no evidence of the heinous crimes. The Americans

intercepted this and decided to act quickly. Around noon-time a large contingent of S.S. men entered the camp and approached block 44, our barrack. A loud speaker announced *alle heftlingen*, all prisoners in barrack 44 line up immediately. The noise and the barking dogs quickly brought all prisoners out.

The Czech Blockaelteste marched in front of the children. He did not abandon us at that critical time. The S.S. on both sides were pushing and shoving us to go faster. As we walked, we felt this was the end because the last few days we could hear shooting coming from the forest. At first we thought

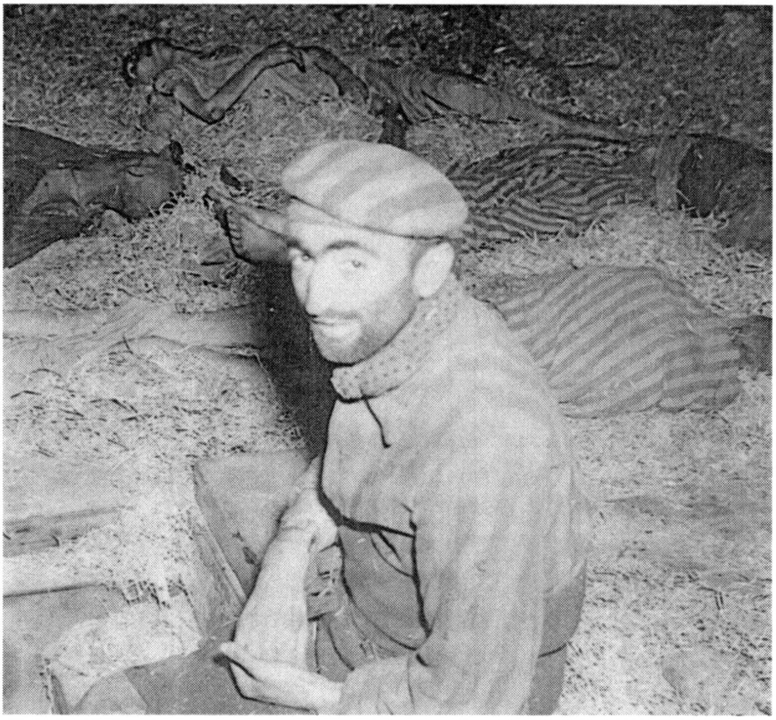

Emaciated human shadows

that this was coming from the allied forces, but when we came closer to the forest we understood that our fate was sealed. I was extremely weak and felt that my end was near. I was praying to G-d and asking for justice and mercy by thinking, "From whence shall my help come?" (Psalm 121:1) I continued to meditate: "Master of the universe, what kind of sin did we children commit, these holy lambs. Why does this flock have to be sacrificed?" I was praying for a miracle. We inched nearer and nearer to the gate. As we got closer, we could now hear clearly the ticking of the machine guns.

It seemed that a miracle did happen. At the moment when the Blockealteste and the first rows of the children were about to exit the gate, the sirens started to wail – as if they were crying. The S.S. ran to take cover and the gate was closed. Our Blockaelteste directed us to return to the barrack quickly. Suddenly American bombers appeared and were crossing the skies of Buchenwald. They were dropping bombs around the camp and strafed the S.S. barracks. This went on for hours. The Germans were shooting at the fighter planes. There was a lot of noise and confusion. Some of us were so weak that we crawled to the nearest barrack to take cover. It took all my resolve and strength to crawl back into the barrack. The prayer of the Biblical Samson entered my thoughts. I prayed and said: "O Lord G-d, remember me, I pray Thee and strengthen me only this once." (Judges 16:28) The explosions shook the entire camp. This was the first time during my incarceration that I saw the master race run for cover. It felt very good, to see them in this situation. We lay low in the barrack and waited. At nightfall it became quiet, there was no movement. We really did not know what was going on around us.

In the morning, units of the S.S. tried for the last time to enter the camp in order to remove the last prisoners. The Americans told us later that as they fought their way towards Buchenwald, they intercepted a train with hundreds of armed Hitler *Jougend*, Hitler youth, who were ordered to Buchenwald to help the S.S. to annihilate all the prisoners and help destroy the camp. At this point, the underground resistance decided to confront the S.S. units. They took up arms, which they hid over the years. The battle lasted a few hours. Through the window cracks, we saw prisoners in striped clothing running with guns in their hands. Suddenly there was silence. Soon after that we saw the S.S. sentries leaving the lookout posts, their watch towers around the camp fences. They left their heavy machine guns on the towers and fled into the forest. Some resistance members hoisted up a white flag on the flagpole on the apell platz. The Germans retreated and the resistance organization took over the running of the camp. Suddenly, American soldiers in jeeps from the Third Army 6th Armored Division entered the camp. Among them were black soldiers. This was the first time in my life that I had seen a black person. Soon after them, a few American tanks rumbled into the camp. Many times during my incarceration I thought that I, too, would not come out

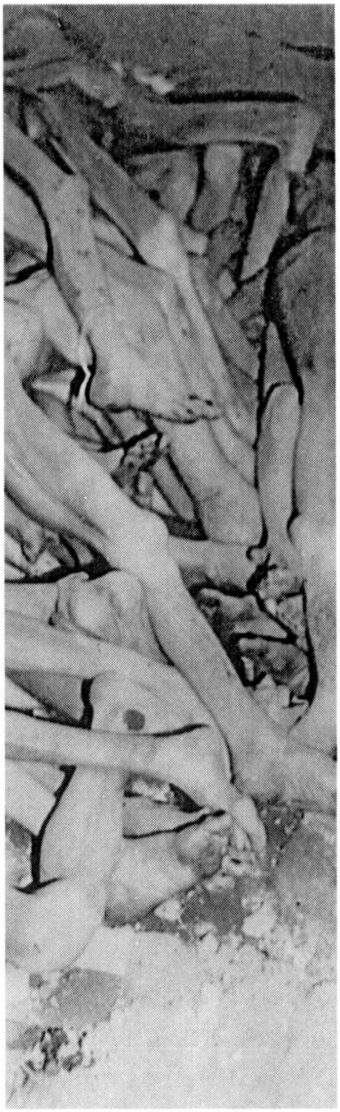

Bodies on top of bodies in Buchenwald.

from this inferno alive. I was very lucky since so many times I was on the verge of death, but somehow I survived.

The Americans were shocked when they saw the piles of dead bodies heaped all over. They did not know what kind of place they had come into. Many of us had no strength to cheer on the Americans; no one was in a position to show emotion. Those of the prisoners who could stand up walked out to see the liberators. When they saw our faces, our skeletons, the dead bodies inside and outside the barracks, they cried. These were our angels for whom we had waited so long. Some of the prisoners were hugging and kissing the American soldiers. They began to distribute chocolate to us, cigarettes and other goodies. Some of us with our last bit of strength tried to catch the gifts. The day of the liberation of Buchenwald was the happiest and the saddest day of my life.

Later on, an entire convoy of American troops arrived in the camp. An officer with a megaphone called out that we were now free men, but that we should listen to the soldiers and obey their instructions. Some prisoners who were not in bad shape, such as the Russians prisoners of war, roamed around the camp and outside the fence. They were looking for hiding S.S. and German officers. Some of them got a hold of cars and weapons and traveled to the nearby city of Weimar to take revenge against the Germans. On the first day of liberation, the Americans did not stop the prisoners from taking revenge on the Germans. On the second day, clear orders were given to the troops not to allow anyone to harm captured S.S. or other German military. Now our tormentors were on the run. For the first time in years, they tasted what it meant to be a prisoner. Many of them were taken to P.O.W. camps where they were now surrounded by barbed wire fences. They were unshaven, hungry, neglected, and deserted by their Nazi idols. But there was still a tremendous difference in

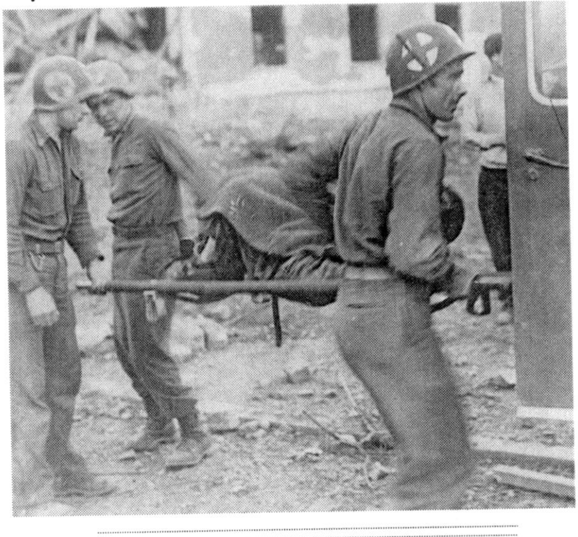

American medics in Buchenwald

the treatment they received by the Allies in comparison to the brutal treatment we experienced by their bloody hands.

One day after the liberation, the supreme commander of the allied forces in Europe, General Dwight Eisenhower and a large delegation of high-ranking allied officers came to Buchenwald. They brought with them all the *Burgermeister*, the mayors of the surrounding towns of the camp, to show them the atrocities their people committed in the camp. The mayors claimed that they had no idea of what was going on inside the camp. They only knew of the imprisoned political prisoners in Buchenwald. They said, "*Wir Haben Garnichts Gewist.*" We knew nothing about it before.

Before the arrival of this delegation, American officers who were stationed in Buchenwald gathered some of the children prisoners to show the German mayors the terrible condition that the children victims were in. Among the children displayed was eight-year-old Lulek, Israel Meir Lau, (later to be elected Chief Rabbi of Israel.) He was the youngest child in Buchenwald, miraculously hidden by his brother, Naftali. One of the American officers approached Lulek and lifted him up and declared, "This is your political prisoner?" After that, the mayors did not dare say anything.

I was very weak and ill. I had to lay in the barrack and could not take part in the joy of the liberation. My body was skeletal and covered with open sores. My legs were swollen from hunger and retaining water. There is a Jewish saying, which says, "*A mensch is shtarker fun eisen und shwacher fun a flieg.*" A person is stronger than iron and weaker than a fly. During the Holocaust, I felt strong like iron because I had this iron will to survive, but on the other hand, there were moments when I felt like a fly because I was weak and helpless. In the meantime, the Americans organized a rescue operation. They dispensed food, registered the living prisoners, and organized the burial of the dead in the camp and in the forest. For that, the Americans forced the Germans from the surrounding towns to take care of the mass graves. They hospitalized as many sick prisoners as they could. They organized makeshift hospitals in the former S.S. quarters. Soldiers, nurses, and doctors set to work to save those who could be saved. I was moved to one of those hospitals, barely alive. American doctors and nurses examined me and prescribed medication and an extremely bland diet of cereal. I was given a hot bath with soap, which I had not had since we left our home in Bilke. They weighed me on a scale. I weighed 70 pounds, which is about 35 kilos. For a while, I was hovering between life and death.

In the hospital, I was fed a spoonful at a time, every day a bit more.

They watched over me very carefully and after a few days, my body began to show signs of improvement. Was there an angel watching over me? The fact that I survived and am able to tell the story is an indication that there was a guardian of Israel.

Unfortunately, the physical liberation from Buchenwald did not bring me mental redemption. I felt that I was left alone in the valley of the slaughter. I wanted to return to my family, to my people, but I did not know where to go or how to do it. There was no one whom I could trust, or ask advice, or to share my anxiety. This loneliness was one of the most difficult situations I found myself in, even after the liberation.

I was alone. I did not know any of the prisoners in the hospital. Because of the confusion that existed in the last days before liberation, and the influx of prisoners from other camps, Buchenwald was in turmoil. At the end, Buchenwald had almost every nationality of Europe including American P.O.W.'s. It was a babble of people and languages. We had only one thing in common and that was that we were all the victims of the cruelest system in the entire history of humanity.

In the first two weeks after the liberation, many prisoners died. Being desperately hungry, many of them grabbed all kinds of food, which was too rich and detrimental to their critical condition. Their stomachs could not digest this kind of food anymore. Our systems were not used to normal food. Some died because they were too weak or sick to be nursed back to health. For others it was too late. No matter what the Americans tried to do, some people died from sheer joy. They had lived and hoped for liberation, and when it finally came, it was too much for them.

One day, I had a pleasant surprise. An American Jewish Chaplain by the name of Rabbi Herschel Schacter came in to see me. I did not know that the American Army had Jewish Chaplains. This was not the only thing I did not know about the Americans. Until then, I did not meet such good-natured people. He asked me my name, how old I was, from where I came in Europe, if I knew anyone in the camp. He was a very pleasant and caring person. You could see in his face that he had seen more than enough in the last few days.

In the military code, there were no specific guidelines of how to treat the survivors. However, the Jewish Chaplains had a wonderful guide for such unprepared situations. This was the Bible. There, one can find many passages of how to kindly treat the poor, the sick, and the downtrodden. There were times when the chaplains had a conflict between their army duties and the needs of the survivors, but their Jewish hearts overcame many obstacles. His

Rabbi Herschel Schacter

visit greatly boosted my strength and my spirits. He gave me much encouragement and he wished me a speedy recovery. Later, I met another Jewish Chaplain. His name was Rabbi Robert Marcus. Later, after my release from the hospital, I had other occasions to meet Rabbi Schacter. Years later, I met him in New York and on one of my visits to Israel, I saw him in a shul in Jerusalem. I even mentioned to him that in Buchenwald, we met on the defiled land, but in Israel we were privileged to meet in the Holy Land. Day by day, I gained strength. The American medical staff worked miracles. They brought me back to life for which I am thankful every day of my life.

Buchenwald Concentration Camp witnessed the deaths of tens of thousands of innocent Jewish victims at the hands of the German criminals through starvation, torture, and disease. On the day of the liberation, April 11, 1945, the American soldiers were shocked by the hell they discovered – tens of thousands of emaciated human shadows, crowded into narrow, filthy barracks, and thousands of unburied corpses throughout the camp and in the forest of Buchenwald. The liberation of the concentration camps came too late for the victims of Germany's war against the Jews. Millions could have been saved had the Western Allies and the Soviet Union, in their strategy for conquest of German-occupied Europe, included plans for the rescue of the Jews. The military maps did not even show the location of the death camps.

Many of the survivors died in the weeks immediately following the liberation from epidemics, diseases, and malnutrition. The uprooted and homeless survivors, despite their suffering and losses, emerged from the valley of death with a strong will to rebuild their lives. These brave survivors emerged from terror and destruction, scared by death, but determined to start a new life.

When the Americans entered Buchenwald, the survivors had to face a grim reality. For the majority of the liberated Jews of the camp, there was no ecstasy, no joy in our liberation. We had lost our families, our homes, our countries. We had no place to go; nobody to hug, nobody who was waiting for us anywhere. We were liberated from death and from the fear of death, but we were not free from fear of life. The Americans wanted initially to classify the

ORPHAN CHILDREN FROM BUCHENWALD NOW IN PARIS

ENFANTS VENUS D'ALLEMAGNE - CONVOI DU 8 JUIN 1945
À ECOUIS (Eure)

Paris List N° 1162

[illegible]	[illegible]	[illegible]	[illegible]		
197	KOCHAN	Henieck	22/3/30	Bendzin	Pol.
198	KOCHAN	Sala	15/3/28	"	"
199	KOHAN	Jona	10/7/29	Felsoiselist	Roum.
200	KOHN	Zoltan	5/6/29	Busting	Tché.
201	KORZENBLATT	Abraham	7/5/31		Pol.
202	KORTUCH	David	6/1/30	Kielce	"
203	KOVAES	Imre	25/3/29	Szalard	Roum/
204	KARPUSINSKI	Israel	25/1/27		
205	KOZUCH	Max	2/3/19	Strzemienyce	Pol.
206	KRAUS	Herman	8/1/30	Uzhorod	Tché.
207	KROUS	Jewo	11/7/31	Miskols-Borzod	Hongr.
208	KUCHARSKI	David	2/12/28	Bendzin	Pol.
209	KULITZ	Moses	7/12/28	Szlakina	Tché.
210	KRAKAUER	Arnold	1/8/39	Chrzanow	Pol.
211	KYBA	Chaim	28/12/28		"
212	LAJTENBERG	Keyt	2/12/25		"
213	LANDAU	Naftali	6/3/28	Banssyhulyad	Roum.
214	LANDAU	Bejniez	6/8/28	Bezesko	Pol.
215	LASZLO	Janos	30/10/28	Oradéa	Roum.
216	LAU	Israel	1/6/37	Piotrkow	Pol.
217	LAU	Naftali	23/6/28	Krakow	"
218	LAUFER	Nathan	16/6/29	Leczyca	"
219	LAZAROWITS	Jakob	10/10/30	Talosremék	Roum.
220	LAZAROWITS	Juda	18/3/29	"	"
221	LEBEWITZ	Frigjes	23/6/28		"
222	LEBOVITZ	Ignac	9/12/28	Szalmar	"
223	LEBOVITZ	Beni	23/8/28	Slatinsko	Tché.
224	LEMPERT	Claudislaus	31/7/28	Oradéa	Roum/
225	LENDER	Jakob	25/9/29	Viseul de Sus	Roum.
226	LENDER	Josef	4/3/28	"	"
227	LERNER	Salomon	9/10/29	Sighet	"
228	LERNER	Chaim	8/5/30	Felsaviso	Hongr.
229	LERNER	Alex	10/12/28	Slatynskie	Tché.
230	LEHRER	Abraham	14/9/27		Pol.
231	LESWZYK	Jakob	10/12/28	Wichau	"
232	LEVENZ	Tibor	8/11/29	Lzirlugos	Hongr.
233	LEWIN	Manfred	27/9/39		Allem.
234	LEWKOWITZ	Léon	20/6/30		Pol.
235	LIBLICH	Szyja	22/3/28	Kra kowie	"
236	LICHTENSTEIN-Arthur		1/1/29		Roum.
237	LIKER	Horsch	30/3/28	Bialisstock	Pol.
238	LIPSITZ	Bernard	5/2/29	Satoralzaribyhely-	Hongr?
239	LIPSITZ	Mozès	18/7/29	Bilke	Tché.
240	LISKER	Henrik	13/2/28	Berlin	Allem.
241	LONDNER	Fishchel	16/5/28	Szokonowiec	Pol.
242	LOWINCZ	Imre	5/10/28	Solizslek	Hong.
243	LOWY	Téodor	16/10/27	Cieszyn	Pol.
244	LURIE	Szane	11/4/30	Wilno	"
245	LUSTIG	Laslo	27/10/28	Oradéa	Roum.
246	MAJER	Salomon	26/4/23	Slatuska	Tché.

This is a page from the list of Jewish orphan children from Buchenwald who were taken to France for recuperation after liberation. The author is number 239 on the list. Also on this list is Israel Lau, number 216, who later became Chief Rabbi of Israel.

> We waited impatiently for the day when we would leave Europe, the continent that devoured our families, which was soaked with so much Jewish blood.

survivors by their nationalities of origin. We demanded to be recognized as sons of the Jewish people, not as Czechs or Poles or Hungarians.

While still in the hospital on May 8, 1945, we heard that the Germans capitulated and that the war was over. People were starting to think about their future, what to do next. Many Gentiles had no problem; they were planning to return to their homeland, to their families. However, we Jews had a great problem since we knew that most of our families had perished, our homes were robbed and all our belongings were plundered. Also the situation all over Europe was very unstable, and most of the East European countries did not want even the handful of Jews who survived back in their countries.

A new term was invented – repatriation – meaning that all should return to their former countries. Day in and day out we heard that the Allies advocated repatriation of all the displaced persons. America and England were not interested in huge immigration to their countries of the displaced persons. England was especially afraid that many Jews would choose to go to Palestine, which would cause them a great headache with the Arabs, and so they pressed for repatriation.

Huge quarries were located around Buchenwald where the prisoners worked. Shortly after the liberation of the camp, the Third Army discovered a great treasure that the Germans had hidden in two tunnels in the stone quarry. There they found all kinds of religious vessels and articles of gold and silver, quantities of gold, silver, coins, wedding rings, watches, diamonds, Torah ornaments, Shabbat candle sticks, menorahs, kiddush cups, Shabbat knives, etrog boxes, Chanukah candelabras, *Pesach kearot* plates, spice boxes, silver trays, and many other valuable articles. All these were looted by the Germans throughout occupied Europe or confiscated from the victims upon their arrival in the ghettos and concentration camps. For days, many military trucks, escorted by armored military police, transported these treasures. Who knows what happened to them and who got rich on account of the Jewish victims. There were a number of organizations, among them the International Red Cross, the U.S. Army, and some Jewish organizations, who compiled lists of survivors and of missing family members, so that people could search for one another. I gave them information about myself and about my missing family, with the hope that maybe some of them survived.

We were told the Buchenwald camp would soon be turned over to the Russians. Those of the prisoners who did not wish to be repatriated to their native country would come under Russian control. Under the auspices of the U.N.R.R.A, United Nations Relief and Rehabilitation Administration, displaced persons were to be sent back to their countries of origin. I had to decide what to do, whether to return to Czechoslovakia, my native country which was then not under Russian domination, or possibly go to Bilke, my former home which was already under Russian occupation, to look for family survivors.

I assumed that my two older brothers Chaim Leib and Nachum Uri perished in Munko Tabor, the forced labor battalions, when the Hungarians shipped them to the Russian front. I saw my father, mother and my two sisters with their children in Auschwitz sent to the left, meaning certain death. I knew my brother, Shmuel Tzvi, had been in Palestine since 1937 because he was an ardent Zionist. I heard from Bilker Landsleit in Buchenwald that my brother Joseph perished in December of 1944 in Plaszow, when he entered the infirmary hospital. It was a tragic irony. All over the world people seek medical help in a hospital in order to be helped. In the German infirmary in the camps, whoever arrived there seeking help never left the place alive. No one marked down the victims names, and thus millions of Jews disappeared without a trace, as if they had never been born or existed.

The only ones I had no definite information about were my three sisters Feige, Mani (Miriam), and Reise and my brother Shlomo, who was also taken to a Munko Tabor in Hungary.

The Carpathians, the Eastern part of Czechoslovakia from were I came, was then under Russian occupation. It was very complicated to get there and it was dangerous because once you were there, the Russians would not let you out.

In the meantime, a Czech diplomat came to Buchenwald to try to convince Czech nationals to return home. Since I was still in the hospital, he came to talk to me. He urged me to return, offered me financial assistance and good opportunities of continuing my education. I thanked him very much and told him that I would soon make up my mind.

The holiday of *Shavuot*, Pentecost, was approaching and it reminded me of my hometown, which was always in full bloom at that time of the year. There were the preparations at home for the holiday, my mother baking all kinds of pastries, especially the cheesecakes, and the wonderful spring air in the mountains. Just before Shavuot, the chaplains Rabbi Robert Marcus and Rabbi Herschel Schacter took over a German recreation hall in Buchenwald

Rabbi Herschel Schacter leads Shavuot services in Buchenwald after liberation. He was among the first to enter Buchenwald on April 11, 1945. Rabbi Schacter provided the much needed spiritual sustenance for the Jewish survivors.

and made it into a Synagogue for the holiday. By this time, I was able to walk outside and so I went to the service. Hundreds of former Jewish prisoners, among them young boys, gathered to celebrate the holiday of Shavuot, the giving of the Torah to the Jewish people at Mt. Sinai. This was the first Jewish holiday we celebrated as free people. It was an inspiration, but also very sad.

I was hoping to leave the cursed German land and make my way to the Land of Israel where my only brother was still alive. I felt that this was the only place on this planet where I would be able to find peace. After seven weeks in the hospital, I gained back my strength and my health. We were informed that the children of Buchenwald would leave the camp in the beginning of June to a recuperation center in France.

Part 4

From The Gates Of Hell To The Gates Of Hope

They shall come back from the land of the enemy and there is hope for thy future saith the Lord; and thy children shall return to their own border.

(Jeremiah 31:16-17)

The Children Of Buchenwald

On June 2, 1945, almost eight weeks after the liberation, we were given regular civilian clothing. These were made of green-gray material. I think it was material that was found in the German storerooms in camp and tailors sewed the clothing for us. Approximately 500 children and teenagers from Buchenwald were taken to the train station. A passenger train was waiting for us. It was quite a difference from the boxcars we were shoved into by the S.S. beasts. Rabbi Robert Marcus, the American Army Chaplain, other American officers, and representatives of The International Red Cross escorted us. On the train there was a large sign – Children of Buchenwald.

The Children of Buchenwald leave the concentration camp on their way to France.

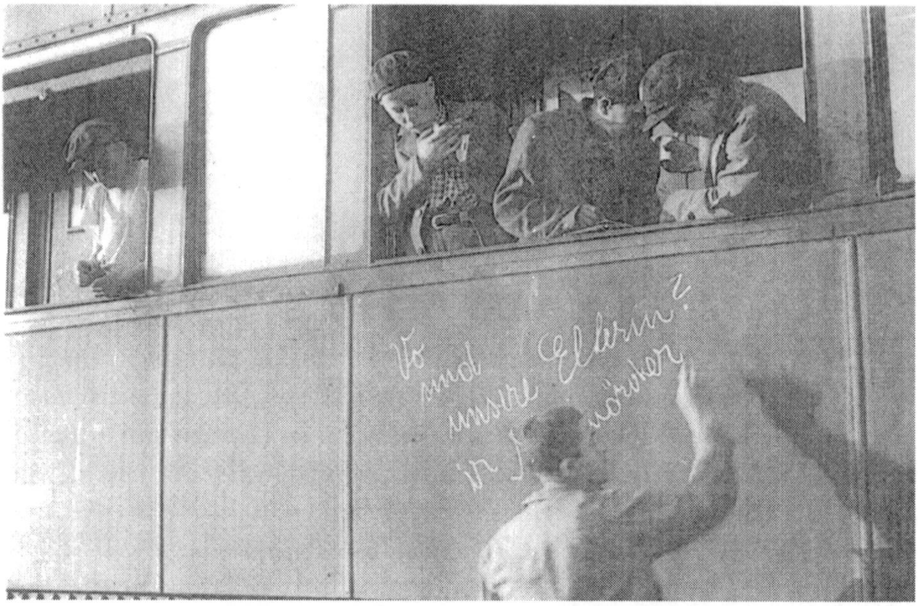

The Children of Buchenwald on the train to Ecouis

Each one of us was given a package of food for the journey. This was the only possession we had. We did not know how long the journey would take because much of the rail system was in ruins, or where this trip would take us. We only knew we were going to France for recuperation. I was only 16 years old. The train traveled slowly, and made many stops. It took a couple of days before we reached our destination. We arrived in Normandy in northwestern France. A delegation of mayors and other French dignitaries greeted us upon our arrival. The leadership of the O.S.E., the Jewish French organization for the welfare of the Jewish children from the Holocaust, also waited for us. From the train station, we were taken in a convoy of buses to a Chateau for

recuperation in the village of Ecouis. It almost looked like a palace to us.

Moshe, a few weeks after liberation.

It was a beautiful and pleasant place. In the complex, there were several buildings. The rooms inside were very spacious and full of light. We were given bedding, pillows, blankets, and towels. This type of an arrangement reminded me of home in Bilke. The estate had beautiful green grass, a great variety of trees, bushes, and flowers. Most of the staff spoke French, but some knew German and Yiddish. A lot of the staff was Jewish. We received very good care there. We were examined by a doctor and received necessary medical treatment. Our stay in Ecouis was sponsored by Jewish organizations in France and the U.N.R.R.A., an organization of the United Nations.

The food that was provided was very good. Every morning we ate fresh French bread, vegetables (which I hadn't had since Bilke) and eggs and meat. Of course everything was Kosher. We utilized the time for rest, study, and socializing. We learned the Hebrew language, Zionism, Hebrew songs, Bible, Jewish History and other subjects. We took strolls into the village and the vicinity. But we waited impatiently for the day when we would leave Europe, the continent that devoured our families, which was soaked with so much Jewish blood.

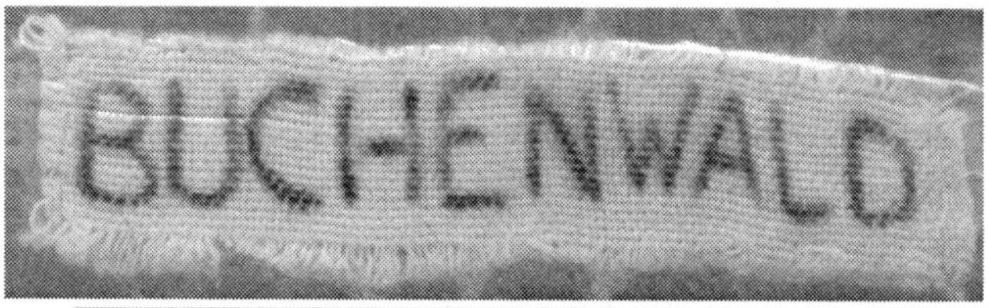

This patch was sewn on each child's jacket sleeve when they left Buchenwald for France.

The *Brichah* Organization, which organized liberated Jews to get to the South of France and Italy, was secretly run by the Jewish Brigade. This was a Jewish unit within the British military, which volunteered to fight against Germany, and after the war, devoted themselves to save Jews all over Europe, and ship them clandestinely to the Land of Israel. They came to Ecouis, led discussions with us, told us about life in Israel, about the *kibbutzim*, cooperative settlements, about the *moshavim,* the agricultural villages, and about the *yishuv*, the organized Jewish community in Palestine. We were told about the Hagannah, and other Jewish underground organizations that were preparing for the day when a Jewish state would be declared. These *shlichim*, emissaries from the Jewish Brigade, elaborated specifically about the struggle of Aliyah Beth, the

The Children of Buchenwald in Ecouis dance the *Horah*, before leaving for Palestine in July 1945.

illegal immigration to Palestine because the British would not permit Jews to enter into the land. The British were in control of Palestine and forcefully blocked the entry into the land for survivors of the Holocaust, at a time when the Germans were decimating the Jews of Europe. This policy continued after the war until they finally withdrew from Palestine.

I was now a person without any documents, without a birth certificate to identify myself, without a family, without a country – alone. Everything was confiscated from us by the Hungarians before we were deported to Auschwitz. I felt I had nothing to return to in my native country. I wondered what kind of a life I could create for myself in post war Czechoslovakia where there were almost no Jews. Most of us teenage survivors were interested in leaving for Eretz Yisrael.

The people who took care of us in Ecouis tried to discourage us from going there. We were told we would be better off staying in France or immigrating to America. Among us were some who wanted to assimilate and leave the Jewish fold. Who could actually blame them after what they went through? In my opinion that was not a solution for any Jewish boy, especially not for me. Even though I carried in me quite a bit of anger and frustration, for me to become a part of another nation was out of the question, especially after no nation lifted a finger to help our people. On the contrary, all of the European nations had a hand in the persecution of our people during the Holocaust. Some more and some less, but they had a share in it. So I surely was not going to join the evil forces of Europe.

U.S. Army Colonel Rozen addresses the Children of Buchenwald in Ecouis in July 1945.

Some of the French Jewish community leaders were eager for us to stay in France and become a part of their community. Some of the French Jewish women who took care of us in Ecouis were like mothers to us. A few youths from Buchenwald later stayed in France, among them Elie Wiesel. The majority of the Buchenwald Children became ardent Zionists and were determined to find a way to get to the Land of Israel, by any means. Our slogan was, "We will not help the Germans and their collaborators to complete the job."

The leaders of the French Zionist movement came to visit us in Ecouis and 350 of us expressed a desire to go on aliyah. A few days later, we were informed that in the beginning of July 1945, the group would be able to leave. Although just a few months had passed since the war ended, we survivors had been largely forgotten by the world at large, and even by the Jewish communities of the free world. We had to struggle ourselves to get somewhere. To most people, the Holocaust was an event they preferred to forget.

Since the British refused to allow survivors to immigrate to Palestine, a massive illegal immigration effort began by the Brichah, Aliyah Beth, and The Jewish Brigade. Large groups of displaced persons, Holocaust survivors, were moved by secret transports to France and Italy. From there they were shipped on obsolete sailing vessels towards the Jewish Homeland.

One night in July of 1945, a convoy of British military vehicles, which were organized and driven by The Jewish Brigade soldiers, arrived in Ecouis at the Chateau. They had the list of those of us who had registered to go to the Land of Israel. The leaders of the Brichah instructed us to take small packages with us and to board the trucks. The vehicles were covered with canvas, so that the French and possibly British agents would not discover what was going on. We said good-bye to Ecouis and in our hearts we thanked the wonderful people who took care of us, helped us to grow, and develop again into normal human beings.

Destination Palestine

During the night, our convoy with the 350 youths from Ecouis arrived in a French port. Nobody told us the name of the port. We were loaded onto a fairly large vessel, which used to haul cargo. This ship was converted by the Hagannah into a *Maapilim*, illegal immigrant vessel. It was renamed Yaldei Buchenwald, The Children of Buchenwald. On the ship we already found more young people from other camps. We sailed from France to Italy to a small port hidden away where more survivors boarded the ship. Now the ship was filled to capacity. We ended up having 1,100 young survivors on board.

It was very crowded on the ship. During the daytime we were not allowed to be on the deck of the ship because British ships cruised the Mediterranean Sea and British planes flew reconnaissance flights to make sure that Jewish refugee ships did not sneak into Palestine. Only during the evenings and nights were we allowed to go up on the deck. We had to go in shifts because there were so many of us. Food and water was rationed because the ship could not hold much cargo weight in addition to its passengers. Also the Aliyah Beth leaders were not sure of the length of the journey. Down below the decks, the air was heavy. Also, it was the month of July when the daytime weather was quite hot. Only the evenings and nights gave us some relief.

The ship's crew, the captain, and all the leaders of the ship were Hagannah members who devoted their lives to rescuing Jews from Europe. They instructed us what to do if we were caught by the British Navy. We had a few drills and we learned some defense tactics.

Our journey lasted 10 days, but it seemed much longer, due to the conditions on the ship and the tension we felt. But we all accepted it with understanding, because every day we came closer to the Land of our Fathers where we would realize our hopes and dreams. I was especially looking forward to seeing my brother Shmuel Tzvi again, his wife Channah and their children, which I assumed they had by now. I had not seen my brother since

1937 when he left for Palestine. At that time I was eight years old. A lot had happened since then, and I was waiting impatiently for the moment of our reunion. Until the war, my brother wrote very often. His letters were wonderful. He described to us the Land and everything that was happening there. Through his letters, although still a young boy, I learned about the country of our Fathers and became familiar with many places, people, and events.

As our ship was nearing the coast of Palestine, the British Navy, which blocked the shores, intercepted our boat. They encircled our ship and followed us towards the shore. In the morning, as we were able to see the mountain range of the Carmel, the British ships closed in on us. Through a loud speaker they ordered the ship to proceed to Haifa under their guard. The captain of our ship hoisted the Jewish flag. Up until that moment we were sailing under a fictitious flag. We also raised banners of rage against the British, such as "We survived Hitler – We will survive the British" and "Death is not a stranger to us." Our captain instructed us to keep calm and not engage the British. The Aliyah Beth leadership on the boat realized that they could not fight the mighty British Navy. They also knew they had 1,100 precious youngsters who miraculously survived the Holocaust. They thought it would be in vain to shed blood. They wanted to make sure these orphans, this precious cargo, arrived in Palestine unharmed.

The ship arrived in Haifa Harbor, where British soldiers and British police boarded our ship. On the ship, they recorded our names, ages, places of birth, names of parents, and other important information. On the one hand we were very happy that our long journey had come to an end and that we were finally in the Land of our Fathers. But on the other hand, we were worried because we did not know what the British had planned for us.

We disembarked the ship under heavy military guard. Military trucks were waiting for us on the pier. We boarded the trucks, and with heavy military escort, proceeded to the internment camp of Atlit near Haifa. So once again, I ended up in a camp, not as bad as a concentration camp, but still a camp and not a free person. The camp was a typical British military camp, clean and in good sanitary condition. We were placed in barracks with military beds, mattresses, blankets, sheets, and all the usual military equipment. We had showers, bathrooms, a dining room, and other installations. The camp at Atlit was surrounded by unelectrified barbed wire, and watch towers, which guarded the camp. In comparison to the concentration camps, this was a four star hotel. But we still were prisoners.

The Jewish Agency for Palestine personnel had access to the camp.

They came and interviewed every one of us to find out who we were and if we had relatives in Palestine. With this information *Kol Yisrael*, the Jewish broadcasting station, announced who the Maapilim, illegal immigrants, were and for whom they were looking. One of my landsleit, Isaac Friedman, heard on the radio that Moshe Doft-Lipschitz (this was my family name at the time) was looking for his brother Shmuel Tzvi Doft-Lipschitz. Isaac Friedman immediately informed my brother that his youngest brother Moshe had arrived on the ship Yaldei Buchenwald, and that he was detained in Atlit.

Moshe, at 16 in Atlit, when he was reunited with his brother, Shmuel Tzvi

The next day, while I was in the barrack someone came in and asked who was Moshe Doft-Lipschitz. I said I was. He said my brother was waiting for me at the gate. The British did not allow visits, but one could stand at the gate. I rushed to the gate. I recognized my brother right away because he was 18 years old when he left home. He had not changed much and he had also sent pictures home from Palestine. My brother did not recognize me because I had changed a lot. When he left home I was only 8 years old and now I was 16. I looked very different. Also it was hard for him to believe that Moshe'leh, the child that he had left, could have survived the Holocaust. My brother asked me all kinds of questions about the family to make sure I was really his brother. He asked me the names of our father and mother, the names of our brothers and sisters, from what town I came, what our father did. Only after this thorough quiz did he come to the conclusion that I was really his youngest brother.

Both of us cried. This reunion was extremely emotional. He wanted to know what happened to our parents and our brothers and sisters, and about all the Jews in Bilke. Isaac Friedman accompanied my brother. He, too, was inquiring about his family. I told him as much as I knew about them. I had to tell him his entire family was deported to Kamenets-Podolsk in 1941 in the Ukraine, where they and other Bilker Jews were all massacred. My brother told me he would do everything possible to free me from the Atlit camp.

The Jewish Agency negotiated with the British about our release, but they had their policy of the White Paper, which did not allow Jewish immigration to Palestine. After three weeks in Atlit, the first week in August 1945, we were awakened at night by people whom we had never before seen. These were Hagannah, members of the Jewish underground. They had successfully overtaken the camp by tying up the guards. They said that they came to free us. They led us out of the camp through a hole they cut in the barbed wire. I looked at my liberators as if they were super human or angels. We walked a while behind a mountain where trucks were waiting for us. The Hagannah rescuers distributed us in various kibbutzim and gave us documents. They told us to stay put in the kibbutz until the British stopped looking for us. Overnight, I became a Palestinian with a new identity. I was sent to *Kibbutz Yavneh*, a religious settlement in the south. When the British discovered what happened the next morning, they declared a curfew in the entire country. Thousands of British soldiers and police started a search for the escapees. They put up roadblocks and turned the country upside down. After a few days, the British lifted the curfew, lifted the roadblocks, and the country returned to normal. As far as I can remember, the British did not catch anyone of the Children of Buchenwald. However they learned a lesson from this setback. They learned that they would be unable to keep illegal immigrants that they intercepted in a detention camp in Palestine. From then on, all the *Maapilim* ships that the British Navy was successful in overtaking were either returned to Europe or sent to the island of Cyprus where they established huge areas of detention camps. They also returned some ships to Germany such as the ship Exodus. As soon as my brother found out what the Hagannah had accomplished, and that I was safe in Kibbutz Yavneh, he was elated. I informed him that I would come to Jerusalem to visit him as soon as it was safe. I was privileged to do what Moses was not privileged to do. I was able to enter the Land of Israel, a great dream fulfilled.

From the tragic end of the voyage of the 778 illegal immigrants, maapilim, on the ship Struma, to the Land of Israel, I learned that we, the survivors of the ship Yaldei Buchenwald, were very lucky. One can learn from this that powerful forces joined hands against the Jews during and after the Holocaust years. The Struma left the Rumanian port of Constanta on December 11, 1941, carrying 778 Rumanian Jews fleeing persecution of the Rumanian Fascist Government, heading for the Land of Israel. Its engine failed on the Black Sea and it was towed into Istanbul, Turkey. The Turkish government refused to allow anyone off the ship. The British, who controlled Palestine at that time, refused entry to Jews because of the White Paper they issued, forbidding Jewish immigration to Palestine.

The Struma sat in Istanbul for 70 days. The ship had only one outlet for fresh water. The only food came from the Jews of Istanbul. Efforts to repair the engine failed. On February 23, 1942, the Turkish police towed the

Struma with its Jewish passengers up the Bosporus. The ship was set adrift in the Black Sea. At dawn the next day, it was sunk by a Russian submarine. Only one of the refugees survived. It was the biggest loss of life in the illegal immigration to the Land of Israel. Not only was the world silent during those tragic years, but there was a convergence of direct participants of individuals and governments in the destruction of European Jewry.

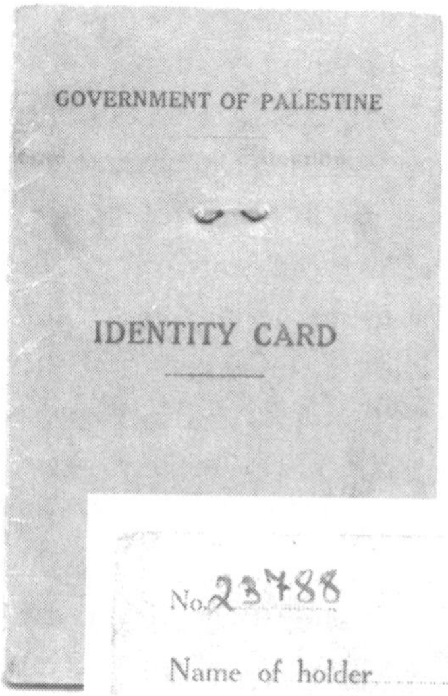

In the case of the Struma, the Rumanians were persecuting them. The Germans wanted to lay their hands on them to annihilate them. The Turkish had no human compassion for those poor Jews, either. The British blocked every path on the way to Palestine and the Russians were trigger happy, because to the communists, human beings meant very little. The brutal British treatment of Jewish survivors after the Holocaust and their prevention from entering Palestine during and

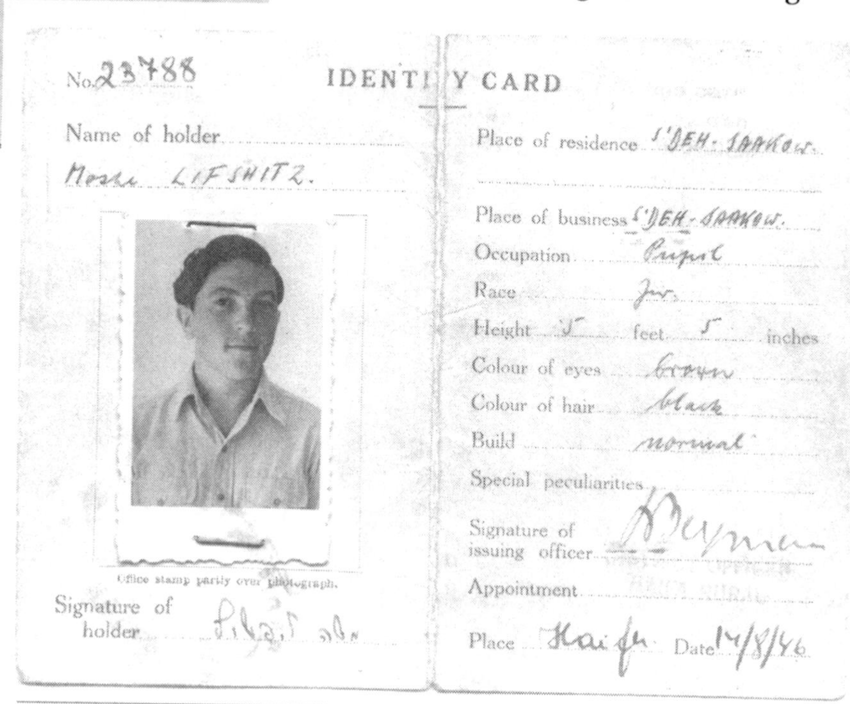

Moshe Lipschitz Avital's identity card, issued by the British in Haifa in 1946.

after the second world war, the silence of the Royal House of Windsor, the British Press, and the British people will remain an everlasting stain on a nation who gave the world the Magna Carta.

We Jews will forever have contempt for the big powers – Britain, France, and America for their hindrance and cold political calculations and self interests at a time when a small remnant of Jewish Holocaust survivors were struggling to reach their ancient homeland. The silence of the Christian Church, the world press, and the liberal intellectuals, when they saw Jewish refugees forcefully returned to the cursed land of Germany, will remain a dark chapter in the annals of world history.

Starting A New Life In Our Homeland

As soon it was safe for me to move around, I was transferred from Kibbutz Yavneh to a Youth Aliyah village at *Sdeh Yaakov* in the valley of Jezreel. In this village there were about 100 boys and girls, all teenagers, who lost their parents in the Shoah and they somehow survived. We lived in dormitories or in tents because they were short on accommodations. Each one of us was assigned to a family in the Moshav, to help work on the farm. We worked on the farm from early in the morning until noon. Of course we were never farmers before, but we learned fast. We milked cows, cleaned out the cow shed, fed the chickens, cows, and horses. In the field, we plowed and sowed all kinds of grain, wheat, and corn. We cut the hay and made bundles. In short, we did all the chores of a farm hand. In return, we received three meals a day from the farmer. I was very lucky to have been assigned to the family of Shlomo Mitzmacher, a fine family who took good care of me. They had two daughters and a son, who was killed in the Six Day War in 1967. The farmer's wife was a very good cook and there was plenty of food. For a concentration camp survivor who was almost starved to death, this was a real feast. I was a good and devoted worker so we got along very well. Their daughter Yonah supplied me with books to read, which I read with great thirst. Not all the boys and girls were as lucky as I was, and some of the farmers took advantage of these teenagers and did not provide them with good food.

In the afternoon, we studied in classrooms at the youth village, secular as well as Judaic studies. All the classes were conducted in Hebrew by professional teachers. We had a lot to catch up on since we lost years of schooling because of the Shoah. We studied the following subjects: The Hebrew language, Bible, Jewish history, Zionism, Hebrew literature, prayers, world history, arithmetic, geography, and others. The evenings were designated for socializing and discussions on burning issues of the times. As a part of our cultural activities, we attended the *Habimah*, Hebrew theater performances, in Haifa.

Since it was a religious village, we observed the Shabbat and Holidays, participated in services, mornings and evenings. On Shabbat, we all ate together in our dining room. We served as waiters, helped out in the kitchen, washed dishes, and cleaned up as well.

During the Shabbat and Holiday meals, we sang *zemirot*, religious songs, and learned many other popular songs, especially nationalistic ones, which gave us a great spiritual feeling and uplift. We took a great interest in the politics of the time, especially the feelings against the British, who put tremendous obstacles on the road to creating a Jewish State. We also had discussions about the Arabs, their mentality, their hatred for the Jews, and their preparations for war against the Jews of Palestine. The British favored the Arabs, and many times turned a blind eye to the activities of Arab gangs who were gathering weapons and ammunition, but when it came to the Hagannah, the British were constantly searching for concealed places of weapons and ammunition.

There was a wonderful spirit among us survivors. We had something special, which was acquired only through suffering. We were an exceptional breed of youth – we, who went through seven degrees of hell, who had an excellent Jewish background and who valued the fact that we were privileged to reach the Land of Israel after so much suffering. In our eyes this was a real miracle. We saw in this some compensation for all the suffering we endured. The spirit and special atmosphere strengthened our spirits and allowed us to begin to build a new life. Of course we became ardent Zionists and we were ready to fight the British oppressor or any enemy of the Jewish people who was putting obstacles in the way of the establishment of a Jewish State in Eretz Yisrael. The Zionist movement in the Land of Israel had forged a new prototype of Jew. It created soldiers and farmers – Jews who felt that they were citizens of their own homeland in which the Diaspora mentality had no place. The *chalutzim*, the pioneers, came to Eretz Yisrael to build and be rebuilt. That period in the history of Israel was something very pure, so idealistic, so vibrant. All this time I was in close touch with my brother and his family who lived in Jerusalem. Whenever I had a few days off from Sdeh Yaakov, I visited them. My first pilgrimage to Jerusalem had special meaning for me. It took a few hours to reach Jerusalem from Sdeh Yaakov. First I had to take a local bus to Haifa, and from there, an express bus to Jerusalem. In 1945, the roads were not very developed and the buses were not the latest models.

As the bus was climbing slowly up the road to Jerusalem, I was thinking how privileged I was. I, the little boy Moshe'leh from a small East European town, who almost died in the Shoah, merited to go up to Jerusalem, to

Sdeh Yaakov – Just a teenager, Moshe begins rebuilding his life in Eretz Yisrael.

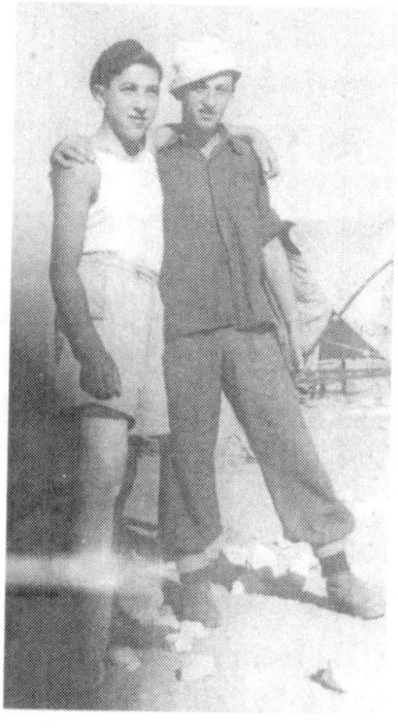

the city of King David of the Holy Temple of the Temple Mount, where Jewish Kings, Prophets, great scholars, and the Supreme Court presided, where great battles took place, where the Jewish defenders gave their lives to protect our eternal Capital. In my head I was reviewing many chapters of the Bible and other history books in connection with the city that I was about to see for the first time in my life. Shmuel Tzvi waited for me on Jaffa Street at the main bus station. Again it was a very emotional meeting, but now I was a free person. We took a city bus to his apartment.

For the first time I met Channah, my sister-in-law, who was a *Sabra*, someone born in Israel, and their two children, Mordechai and Nili. My sister-in-law was a tall good-looking woman. She was a wonderful wife, mother, and a gracious hostess.

Being in my brother's home in Jerusalem, we had more time to reminisce about our family, our home in Bilke, about the Jewish community in Bilke, and about my experiences in the Shoah. A few Bilker Landsleit who made aliyah in the 1930s, lived in Jerusalem. Among them were Isaac Friedman, the two brothers Moshe and Bumy Newman, and Chaim Gevaryahu. I had to tell again some of the stories about our town, what happened since they left Bilke, and whatever I knew about their families, and their whereabouts. I had a wonderful time in my brother's home and I greatly enjoyed playing with the children. Although my Hebrew was still not very good, somehow I made myself understood to the children and Channah. I spoke Yiddish at that time with my brother and the Bilker landsleit. My brother, who was a very educated person, both in secular and Jewish studies, was working in the post office administration. After a few days in Jerusalem, I returned to Sdeh Yaakov, to my studies, farming, and my friends.

The British gave permission, in each of the Jewish villages and kibbutzim, to operate a small police station. It was something like a sheriff's office. The head of the station was called *Noter*, policeman. These *Notrim* were trained and armed by the British, and they were in constant communication with their British headquarters by telephone and short wave radio. These Notrim were all Jewish and secret members of the Hagannah. They utilized their positions to inform the Hagannah leadership of what was going on in the British offices, and they also utilized the weapons that were stored in their stations for secret training with the Hagannah members in their villages and Kibbutzim. This was a tremendous network.

After a few months in Sdeh Yaakov, I and a few of my friends, survivors of the Holocaust, approached the Noter of Sdeh Yaakov and told him

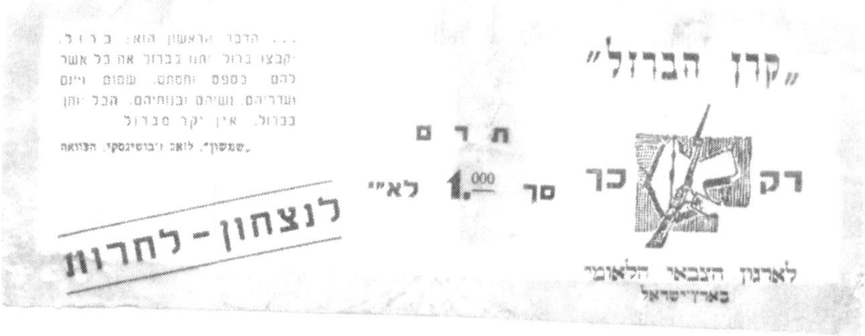

This is a receipt for one Eretz Yisrael (British/Palestinian) pound given to Moshe for his donation to the Irgun for purchasing weapons. It has the symbol of the Irgun, which represented the map of the historic boundaries of the complete Land of Israel. It reads, "To victory and to freedom."

that we would like to volunteer and enlist in the Hagannah and help with the national struggle against the British. At the next meeting, he approved our membership. We went through a swearing-in ceremony with our hands on a Bible, promising to be loyal to the Hagannah, obey the orders of its leaders, and be ready to sacrifice our lives for our homeland. I knew that this was a matter of life and death. However, as a Holocaust survivor I felt obligated to fight the British oppressor. Some of my friends were of the opinion that this was not the right thing to do. They said to me, "You were snatched from the inferno of the Shoah and you should not endanger your life." Now I was an enlisted member of the Hagannah, although, I greatly sympathized with the *Irgun Tzvai Leumi*, known in short as *Etzel* or *Irgun* and the *Lechi*, the other two Jewish underground fighter organizations that were more aggressive against the British. There were times when the three underground organizations worked together as a cooperative venture. It was called *Tenuat Hameri*, the rebellious movement.

After the British executed prisoners of the Irgun and Lechi in the winter and spring of 1947, it fueled great anger among all Jews in Eretz Yisrael. That's when the Tenuat Hameri was activated, and a series of operations against the British were executed, such as the bombing of the King David Hotel in Jerusalem, where one of its wings was used by the British intelligence services as their headquarters.

Three of my friends and I were approached by the Noter in Sdeh Yaakov and asked if we wanted to participate in a two month military training exercise at which time we would learn tactics of war. We accepted the invitation and reported to a camp made up of tents deep inside *Yaar Landau*, a forest near Tivon. Officially this camp was supposed to be a sport training camp in the event that the British showed up. Sixty young men participated in the training. The instructors were all Notrim. Not only did they instruct us, they also secretly brought along with them, all kinds of weapons, such as hand grenades of various types, pistols, rifles, submachine guns and a small mortar for shooting shells. The commander of the training camp was Tzvi Chera, a Hagannah commander who changed his name to Tzvi Tzur and who later on became Chief of Staff of the I.D.F. - Israeli Defense Forces.

We learned field tactics, how to find our way at night according to various objects even the stars. During one of our exercises, we were in a field in the Valley of Jezreel. Suddenly we saw from a distance British paratroopers combing the area. Our leader ordered us to lie low, deep in a cornfield, until the British passed. From time to time the British conducted sudden searches for weapons and ammunition caches belonging to the Jewish underground organizations. We trained in face-to-face combat. We used a shepherd's rod, which could be used very effectively to control Arab gangs when we had no arms. Since we could not use arms openly during the British rule, we learned how to use a compass and how to subdue the enemy with Judo tactics. We learned how to cross natural obstacles such as rivers and hills. We learned how to descend from buildings, and how to utilize ropes with an omega. We learned how to prepare bridges from ropes and how to erect tents. In short we learned a great deal; how to survive in action and how to be good fighters and well-trained leaders and how to outsmart the enemy. It was quite difficult for me in the beginning of training camp. It was a great physical strain and all my muscles ached. At first I thought I would not be able to make it, but after a few days, we got used to it and we also received a lot of encouragement from the Notrim instructors. These were very special people. For me it was a privilege to be under their command. I was very happy that I, little Moshe'leh from Bilke, who went through the hell of the Shoah, was chosen to participate in training for the future Jewish Army in the Land of our Fathers.

At the end of the training course, we got the rank of *Mefaked Kitach*, a group leader. I returned to Sdeh Yaakov where I completed the two-year customary stay in a youth aliyah village. Whenever I had free time, I read books. I had a great thirst for knowledge. Perhaps because I lost such precious time during my youth, I felt my soul needed spiritual sustenance.

Among our group in Sdeh Yaakov, a *gareen*, a nucleus of a farming group began to form. The purpose of the Gareen was to prepare for establishing a new settlement in a part of Israel where settlements were needed. Some 50 members signed up. They established Moshav Tekumah in the Negev, the southern part of Israel. I felt I would be better suited for city life and I wanted to be near my brother and his family in Jerusalem, the city I enjoyed so much. There was a special magnet that pulled me to Jerusalem and I ended up settling in the Holy City. While I was looking for a job, I stayed with my brother and his family. I temporarily took a job in a pastry bakery, which was arranged for me by my landsman Isaac Friedman, who also worked in the Sichel Bakery.

Meanwhile, my brother Shmuel Tzvi received a letter, via a soldier of the Jewish Brigade, who was stationed in Austria, from our brother Shlomo, who had survived the forced labor camps. In the letter he informed Shmuel Tzvi that three of our sisters, Feige, Mani (Miriam), and Reise had also survived the concentration camps. They were now together in a Displaced Persons camp, near Gratz, Austria and that they had applied for visas to the United States. They still had no idea that I survived the Shoah. My brother and I received the good news with great joy. To us, the discovery of our living brother and three sisters was another miracle. We wrote a letter to them, via this soldier who was going back to Europe to his unit. From then on, we corresponded with them frequently. In 1948, they arrived in the United States and settled in Brooklyn, New York where other Shoah survivors established new congregations.

Now that I lived in Jerusalem, my brother Shmuel Tzvi and I, with our friends, used to go to the *Kotel*, the Western Wall. This was a shrine of huge stones, venerated by Jews for centuries, a remnant of a wall that surrounded a plateau where the *Beit Hamikdash*, the Holy Ancient Jewish Temple, stood before it was destroyed by the Romans in A.D. 70. In those days, it was a very narrow place that was located in an alley. Most of the time, one could meet elderly Jews praying there. The place was neglected and very depressing. For many years under the Turkish rule in Palestine, it was purposely kept in a poor degrading state. It was their policy to minimize the rights of the Jewish people to the Temple Mount and its surroundings. The British also left the area in a non-appealing state. This was the only remnant of the great and beautiful Temple we Jews once had. The British discouraged Jews from worshiping at the *Kotel*, because for Jews it was always dangerous going through the narrow streets in the Old City. The Arabs wanted Jerusalem for themselves.

There was a custom in Jerusalem to sound the *Shofar*, the ram's horn, at

Shmuel Tzvi (L) at the Kotel

the Kotel after *Neilah*, the closing service of Yom Kippur, the Day of Atonement. Since the Kotel was the last vestige of the glorious times of Jewish independence, the British forbade the Jews from sounding the Shofar at the Kotel. There was a legend that if the Shofar was sounded at the Kotel, at the moment when the Gates of Heaven opened up, the redemption would surely come. This act also aroused nationalistic feelings, which the British wanted to suppress.

The *Irgun* and *Lechi*, the nationalistic underground with a number of traditional Jews as members, made it their goal to spite and prove to the British that they could not prevent the Jews from practicing their customs by sounding the Shofar in an ingenious way. Towards Neilah, a large number of young people imbued with national pride, streamed into the narrow alley where the Kotel was located. Rabbi Moshe Segal hid the Shofar under his clothes. The British police also made its presence felt. They were watching the worshipers very carefully, so that they would not dare attempt to do it. At the appropriate time, Rabbi Moshe Segal, one of the Lechi members, took out a Shofar and sounded a *Tekiah Gedolah*, a strong and long blast for the hope that the G-d of Israel would accept the prayers of the Jewish people and bring the long awaited redemption of Israel. At that moment, the British police were shoving and pushing the worshipers trying to catch the culprit, however, the young worshipers, whose goal was to defy the British, created a lot of confusion which made it possible for the Shofar blower to get away. For the next few days, this heroic act was the talk of Jewish Jerusalem.

The Glorious I.D.F.

In November 1947, prior to the United Nations vote on the partition plan of Palestine, there was great tension among the British, the Arabs, and the Jews. The Underground increased their activities to put pressure on the British and the Arabs. In those days, the British were openly pro-Arab. The underground organizations publicized their heroic acts through their clandestine radio broadcasts and newspaper wall posters which were glued to billboards during the night all over Israel. Since I worked in a bakery, I went to work very early in the morning. On Strauss Street in Jerusalem, I saw new posters on the billboard. I stopped to read them. I always liked to read them since it gave me a lot of information about what was really going on behind the scenes and it made me proud to be a Jew. The Hagannah paper was called *Hachomah*, the Fortress; the Irgun's paper was *Ha-Maas*, The Deed; and the Lechi paper was called, *Hechazit*, The Front. As I was standing there and reading intensely, I did not notice that a British police armored patrol vehicle pulled up. A British officer stepped out, demanded my identification. After he examined it, he ordered me to accompany him to the armored car. They took me to the police station in *Machaneh Yehudah*, on Jaffa Street where they interrogated me. They wanted to know to which underground organization I belonged, because they saw me reading the underground newspapers. I did not understand any English, so they brought an Arab policeman who knew Hebrew and he asked me all kinds of questions. I denied belonging to any organization. I told them that I was on my way to work at the Sichel Bakery, which was not far from the police station. I told them to call the bakery and verify that I was telling the truth. After a while Mr. Sichel, the bakery owner came and verified my story and so they let me go. Even though it was a bit scary because the British frequently committed brutal acts against the Jews in Palestine, after my experiences during the Shoah, I stood up to them pretty well.

On November 29, 1947, the U.N. Special Session in Lake Success, New York voted to accept the recommendation of the U.N. Special Commission to partition the country into two states, Jewish and Arab with Jerusalem as an international city. A wave of euphoria sent the masses into the streets singing and dancing. Everyone ran to the building of the *Sochnut*, the Jewish Agency for Israel headquarters. People were reciting the *Shehecheyanu*, a prayer thanking G-d that he kept us alive and sustained us and enabled us to reach such a historic occasion. The multitudes were waiting for David Ben Gurion, the Chairman of the Sochnut, to address them.

The next day I was fully mobilized as a Hagannah member and assigned to *Palam*, an elite local force in Jerusalem, stationed in the Gymnasium building of *Beit Hakerem*. We were given some weapons, old Italian rifles, submachine guns produced by the Hagannah Secret Weapon Industry, hand grenades, pistols, and clubs.

The Arabs in Israel began armed assaults upon Jewish settlements and Jewish transportation systems traveling through Arab districts from the coast to Jerusalem. The first major encounter between Arabs and Jews broke out in Jerusalem. An Arab mob from Jaffa Gate of the Old City stormed and attacked the Jewish commercial center. They reached *Mamilah* Street and entered Princess Mary Street, today *Shlomzion* Street, which housed many Jewish

דוגמת חתימתו של בעל התעודה

מספר אישי מ/ 105552 חיל רגלים

שם משפחה ליפסיץ

שם פרטי משה

תעודת זיהוי ממשלתית מס' 191586

תאריך לידה 1928

תאריך חיול לצ.ה.ל. 1.5.48

מספר התעודה № 173812

דף 1

הוראות לחייל בכחות המלואים

1. הנך אחראי אישית לשלמותה של תעודה זו.
2. הנך חייב להציג תעודה זו בכל עת שתדרש לכך ע"י רשות מוסמכת.
3. במקרה של אבדן התעודה עליך להודיע על כך מיד למפקד יחידתך ולמשטרה האזרחית.
4. רשומים בתעודה זו יעשו ע"י רשות מוסמכת לכך בלבד. אסור לך להוסיף, לגרוע או לשנות רשום כל שהוא בתעודה זו.
5. במקרה של גיוס יחידתך או גיוס כללי, עליך להתיצב מיד במקום שנקבע ע"י מפקדך. במקרה ואתה מנותק מיחידתך, עליך להתיצב בפני הרשות הצבאית הקרובה ביותר למקום המצאך.
6. אי מלוי ההוראות דלעיל מהוה עבירה על חוק שרות הבטחון תש"ט - 1949. באם תעבור עבירה כנ"ל - תהיה צפוי לענש בהתאם לסעיף 16 (א), (ב) של החוק.

טופס 410 (1/50)

דף 2

The Israel Defense Force's identity booklet for Moshe Avital

צבא ההגנה לישראל
מפקדת מחוז ירושלים
1710
תעודת שרות זמנית
שם פרטי
שם משפחה
כתובת פרטית
שם היחידה
מגויס (מלא, חלקית)
14 VII 48
תאריך הוצאת התעודה

Moshe Avital and his identity card in the Hagannah.

stores. They attacked the Jews and looted at will. Two dozen Jews were wounded. Present on the scene was an armored car with British police, ostensibly there to prevent any Arab Pogrom. They did not raise a finger. The British Mandatory authorities remained neutral. This was a very one sided neutrality which really supported the Arab interests, because whenever the Hagannah attempted to rush to the rescue of their brethren, they were arrested and thrown into prison. Later in the day, Jewish forces with clubs drove off the Arab mob.

At first, our unit, which was a part of the *Etzyon* brigade, served in a defense capacity. We patrolled, especially at night, the Jewish neighborhoods of Beit Hakerem, and *Bayit Vegan*, which bordered Arab neighborhoods, to deter the Arabs from harming Jews, and prevent destruction and looting. When the high command of the Hagannah realized that the Arabs meant all out war, a new policy was instituted. Units of the Jewish forces started to clear out pockets of Arab houses and fortifications near Jewish areas because these Arab areas constituted a danger to the Jewish population and also to improve the positions of the Jewish forces in these areas.

Our unit was active night after night. We conquered the Arab neighborhoods of *Sheik Badar*, *Malcha*, *Miss-Cury*, and the area of *A-Sharfa*, which was designated to be *Har Herzl* - Mount Herzl, and others. The city of Jerusalem

In the I.D.F. – Moshe Avital defends the Jewish homeland

was completely surrounded by hostile Arab villages. It was under total siege. The road to the coastal plain with a larger Jewish population was completely cut off. The hunger in the city was a major problem. There was very little food, no medical supplies, very little water, no electricity. There was a great shortage of all the basic necessities for normal life. The Jordanians, with the help of the British, surrounded the Jewish neighborhoods in Jerusalem from the surrounding hills. My brother Shmuel Tzvi and his family had to leave their apartment on Shmuel Hanavi Street because the Arabs across from neighboring *Sheik Jerach* were constantly sniping at the building. The Jewish authorities assigned to them another apartment in an Arab house that was abandoned by the Arabs in the Schneler section. The mobilized Jewish forces somehow managed to get food, while the civilian population was suffering greatly. Sometimes we found food in the Arab houses, which were abandoned when they were told by their leadership to flee. At times, I brought oil, eggs, chicken, sugar, olives, and other staples to my brother's family. This kept them going during the siege.

Just before the British evacuated Jerusalem and their fortress called *Bevingrad*, named by the Jews after the anti-Semitic British Foreign Secretary Ernest Bevin, our unit was dispatched to *Kibbutz Ramat Rachel*, which was the southernmost outpost for Jerusalem. The women and children from the Kibbutz were evacuated. Only the men stayed to take care of the livestock. Our platoon was sent as reinforcement to the Kibbutz, because there were not enough military trained men among the members of the Kibbutz.

On Friday, the 5th day of *Iyar* 5708, May 14, 1948, just a few hours before Shabbat began, the British Mandate on Palestine was to expire. Our unit was ready in positions around Kibbutz Ramat Rachel. We listened to the Hagannah radio station when it was announced that the leaders of the Yishuv, the Jewish community in Eretz Yisrael, gathered in the assembly hall of the Tel Aviv Museum. On the platform stood David Ben Gurion, the chairman of the provisional government.

In a joyous voice, Ben Gurion began saying, "We, the members of the People's Council, representatives of the Jewish community of Eretz Yisrael and the Zionist Movement, are here assembled on the day of the termination of the British Mandate over Eretz Yisrael, and by the virtue of our natural and historic right, and on the basis of the resolution of the United Nations, hereby declare the establishment of a Jewish State in Eretz Yisrael to be known as the State of Israel."

The 37 representatives of the various movements of the Jewish

> "We... hereby declare the establishment of a Jewish State in Eretz Yisrael to be known as the State of Israel."
>
> *David Ben Gurion*
> *5th of Iyar 5708*
> *May 14, 1948*

community in Eretz Israel stepped forward, one after another, and signed the Declaration of Independence. We, in the trenches of the Kibbutz, held our breath at this historic moment, a moment the Jewish people dreamed of for thousands of years. This announcement would never have happened were it not for years of yearning, praying, hard labor, pioneering, and creativity, which led to the building of cities, towns, villages, and kibbutzim; making a desolate country once again into a flourishing land; the renaissance of the Hebrew language and culture, the development of agriculture, industry, and transportation by land, sea, and in the air, as well as the revelation of the ability of Jewish national survival and self-defense. One should not wonder because we had accumulated thousands of years of spirit, culture, love for learning, and devotion to a faith from which to draw strength.

Immediately after midnight on that Friday, now May 15, 1948, the Arabs openly declared war against the newborn state and ordered the armies of Egypt, Jordan, Iraq, Syria, and Lebanon, as well as units from other Arab countries, to invade Eretz Yisrael. In the south, the Egyptians sent their regular army with tanks, artillery, armored vehicles, and all kinds of weapons. All around the country, the other Arab armies did the same. Their plan was to choke and destroy the fledgling Jewish state with a *Blitz Krieg*, and throw the Jews into the sea. Egyptian aircraft attacked in waves and bombed Tel Aviv, its harbor, and its airport. They dropped leaflets calling upon the Jews to surrender. On that day, 41 Jews were killed and scores wounded. The Jewish forces organized themselves quickly to repel the invasion.

We in Kibbutz Ramat Rachel received word that an Egyptian Brigade was advancing from the Negev, south on the Hebron – Bethlehem Highway, and that their destination was Jerusalem, entering from the south. There was a race between the Jordanian and Egyptian Armies as to who would be first to capture Jerusalem. This would have been the biggest prize of the war. Although we were only a platoon, 38 soldiers, plus 24 members of the Kibbutz who were combat ready, we did not panic. Even though the Egyptian Brigade was heavily equipped with tanks, artillery, heavy machine guns, mortars and more, we were ready to fight. We had our Italian rifles, sub machine guns, hand grenades, Molotov cocktails, pistols, and one 2 inch mortar. We also had a secret weapon called *General Ain Breira*, no alternative, which meant we had a unique fighting spirit. We knew it was our task to prevent the Egyptians from entering Jerusalem at all costs, even with our own bodies. We knew we were fighting not only for our platoon, and for Kibbutz Ramat Rachel, which was named after our Matriarch, Rachel. We knew this was a matter of life and death for Jerusalem and the future of the Jewish people. We knew this was the last place we Jews had. If we lost, there would be no future for our people. Especially we, the Holocaust survivors, were ready to give our lives for Eretz Yisrael. We survivors were among the most daring fighters. That's why 1,500 Holocaust survivors fell during the War of Liberation. This was a very high percentage of the total Jewish casualties.

The next day, the Egyptian column appeared on the horizon. They were closing in on the Kibbutz. They started to shell the buildings in the compound. The cow shed was hit directly and a number of cows were killed. Our platoon commander gave us an order not to open fire until the Egyptians reached the barbed wire fence in order to conserve our very limited ammunition. We did not know whether we would be able to get reinforcements of men or weapons. There was not even one direction in Jerusalem – east, west, north or south that was not a front line. The Arabs were attacking simultaneously from all directions.

We noticed that the Egyptian infantry was marching, standing up, towards our trenches near the fence. They did not even try to walk low or to use usual battle techniques. They marched as if they were going on a stroll. Perhaps they were told by the officers, since they never went in front of the soldiers to lead them, that there would be no resistance. When they were almost on top of us, the order came from our platoon commander, "*aish*," fire. We opened fire with everything we had. We gave them a real welcoming surprise. Scores of Egyptians fell to the ground; the rest began running back in a panic flight. It was a rout. We ceased firing in order to conserve the ammunition for the next round. We knew that after they licked their wounds, they would regroup and attack again. Not one of our soldiers was hit. The Egyptians left their dead in the field. After that, the rest of the day was very quiet. We did not fear for the night because the Egyptian soldiers in those days were not trained for night combat.

The next morning they started with heavy shelling all over. We kept low in our trenches so as not to get hit. The trenches were dug quite deep all around the Kibbutz boundaries so that one could walk in them without being seen. The dining room, which was well built, was fortified inside and outside with sand bags. This was our fortress. It was a symbol of endurance. It was hit heavily many times by bullets, shrapnel, and even shells, but it withstood the main onslaught. (Until this day, one can see the old dining room in the Kibbutz, full of bullet holes, standing as a monument to those heroic days.) This time the Egyptians began an attack with their tanks and armored vehicles. During the bombardment, five soldiers were wounded and the platoon's two-way radio was hit and put out of commission. This was a great loss to us because the radio was our only link to our headquarters in Jerusalem.

Moshe Avital with the captured Egyptian pistol.

I and two other soldiers were stationed in the trench near the gate to the main entrance of the Kibbutz. Suddenly we saw a tank approaching the gate of the Kibbutz. The commander of the tank was standing up with his head sticking out from the trunk of the tank. One of us aimed at him and shot him and all of us threw Molotov cocktails at the tank, which set the tank on fire. The tank crew jumped out of the tank and confronted us. I loaded my sten sub-machine gun, but it did not work. This was a flaw in the sten gun; sometimes it got stuck. My friend near me quickly shot the Egyptian, saving my life. I approached the body of the Egyptian and saw that he had the rank of sergeant and that he had a pistol lying at his side. I could not thank my friend Elimelech Rokach enough for saving my life. I took the pistol and wore it during the rest of my service in the army. I kept it as a sort of a *kameah*, a good omen. We lost four of our comrades and a half a dozen were wounded in this battle.

Our numbers were shrinking, our ammunition was dwindling, and we had lost our contact with headquarters. To get to the city was very dangerous. There were only open fields between the Kibbutz and the nearest Jewish neighborhood, *Arnonah.* One could hear in the distance, the battles raging from all the directions of Jerusalem. Every unit, and there were not many, was engaged in the battle trying to hold the line, not to allow the enemy to get a foothold in Jerusalem. The pressure on Ramat Rachel by the Egyptians increased. On the third day, they attacked again, this time in full force. We had no chance against this overwhelming power. We had dead and wounded; our ammunition was gone. Towards evening, our platoon commander gave us an order to retreat to Arnonah, the nearest Jewish position.

We had to pass through an open field. We used all the techniques of retreat that we had learned. We ran fast in zigzag advances. We laid down and ran again. When the shooting became intense, we crawled on our stomachs so we would not get hit. A few were hit, among them my good friend Elimelech Rokach, who was an only child, brought up by his widowed mother. For me, his death was a terrible loss. We were successful in dragging his body with us to Arnonah. In those days, we had a holy understanding that no soldier wounded or dead was ever left on the battlefield. To our luck and astonishment, the Egyptians did not make any attempt that night or the next day to try to advance further into Arnonah. Maybe they suffered great losses or maybe they were tired, or maybe the officers felt that they had already accomplished enough. We fought like lions. Our morale was high. I felt that I was also fighting for the 6,000,000 of our people and especially for my dear family who were murdered during the Shoah.

The following day we received reinforcements from our company. That evening, those of us who were not hurt, and the reinforcements, made a surprise attack on the Egyptians and recaptured the Kibbutz from them. When we surprised them, we saw that they were broiling meat on a fire. The meat was from cows they slaughtered. Since the Egyptians were afraid to fight at night, they retreated quickly and our casualties were low.

During the time the Egyptians held the Kibbutz, they caused a lot of damage. They looted, killed the cows, and burned the chicken coop with the chickens in it. For the next few days, they tried again, but in the end, the Kibbutz remained in our hands. Thus the most southern position of Jerusalem remained in the hands of the I.D.F. for the next 19 years, until the Six Day War, when the Kibbutz was no longer an outpost but rather a tourist and recreation center. Perhaps because of the merits of our Matriarch, Rachel, the Kibbutz survived the Egyptian onslaught.

There is a very interesting passage in the Book of Jeremiah (31:14-16) where Rachel turns to G-d and is asking for mercy upon the Children of Israel, as they were led away into Babylonian captivity. "Thus saith the Lord, a voice is heard in Ramah – in heaven, lamentation and bitter weeping, Rachel weeping for her children. She refuses to be comforted for her children, because they are not. Thus saith the Lord: Refrain thy voice from weeping and thine eyes from tears; for thy work shall be rewarded saith the Lord; and they shall come back from the land of the enemy and there is hope for thy future saith the Lord; and thy children shall return to their own border."

During the next two years, my unit participated in various battles all around Jerusalem, on Mamila Street on Mount Zion, at the Notredam Monastery, around the walls of old Jerusalem, and other places. During my two and a half years in the war, I was promoted in rank from Corporal to Sergeant to Staff Sergeant to Battalion Sergeant Major. This was the highest non-commissioned officer's rank in the army.

During one of the cease fires I was chosen to go to a military school to train to be an officer. I was sent to *Kfar Yonah*, officers training school. It was a very intensive course. We learned military strategy and tactics, leadership, coordination with larger units, and how to use heavy equipment, especially the heavy Beza, machine guns that Israel acquired during the War of Liberation from Czechoslovakia, as the Western powers refused to sell arms to Israel, due to the United Nations embargo. The Arabs had no such problems acquiring arms since the British equipped and supplied most of their armies. This machine gun helped a great deal to win many battles. At that time, it was the most modern weapon. Not only could it shoot hundreds of bullets rapidly for a distance of four miles, but one did not have to worry that it would get hot and explode. Also it came with an optic instrument, which helped us calculate the distance to shoot in the form of a rainbow, which could suddenly reach the enemy behind a mountain without the enemy knowing what hit him.

Because the cease fire was broken and the hostilities renewed, our training was interrupted and I was ordered to return to my company in the Etzyon brigade. Since I was now an expert in the use of the Beza heavy machine gun, I was placed with such a gun on top of the Anglo Palestine Bank Building in Jerusalem, which overlooked the Old City, inside the walls. I was placed there to give cover and support and backing to the troops who were about to attack the Old City in order to capture it. It was a fierce fight with many casualties on both sides. The attack failed, and after that, no attempts were made to capture the Old City until June 1967. I trained many soldiers in our company how to use this heavy machine gun. In May of 1950, I was transferred to the 63rd Battalion of the Givati Brigade, which was responsible for guarding and patrolling the front lines in the center of Israel, opposite the Jordanian forces at the triangle. I was assigned to lead a platoon stationed on the Beitlit Tul Karem road. I was promoted to the rank of Battalion Sergeant Major.

Our responsibility was to patrol the Arab villages of Taibe, Kalansuah, Kfar Kassem, Um-El-Fachm, among others. This was the period of terrorist infiltrations, from across the border into the Kibbutzim and villages on the Israeli side. They came to murder, to loot, and to steal herds of sheep and cows. Night after night, we went out on patrols and ambush. We caught a number of infiltrators, but many times the Jordanian Army attacked our patrols even though we were on our side of the border. I considered making a military career because I felt the army was the most important place to serve my country. In the meantime, my sister Reise who lived in New York was getting married. She begged me to come to her wedding. In November of 1950, I took a leave of absence from the Army in order to travel to the U.S.A. to her wedding. Little did I know that this trip would change the entire course of my life.

My First Journey To America

On November 15, 1950, I boarded an Air France airplane (El Al, Israel's Airline was not yet in existence) via Paris to New York. My brother Shmuel Tzvi, his wife Channah, and their children accompanied me to Lod Airport. When I said good-bye to my brother, little did I know that I would never see him again. It was hard for me to leave Israel and my family and wander again, first to Paris and from there to New York. On the plane I had time to think, so I reviewed in my mind the things that happened to me during the last five years. Israel was now my country and Jerusalem my home.

During the four and a half years being in the Land, a lot had happened. I was privileged to see the miracle of the establishment of a Jewish State in the Land of our Fathers. I witnessed the great miracle of the defeat of the Arab armies who wanted to annihilate the Jews in Israel, and to destroy the last hope of the Jewish people. I saw the ingathering of hundreds of thousands of our brethren from a multitude of nations. Among them were a few survivors from Bilke. I felt like a newborn person, a proud Jew who would not allow evil forces to do harm to the Jewish people anymore. Also, I had become attached to my brother Shmuel Tzvi and his family. My brother was to me, not only a very devoted brother, but he was

Moshe Avital at Lod Airport in Israel, November 1950, prior to departure on his first trip to the United States.

(L-R) Mordechai, Shmuel Tzvi, Nili, Moshe, Uri, Shmulik (Channah's nephew), Channah

(L-R) Front Row: Reise Doft-Lipschitz, Feige Doft-Lipschitz Schwimmer, Miriam Eidel Doft-Lipschitz
(L-R) Back Row: Shlomo Doft-Lipschitz, Leib Ber Schwimmer

This picture was taken in 1946 in Austria in a Displaced Persons camp.

also my mentor, and a very wise man, who was guiding me during my period of acclimatization in the land. I looked up to him as many other people did for many reasons. He was a sincere, educated person both in Jewish and worldly knowledge, and had a great deal of love for Israel and the Jewish people. I was trying to calm myself in my thoughts, by making up my mind to return to Israel, soon after my sister's wedding.

I arrived the next day in New York's Idlewild Airport (later it was changed to J.F.K.) Upon my arrival, I did not speak any English. At the immigration office at the airport, an official started to ask me questions in English, which I did not understand. They kept me there for a while. In the meantime, my brother Shlomo was waiting for me outside and getting nervous. Finally, they brought an immigration officer who spoke German, so I was able to answer his questions. As I came out, I met my brother Shlomo. The meeting was very emotional, since I had not seen him for seven years. The last time I saw him was in Bilke in our home. In a taxi, we rushed to Brooklyn where my three sisters and two brothers-in-law with a couple of babies were waiting for me impatiently. The two older sisters, Feige and Mani (Miriam), were married after the war in a Displaced Persons camp to men from our area in Ruthenia. Shlomo wasn't married yet.

As I entered the apartment there was a loud scream, "He is here." They hugged me and kissed me and cried for the joy of our reunion and also for sadness, for all the others who did not survive. At first they did not recognize me. When they left me in Auschwitz, I was a little boy. Now I was a full-grown man with a mustache, which I had let grow in the army. This time I was dressed in modern clothes, quite different from what we wore in Bilke. During the first few days we exchanged a lot of information about our experiences

This is more than a traditional wedding picture, which was taken in 1950 in Brooklyn, New York. These Doft children, whose parents were Joshua and Pearl Doft – murdered in Auschwitz six years before – gather for the marriage of their sister, Reise. This picture affirms the strength and resolve of the Doft children, survivors themselves, to rebuild the generation of hundreds of Doft relatives murdered at the hands of the Nazis.

(R-L) Shmuel Rosenbaum and his wife, Miriam Lipschitz Rosenbaum; Moshe Avital; the bride, Reise Lipschitz Moskovitz and the groom, Alter Moskovitz; Shlomo Doft-Lipschitz; Feige Doft-Lipschitz Schwimmer and her husband, Leib Ber Schwimmer.
In front, Yehudit Rosenbaum and Yehoshua Hershele, Moshe's neice and nephew.

since we saw each other last. They wanted to know everything about our brother Shmuel Tzvi and his family in Jerusalem. The next day my sister Reise took me for a ride on the subway, which was a new wonder to me.

On November 19, 1950, I was an honored guest at my sister's wedding. I met a few Bilker Landsleit there who had survived and immigrated to America, and some who had come to America in the 1930s. They all remembered me as a child, and as a soloist in the Great Synagogue, in the choir of my father, the Cantor. Everyone urged me to sing at the wedding. I still had a good voice and felt that I would enhance my sister's wedding. I decided to sing a few Hebrew songs, which were popular in Israel during the war, among them, the song, *Yerushalayim*, Jerusalem. There were a few hundred guests and I received quite a round of applause. Some of the family members and Bilker Landsleit shed tears, because it reminded them of Bilke, and also they were very proud of me, that little Moshe'leh was serving in the Jewish Army. It was a beautiful wedding with a lot of spirit, singing, and dancing, the way the ultra orthodox Jews celebrate.

After the wedding, my family in Brooklyn started to pressure me. They wanted me to stay in the United States. Their argument was that I was a young man who had lost years of education in the Shoah and in the Israeli Army, and they maintained that in America I would have great opportunities. They also argued that my strong and beautiful voice could be further developed, and I could make a career as a Cantor and carry on the tradition of our father. This went on day after day and so I found myself in a great dilemma. On the one hand, I realized their arguments were valid and they were right that in America one had greater choices and possibilities, although I also saw how in America people were enslaved to their work.

I had an uncle in New York, Rabbi Meir Lipschitz, my mother's brother, who came to America early in the 20th century. I went to see him. He was a learned and wise man, and had much experience in life. He said to me, "Moshe, America is a golden country. Gold is lying in the streets. However, when you bend down to pick it up, the back hurts terribly." What he was trying to tell me was, that if one really wanted to succeed in America, one had to work very hard.

On the other hand, I felt that if I stayed there for a few years, I would lose my soul and my unique spirit, which I succeeded in rehabilitating during the five years that I was in Israel after the Shoah. There was a tug of war in my soul, a great struggle in my mind for and against. I decided to ask the advice of my brother, Shmuel Tzvi in Jerusalem. I knew that he had my best interest at heart, although he missed me and wanted me to be near him, so that he would not be the only family member alone. His advice was to stay for a few years, study, and get experience, perhaps save some money and then return. I decided to stay for a few years, not with a full heart because every day I was outside of Israel, I felt uprooted like a tree that is placed on top of soil with its roots exposed.

My visitor's status in the United States changed to that of a student and I was allowed to stay on as long as I was studying at a university. I was accepted as a student at Yeshiva University Teachers Institute for the Spring semester in 1951. Dr. Pinchas Churgin, the Dean of the Teachers Institute, personally interviewed me and placed me in a higher class due to my knowledge of Hebrew. During the years I studied there, he was very nice and friendly towards me. He also lectured in my class in Jewish History, a subject which was his expertise. I studied many subjects such as Education, Talmud, Bible, History, Hebrew literature, Jewish laws and customs, Hebrew songs and others. I became active in the student council, and helped to plan student cultural activities. We published a Hebrew newspaper called, *Hameasef*, and a yearbook called *Nir*. We had student parties with Jewish-Hebrew content. We used to sing both classical Hebrew songs and most of the modern songs that were then popular in Israel. Beny Berhan, a student from Israel, played the accordion and I led the singing. While I was studying at Yeshiva University, I also took voice development lessons with Martin Lawrence, a Metropolitan Opera singer. I studied Cantorial music with Cantor Vigoda. I utilized every moment of the day to study a variety of subjects because in the back of my mind, I kept alive the idea of returning to Israel as soon as possible. I lived with my sisters in Brooklyn and commuted by subway during the week to Washington Heights to school. I developed my Cantorial skills and built on the experience I had in my father's choir and his *nusach*, a mode of melodies, which were unusually beautiful. I took a Cantorial position for the high holidays at Congregation Agudath Achim, in Hartford, Connecticut where Rabbi Abraham Avrutick was the spiritual leader. The Rabbi and the congregation liked my Cantorial style very much. They rehired me year after year. I had great spiritual satisfaction from my Cantorial performances, because it reminded me of my father's renditions, and because of my deep knowledge of the Hebrew language, I was able to musically interpret the contents of the prayers in a special way.

During the summers, I took a position at the famous Massad Camps, Hebrew speaking summer camps, where I held various positions as counselor, division head, head counselor and later, the director of one of the three camps. There I acquired a lot of experience and organizational skills in planning formal and informal educational activities. Through the camp staff, parents of campers, and distinguished visitors, I made contact with many people in high positions in the Jewish community who were helpful at various times. While still at the Teachers Institute at Yeshiva University, I took a teaching position in the Sherman Avenue Talmud Torah, in Jersey City. It was an afternoon school where Jewish children learned two hours a day, four days a week after public school and on Sunday morning. The school had high educational standards, where the students learned a great deal. In this school, I acquired a great deal of experience in actual teaching, which I enjoyed very much. My efforts bore fruit and the three classes I taught accomplished much. When they graduated after six years, quite a few continued in the high school department where I also taught the Prophets and Mishnah. The administration, the parents and the Rabbis of the community treated me graciously, since they were very pleased with my educational and spiritual contributions to the students. I was fresh and full of enthusiasm and I had a great deal to offer to the school in the way of knowledge, organization, Jewish music, Cantorial music, and the spirit of modern Israel. I developed great friendships with the board members and parents as well as with the students who for many years kept in touch with me.

In order for me to be able to stay longer in the United States and be allowed to work, my status had to be changed and I was issued a green card. Even though I was so involved with my family, the university, the school where I taught, the summer camp, and the Cantorial studies as well as the High Holiday position, my longing to return to Israel did not diminish. I kept my contact with Israel through correspondence with my brother Shmuel Tzvi, my friends, by reading local and Israeli papers, through the news and so on. Each time Israel had a problem with its Arab neighbors, I felt I should be there to help. I made up my mind that soon I would return.

In 1955, my brother Shmuel Tzvi became seriously ill. I really wanted to be there with him. He died shortly after that, before I had a chance to return. His heart gave up after the pain he accumulated during the Holocaust years, because he could not save his dear family. He was only 39 years old. His death was a great blow to my spirits and the entire wound of our great losses in the Shoah opened again, because the dwindling of our family members continued. I made preparations to return to Israel in October 1956.

Back To Israel To Fight Another War

During the early months of 1956, newspapers in the United States were carrying daily front-page accounts of growing tension in the Middle East. Egypt nationalized the Suez Canal. I felt compelled to return to my unit in the Israeli army and help if a war broke out. I felt I couldn't sit in the United States and watch the battles on television. I would have gone out of my mind in New York listening to news reports. My willingness to return to the army was connected to my Holocaust experiences. I thought, here we go again. The world will sit idly by as the Egyptians prepare for war with the help of the Soviet Block. The United Nations would certainly not do anything because of politics. All these feelings had been seething and growing in me for quite a while so I booked passage to return to Israel on October 5, 1956 on the passenger ship Israel, from New York to Haifa.

In the news, I learned there were skirmishes between the I.D.F. and Arab forces along the frontiers. The commentators talked about another war in the Middle East. My brother Shlomo, my sisters, and brothers-in-law were not happy at all with my decision. They tried a last moment appeal, but my mind was made up. I made the rounds to many friends to say good-bye, my family, and so on. The ship was sailing on Friday, October 5, 1956. Three days before that, I was invited for a farewell supper at Rabbi Shlomo and Libby Wind's home in Brooklyn. There I met a very charming and beautiful young lady who had *Yiddishe Chen*, Jewish grace, who was asked by Mrs. Wind to take me in her car to another farewell in Flatbush. Her name was Channah Hershman from Boston. I fell in love with her at first sight. I told her it was too bad that I had not met her earlier, since I was sailing for Israel on Friday. She offered to take me to the pier on the day of departure, which I graciously accepted. My brother Shlomo, and my sister Reise came along to the ship where Channah had a chance to meet them. We exchanged addresses and said farewell to each other with moving feelings.

During my voyage on the Israel, I had plenty of time to think about

Channah, our strange meeting and our feelings about each other. I began writing a daily log in letter form telling her what was going on during the voyage with the intention of mailing it at the first port we stopped at, which was Milano, Italy. I also revealed in this letter my strong feelings for her.

On the ship, we listened to the news from Israel since we were anxious to know what the situation was on the front line. We heard that the skirmishes were continuing and that Israel was calling up some of the reserves. The strong feelings that I had for Israel were instilled in me during my youth in my home in Bilke in Cheder, where I learned the Bible and about the covenant G-d made with Abraham, Isaac, and Jacob to give the land to the Israelites. I learned the history of our great Prophets; of Moses redeeming our people from Egypt; and Joshua who conquered the land and portioned it out to the various tribes of Israel. I learned about the problems the neighbors of the Jewish kingdom caused from time to time, and great leaders who arose to save the people from destruction, among them Judges, Kings, and Generals.

After the Holocaust, especially, those strong feeling for Israel became even stronger. I felt that as long as there was a Jewish state with a strong and innovative army, our people had a good chance of surviving. If there had been a Jewish state before the second world war, the Holocaust perhaps might have been prevented, or at least minimized. Since the Holocaust, I did not trust the nations of the world and so, being Jewish, carried with it a certain responsibility. We had to make sure that no matter where on this planet Jews were persecuted, we would be able to rise to their defense. Now that we had a Jewish state, it became a bulwark against homelessness and helplessness; it became a refuge where any Jew could go. When I am in Israel, I feel a part of Jewish history that extends to the early Hebrews, when Jews fought as equals, army against army.

I mailed my letter to Channah and was hoping to hear from her soon. We arrived in Haifa safely after two weeks. My sister-in-law Channah, her children, and friends waited for me at the Haifa port. The reunion was a happy one with a sad undertone because my brother Shmuel Tzvi, may his memory be for a blessing, was not alive anymore. In Jerusalem, I stayed with my brother's family. The next day I reported to the army. During my six years in the United States, I went to the Israeli Consulate and extended my leave of absence from my unit. A couple of days later I was fully mobilized and attached to my unit in the Givati Brigade. With the beginning of the Sinai Campaign on October 29, 1956, our unit entered the Sinai Desert. Within a few days we fought our way to a place called Bir-Gafgafa, only a few miles from the Suez Canal. We

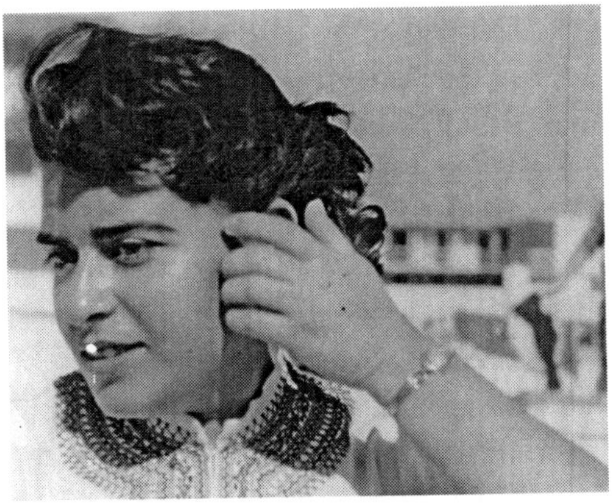

Channah Hershman – a very charming and beautiful young lady

Channah accompanied Moshe to the pier for his voyage to return to Israel.

were involved in a number of battles. At first the Egyptians put up stiff resistance, but then they ran for their lives.

This was at the time when John Foster Dulles, who was not a friend of Israel, was the Secretary of State and the Americans were courting the Arabs. Gamal Abdul Nasser, the President of Egypt, nationalized the Suez Canal. The French and the British felt America was wrong to placate Egypt and decided to take the canal back. Secretly, a pact was made between David Ben Gurion, Israel's Prime Minister, the French Prime Minister, and the British Prime Minister, to join forces in order to strike at Egypt and teach her a lesson. The three nations had a common interest in the region. Israel knew then that it couldn't rely on the Americans to lift the blockade of Israeli ships that had to pass through the Suez Canal.

While I was in the war in Sinai, I wrote more letters to Channah giving her eyewitness reports about the war. When the British, the French and the I.D.F. reached their goal of taking the Sinai and the canal, a cease-fire was declared. This broke the Egyptian blockade of the port of Eilat on the Red Sea and removed the terrorist threat emanating from Egypt and Gaza. The Russians and U.S. President Dwight Eisenhower pressured Israel to withdraw from the territory it captured from the Egyptians.

During a few days of leave, I went to Jerusalem to see my brother's family. There I found a few letters from Channah from New York, and a letter from my sister Reise. Both worried about me being in the war. From a distance, it sounded even worse than on location. Channah was happy to get my letters and she sent me a couple of pictures of herself, which was a pleasant surprise. My sister was very worried about me and begged me to return to New York for two reasons. She was afraid that I might get killed, that our family had lost enough, and she felt that Channah was a perfect match for me.

After a few weeks in the Sinai, our unit was ordered to move to the Gaza strip into a military camp near the city of Rafah. Our duty was to keep order in the area. Ben Gurion agreed to relinquish the Sinai Peninsula, but refused at first to return Gaza to the Egyptians, since Gaza was never Egyptian territory. They captured it in the 1948 War because it was a part of the British Mandate over Palestine. After heavy pressure by the Russians, the United Nations, and the United States, Ben Gurion ordered the I.D.F. to withdraw to previous lines. The Egyptians re-occupied the Gaza Strip, which later became a terrorist base again.

After five months, other reservists and I were discharged from the army and I returned to Jerusalem. I found more letters from Channah and

The Givati Brigade – in Rafah in Gaza. Moshe Avital's unit fought in the Sinai Desert during the Sinai Campaign, which began October 29, 1956.

another letter from my sister Reise. The feelings between Channah and I grew stronger and stronger. It became very serious. At the same time I did not want to leave Israel. I asked Channah in one of my letters, whether she would consider coming for a visit to Israel in order to see whether we were really serious, and whether we were right for each other. At that time, though, the United States restricted its citizens from visiting the Middle East. Channah was not allowed to make the trip. I received another letter from my sister Reise in which she scolded me, telling me in Yiddish that, "If I do not come, I should be given straw to eat," which meant that I was a fool.

My friends in Israel and my sister-in-law encouraged me to make the trip. It was February 1957. I realized that I had to make a fast, and at the same time, fateful decision. After much thought, I decided that this whole situation had a touch of providential intervention. I searched the Bible for guidance as to my dilemma, whether a Jewish person is allowed to leave the Land of Israel and under what circumstances. Abraham instructed his servant Eliezer when he sent him to his native land, Haran, to look for a wife for his son Isaac, not to agree for Isaac to go to live there.

Abraham said unto him: "Beware thou that thou bring not my son back thither... If the woman be not willing to follow thee, then thou shalt be clear from this my oath," (Genesis 24:6-8). Also during the famine in Isaac's time in the land of Canaan, G-d instructs Isaac not to go down to Egypt though Abraham did in his time, but rather stay in the Land. Our sages say that this restriction was meant only for Isaac, because he was an *Olah Temimah*, unblemished and innocent person.

However, we see that Isaac blesses and sends his son Jacob to his family in Haran to take a wife, "Isaac had blessed Jacob and sent him away to Padan-Aram to take him a wife from thence." (Genesis 28:5-6) Maybe we survivors should also be thought of as an *Olah Temimah*, as innocent victims. With Jacob being sent to Padan-Aram, we see that there is a precedent, that under certain circumstances, a person may leave the Land of Israel to find a wife.

So I decided that before I would accept a position in education in Israel, or possibly pursue a promising military career, I had better see what Channah and I meant to each other. I had no problem going to the States because I had a green card and I could always return if it did not work out.

I informed Channah and my family in Brooklyn, New York that I would return to the United States for a visit for the holiday of Pesach, which was approaching.

Moshe Avital, in Jerusalem, ponders leaving Israel for a wife.

Before sailing back to America, I visited my brother's grave in the cemetery on *Har Hamenuchoth*, which my unit and I captured from the Arabs in 1948, to say farewell to him. I missed him a great deal, especially at this critical juncture of my life when I could have used his wise advice. Since then, every year on my trip to Israel, I visit his and my sister-in-law's graves.

Leaving Israel was very hard for me. My friends with whom I fought in the army did not look favorably on my going to America. They said to me, "Don't you see that people like you are needed here? Don't you know that a Jew can never be secure in the Diaspora? How is it that one who lived through the horrors of the Holocaust cannot understand that Israel is the only place and the only solution for the Jews?"

Once more I took a leave of absence from the reserves. I sailed by ship to New York and arrived two weeks before Pesach. With this trip, I actually ended my military career after fighting in two wars.

Marriage And Raising A Family

On the way back to America, my mind was working and thinking in different directions. If I found that Channah and I were not meant for each other, then I had no problem. After the holiday of Pesach, I would return to Israel and start building my life there. But, what if we were meant for each other and Channah did not agree to settle in Israel? What then?

When I arrived and saw Channah again, I had a feeling that this was it. I knew what I felt for her was real and not just my imagination. She was very attractive. Her beautiful Jewish face, her grace, her mannerisms, were attracting me to her. Although she was born in the United States, and I in Czechoslovakia, two entirely different worlds and different personalities, she an extrovert and I an introvert, we had a lot in common. She came from a very fine Jewish family who immigrated to the United States in 1922 from the Soviet Union. Her parents were steeped in Jewish tradition and very proud Jews. Channah spoke Hebrew well. She graduated from the Hebrew Teachers College in Boston and was very musical. She played the piano, was a Hebrew teacher, and was a staunch supporter of Israel. In many ways, she was very different from most American-born Jewish girls. I also saw how she loved children, which was an indication to me that she would be an excellent and devoted mother. She was clever and well educated, and above all, she had an extremely good heart. I thought, "What else could a man desire?" Maybe my sister Reise was right after all.

My family was very happy to see me again, especially my sister Reise. Channah and I saw each other a few times before Pesach. She went home to Boston for the first two days of Pesach to her parents and family and I celebrated the holiday with my family in Brooklyn. During *Chol Hamoed*, the intermediate days, Channah picked me up with her car and we drove to Boston to meet her parents and family. Meyer and Rebecca Hershman lived in Dorchester at that time. They lived in a nice and spacious apartment in a three family house, which they owned. As soon as I met her father and mother, I hit

Mr. and Mrs. Meyer Hershman
Jack, Channah, Hy

it off with them. They were very fine and gracious people. It reminded me of our own people in Bilke. I spoke Yiddish with them, which they knew well. Especially Mrs. Rebecca Hershman, Channah's mother, did not know what to do to care for me. She was a real *Yiddishe mame*, a Jewish mother, which I had missed since I was separated from my own mother in Auschwitz. She was a terrific cook and a gracious hostess. Channah's two married brothers and their wives and some cousins came over for a festive supper to meet me. From what I saw, I passed the test and I was also pleased to meet Channah's brothers and their wives. Her middle brother Jack and his wife Bebe were very outgoing and very friendly to me. This continued all the years until Jack died at a very young age. Channah and I talked into the wee hours about our feelings and how to proceed with our plans. The next day I told Channah's parents that I wanted to marry Channah, with their permission. They were elated and overjoyed. I called my family in New York and informed them that Channah and I were engaged. They were very happy for us and wished us Mazal Tov.

Meyer Hershman

Rebecca Hershman

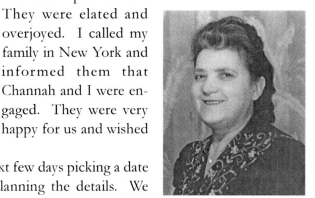

We spent the next few days picking a date for the wedding and planning the details. We picked June 16th. In the Hebrew calendar, the date was the 17th day of *Sivan*, which means *tov*, good, in Hebrew numerical value. It was also Channah's birthday and that year, 1957, it was also Fathers Day, which was a nice gift to my father-in-law, Meyer Hershman. We hired a band, met with them and gave the band leader a list of Jewish and Hebrew songs and other music we wanted them to play at our wedding. We had to do things quickly because our wedding was just eight weeks away. We returned to New York right after the holiday. Channah returned to her teaching position at the Great Neck Synagogue. I called the chairman of the Sherman Avenue Talmud Torah in Jersey City and its principal, Dr. David Greenberg. I informed them of my plans. They immediately asked me to return to the school to my previous position, which I accepted. Now I had additional responsibilities and therefore they gave me a substantial raise. I also called Rabbi Avrutick in Hartford and secured my High Holiday Cantorial position in his Synagogue.

Cantor Moshe Avital

Shlomo Shulsinger, the director of Camp Massad, was happy to have me back and also offered Channah the position of girl's head counselor. I was very preoccupied with the wedding, my positions, and many other arrangements including finding an apartment. At the same time, I was thinking to myself, what a transformation I went through from wanting to live in Israel to getting married in America. The Yiddish saying came to mind, *A Mensch Tracht Und Gott Lacht,* a person thinks that he knows what he is doing, but G-d laughs or in other words, "Many designs are in man's heart, but the counsel of G-d, only it will prevail." (Proverbs 19:21)

I was hoping that this detour in my life would only be temporary, that someday I would still fulfill my dream to live in Israel. In the meantime, I rationalized that I was needed in America, too, to contribute to the Jewish community in the three areas to which I devoted myself, Jewish education, Hebrew camping and Cantorial services. I felt that as a Holocaust survivor, I wanted to make sure that the next Jewish generation got the much needed Jewish and Hebrew substance, so that the link of the generations would continue. Being in these three roles, I also sustained my spirits because I saw in this building a live bridge between the Jewish community in America and Israel. I felt that I had to be the torchbearer of the Hebrew language, culture, and Judaic scholarship. Also, I thought about my name. I wanted to change it back to my father's name, Doft, but I wanted there to be a Hebrew connection.

The newlyweds, Moshe and Channah Avital

So I considered that Doft, in German, means dew and in Hebrew, *Tal* means dew. *Avi* means my father. Thus by combining Avi and Tal, my name became Avital.

Later on, I wrote many articles in the Hebrew press in the United States and in Israel, subjects which dealt with Jewish education, the legacy of the Shoah, Zionism, and Israel, American Jewry, great Jewish personalities, about Jewish holidays, and other subjects and issues in Jewish life.

Our wedding took place in Dorchester, Boston in Congregation Kehilat Jacob. My family from New York with their children came, as well as a few close friends of mine – Dr. Joel Schwartz, Larry Kobrin, and others. A few of the Board members from the Sherman Avenue Talmud Torah in Jersey City came, some of my cousins, Rabbi and Mrs. Shlomo Wind, and my Cantorial teacher Cantor Vigoda. Also Channah's friends from New York and Boston came, Rabbi Samuel and Sarah Rothstein, Dr. Yitzchak Twersky, members of the faculty of the Boston Hebrew Teachers college, Dr. Saul and Rochelle Isserow, Nachum Twersky and his wife, and scores of others, approximately 200 guests. It was a real Jewish wedding in spirit and in Jewish tradition. The food was delicious, the band played all the songs we requested of them, and the Jewish music we gave them including the *Krentzel Tanz*, a dance that is done when the *Mezinkeh*, the youngest child in the family is married. Since Channah and I both were the youngest in our families, it was most appropriate, although it was very sad that my parents and many of my family were not there since they perished in the Shoah. My brother Shlomo, who was married a few years before, and his wife Zlaty, took the place of my beloved parents as *uterfierer*, those who led me to the *chupah*, the wedding ceremony.

Moshe and Channah Avital in Sharon, Massachusetts

Channah and I spent a short honeymoon in New York City and immediately

Moshe and Channah Avital with their daughters, Leora, Reva, and Sheara

Moshe Avital as the Director of the Department of Education and Culture of the Jewish Agency for Israel in the United States and Canada.

after that, we went to Camp Massad for the summer. From then on, the both of us devoted ourselves to Jewish education. For 40 years, I served in Jewish education in various capacities, as teacher, assistant principal, and principal. In camping, I was promoted through the ranks as counselor, division head, head counselor, educational director and then overall director. The positions I held were in Jersey City, Boston, and New York. I also served as the executive director of the Forest Hills Jewish Center. As a Hebrew educator, both

Ross Photo

Moshe Avital with Zalman Shazar, the President of Israel - 1970.

in the Hebrew schools and in summer Hebrew camps, my creativity and contribution to the education of two generations was phenomenal. I helped raise two generations of faithful Jews who became devoted to our people, our traditions, observances, and to Israel. Those days were full of satisfaction for me upon which I can look back with pride.

My most spiritually satisfying position for 12 years was as the Director of the Department of Education and Culture of the Jewish Agency for Israel in the United States and Canada. This position provided me with an unusual channel for utilizing my intellectual and educational talents as well as direct contact with Israel by visiting Israel officially, quite frequently, the land I became so much attached to and longed for. It also gave me many opportunities to meet in Israel with personalities in high positions such as President Zalman Shazar, President Yitzchak Navon, Prime Minister Menachem Begin, and others.

Channah and I established a family of which we are very proud. We are blessed with three wonderful daughters, Leora, Sheara, and Reva Miriam. When they were born, I felt that my daughters were partial compensation for the suffering I experienced during the Holocaust. We named our first daughter Leora, which means a new ray of light came into our home. Our second daughter was named Sheara, which means a song, a melody or music, which filled our home. Mrs. Rebecca Hershman, Channah's mother, became ill and lapsed into a coma. After three weeks, she opened her eyes and little by little, she gained strength but never returned to herself. Two years later, she passed away.

Channah's mother's death was a great blow to the entire family, especially to Channah and her father. Mrs. Hershman was the pillar of the family. During the Jewish holidays, it was always a special time in her home. For me it was a blow; I loved her very much. We had a unique relationship. She treated me like a son and I felt that she was like a mother to me. Then we were blessed with a third daughter who was named Reva Miriam, after Channah's mother. We decided to raise our children with great care and devotion. We were the

Moshe Avital with Israeli Prime Minister Menachem Begin in 1982.

happiest parents there were. As young parents, we watched every moment of their development, their smiles, their movements, their utterances, their first steps, and so on. We decided to speak to them in the Hebrew language. From my experience, I learned that a young child could learn several languages simultaneously. All these happy developments increased our joy and strengthened our love for each other and for our daughters. Every one of them was beautiful, good looking, and full of Jewish grace. After each birth of yet another daughter, our joy and happiness skyrocketed and with the third one our joy tripled.

As they reached school age, nursery, kindergarten, elementary, and high school, we made sure they attended the best Jewish private schools, where we carefully watched their outstanding accomplishments. At every stage of their schooling, we thanked G-d for all the *nachat*, the joy He showered upon us. We were thankful for all their talents and the wonderful qualities with which they were blessed.

When Channah and I, with our children, would visit my sister Feige, it was like a holiday to us. As I write these words about her, so many memories enter my mind, which I will never forget. She lived through the horrors of the Shoah, established a family and gave birth to a son. She was a wonderful person, very charitable, a devoted wife and mother, and a close sister. Her hospitality knew no boundaries.

In 1987, I lost my sister Feige. Tragically she developed heart problems in the concentration camps, which plagued her all her years in the United States. She took great pride in our accomplishments and derived great joy from our children. Her death saddened me greatly and further diminished the few of us who survived the Shoah

During our daughters' college and graduate studies, they were among the excellent students and were put on the Dean's List. They attended Ivy League Schools. All three of them graduated with distinction, Leora and Sheara as attorneys, and Reva as a Judaic instructor. Our friends say that one is prettier than the other, and all of them together are most charming. Many families wish that they could have such exceptional daughters. All three of them married wonderful Jewish men, to our great satisfaction.

Leora, our oldest daughter made aliyah and lives in Israel. She is married to Dov Abramowitz, an American, who also made aliyah. Both are practicing law in Jerusalem. They have two daughters and two sons. Leora fulfilled my dream by living in Israel. She represents our family in the land of our ancestors.

Sheara, our middle daughter, practices law in New Jersey. She is married to Dr. David Arbit, a physician. They have two daughters and a son. They live and work in New Jersey.

Our youngest daughter, Reva Miriam, is a Judaic instructor. She is married to Ilan Slasky, who is a chief financial officer in a thriving technology company. They have two daughters and a son. They reside in Westchester, New York, near us.

Our three children, the first generation, and our ten grandchildren, the second generation of a Holocaust survivor, are my miracle children. To see our grandchildren follow the Jewish traditions and hear them speaking our Hebrew language is my greatest personal pride and joy. They are my greatest revenge against the evil forces in Europe who tried to annihilate the Jewish people. They and hundreds of thousands like them are definite proof that, "the glory of Israel shall not lie," (First Samuel 15:29), that no enemy of the Jewish people can ever annihilate us.

Our Miracle Children...
A Family Of Which We Are Very Proud

Leora and Dov Abramowitz
Sheara and David Arbit
Reva Miriam and Ilan Slasky
and all of our Grandchildren!

The Foundation For My Thinking

As a Holocaust survivor, I, Moshe Doft Lipschitz Avital, went through a fiery furnace, or if you will, a melting from which I survived and came out purified. My experiences taught me how important and sacred the meaning of life is. I will always be on guard to protect my freedom, the freedom of my family and the Jewish people.

Looking back, my life can be subdivided into four periods that have created the foundation for my thinking.

It was in the first period of my life as a child in Bilke, Czechoslovakia, when my basic character was formed and where I acquired my rich Jewish foundation.

The second period was during the second world war, especially during the Holocaust years, as I went through the seven degrees of hell (the ghetto and six concentration camps) on this earth when I discovered the brutal behavior of the Gentile world toward our people during the time when most of my family perished.

The third period in Eretz Yisrael, where a new era began in my life, as a pioneer, as a freedom fighter, as a soldier, and as a defender of the rights of the Jewish people. This period, from July 1945 through November 1950, was one of the decisive periods in my life because it was then when I formulated my adult thinking, my nationalistic feelings, which nourishes me spiritually until this very day.

The fourth period and last one, as I settled in America, building a family and acquiring higher education. Here is where my thinking was set and finalized. Here, I discovered a different world altogether, in contrast to the others – a world with much goodness and decency, but also a false society.

During my adulthood, I have experienced the great inner struggle as to what should be the proper and true pathway in my life. What should be the way of my life as a nationalistic Jew? There were religious and spiritual inner struggles, which fermented and agitated my heart and mind. It has been said

Moshe Avital, a graduate of Yeshiva University.

that a person lives as long as he remembers his past. Once he forgets it, he stops living. Many times in my deliberations, I find myself returning to my original source, to my family and my hometown, Bilke, Czechoslovakia, and my childhood. Certain characteristics of activities that I am involved in are a part of my personality, interwoven with memories of my family and the environment I came from. However, I feel that I also have personal and spiritual freedom, which is not subordinate to the environment of my childhood, or to public opinion during those various periods of my life. I find myself many times going against popular public opinion, even though it is not simple and at times causes me problems. Over the years, I learned to be myself, to do what I believed in, and not to be concerned with the consequences.

After the Shoah, there was a tug of war in my mind. My thinking after the war did not agree with the young lad before the war. Actually, within me two worlds existed, the past with a happy childhood at home and the other, the cruel world of the Holocaust. Sometimes I found a compromise in my mind between these two opposites or sort of a bridge on which I tried to walk so that I would not fall into the abyss. I had a religious upbringing from which I could not part, a whole range of implanted traditions.

During this period, I reached my adult spiritual Jewish intellectual development after a long and intensive struggle. This struggle was about important matters that affected my life, like my desire to live in Israel and not in the Diaspora. I also felt that after the Shoah, I had my doubts about real justice in the world. But at the same time, I remained with a very strong longing and feeling for the Jewish religion and tradition. I came to the conclusion that Jewish tradition was uniquely beautiful, inspiring and had great cultural and spiritual treasures. Deep inside me, my past is firmly embedded. As Solomon the Wise said: "Train up a child in the way he should go and even when he is old, he will not depart from it." (Proverbs 22:6)

I was never a conformist and I did not follow other theories and opinions blindly. I never tried to fit, or adjust to the prevailing fads. I did not feel a necessity to belong to a certain party or movement, only to *Klal Yisrael,* the entire Jewish People. A durable spiritual strength which I acquired while I was still at home in Bilke, when I was young, helped me a great deal to overcome very difficult times with which I was confronted in my lifetime. I came to the conclusion that a person can overcome obstacles inside himself and still remain a free-thinking person, without becoming a slave to others or ideas.

Since the Holocaust, I do not trust the Gentile world. I have lost my respect for them and faith in them. Our people were not interested in museums, monuments, or memorials which some established in their capitals, to exhibit the horrors of their actions.

We demand justice for the Jewish people. We demand punishment for the German war criminals and their collaborators, for their despicable actions because of causeless hatred. We also demand the return of Jewish property and full compensation for our suffering and loss of our families. We demand that the Gentile world leave us alone, to live in peace, and once and for all, stop meddling in the affairs of the State of Israel, the land of our ancestors, which was given to the Jewish people by the Divine promise to our Patriarchs, which was the homeland of the Jewish people for over 3,000 years.

Only when other nations stop hindering the Jewish people from settling and developing the entire land of Eretz Yisrael and adopt a policy of friendship toward the Jewish people, only then, should we consider calling a truce with the Gentile world. However, we can never forgive them for the great suffering and losses they caused our people. Only the victims themselves and G-d Almighty can pardon them. We can only pledge normal relations with them without embracing them.

In the meantime, I urge our people and leave this as a sacred last will and testament to the coming generations:

> *Do not forget what the modern Amalek did to our people.*
>
> *Remember the annihilation of the 6,000,000 of our brethren, the innocent men, women, and children who were murdered because of baseless hatred. Otherwise, there might come another day when our people become complacent and some Jew hater will again, G-d forbid, drown our people in blood and finish the process that Hitler did not succeed in accomplishing during the tragic Holocaust.*

Part 5

Reflections And Analyses

The Jews are a people that shall dwell alone
and shall not be reckoned among the nations.

(Numbers 23:9)

In the previous pages, the author, Dr. Moshe Avital, has presented the personal account of his life before, during, and after the Holocaust.

After more than 50 years since he was liberated from the Buchenwald Concentration Camp, Dr. Avital presents in the coming pages, psychological, philosophical, and theological analyses and reflections regarding the perpetrators of and bystanders in the Holocaust. He reviews their policies, practices, and responsibilities to shed light on how and why the Holocaust occurred.

Dr. Avital, a recognized authority in education, presents his curriculum to teach the generations that did not live through the Holocaust years about the tragedy that befell European Jewry from 1933 to 1945.

Dr. Avital's observations and conclusions come with poignancy and authority, supported by his firsthand experiences in the Holocaust and his educational background.

The Publisher

Reflecting On The Holocaust

More than 50 years have passed since the allied victory over Nazi Germany and only then did the Jewish people discover the tremendous losses they endured during the Holocaust years. Until this day, the sorrow, the pain, and the great effect of the destruction has not diminished; the wound is still open and bleeding. Who knows if it will ever heal? The usual concept of mourning cannot exhaust the deep pain about the destruction of European Jewry in the hands of evil forces, the German demons. The great pain and sorrow at the loss of parents, husbands, wives, brothers, sisters, uncles, aunts, cousins, nephews, neighbors, friends, *landsleit,* and one third of our nation will linger for along time.

There are many survivors who keep this terrible trauma to themselves. It is actually a story of thousands of people who function daily like any other people who have not experienced the terror of the Holocaust. They go to sleep like other people, however, many have sleepless nights because of the memories that haunt them. In the morning their pillows are wet from their tears. Many of us were abruptly torn away from our families and until this day remain without information as to what happened to them. The survivors feel guilty that they survived. Others, especially those who were very young, have a feeling of rage because their parents left them in limbo. The Holocaust causes many survivors mental anxiety, since they cannot overcome the depth of the tragedy. A heavy cloud hangs over the survivor's soul. This problem is not only an individual problem. It is a Jewish national problem, because the entire nation of Israel has been traumatized.

The mourning is not only that of individual survivors but of the entire people of Israel, because the national pain and sadness is not less than that of the individual who lost his family. The Jewish people will probably never be able to assess and describe the great destruction of the spiritual and cultural treasures, which were lost for our people. The German scoundrels and their collaborators cut off the great and rich creativity of thousands of years that was produced on the European continent.

If the pain of the entire nation of Israel is huge, the pain of the survivors is tenfold greater. These brands, plucked out of the fire of the Holocaust, the precious remnant who survived by miracles, continue to carry the pain deep in their hearts and the tragedy of their families of their relatives and their dear ones. We, the survivors, carry not only our own pain and suffering of the concentration camps, but also the decree which was imposed on us to carry the burden of the eternal painful question which does not diminish, "In what way are we more worthy than our dear ones who were sacrificed?"

Those of us who suffered during the Shoah are not eager to speak about the terrible years; perhaps because we are reluctant to uncover our wounded souls, and the scroll of agony of those horrible days. However, as the Holocaust era is becoming a distant past, I wonder if our silence is wise. I feel that it is our obligation, those of us who have survived, to raise our voices incessantly and remind the nations of the world what terrible tragedy they inflicted upon the Jewish people. Also to inculcate to the Jews who did not taste the bitter cup of the Holocaust, the decree: "Remember what the modern Amalek did to us."

There was a period of time after the Shoah that European Jewry was an object of scorn and derision, as if to say they went like sheep to the slaughter, although, since then, there has been a radical change in this kind of thinking. During the immediate years after the Holocaust, the survivors felt like strangers on this planet. Many doors were shut for them, even among our Jewish brethren; some looked down at the survivors. Maybe there was this attitude because of a guilty feeling people had about what happened in the Holocaust. Therefore, they tried to keep a distance from the survivors who reminded everybody of the sin of silence during the Shoah. Even in Israel, the young generation who were born after the establishment of the State of Israel, looked down upon the Jewish refugee survivors. They thought that we were strange and different from normal human beings. To them, the Shoah was a source of shame and they did not want to hear about that period in history. In Israel, the initial reaction to the Shoah was evasive because the Holocaust provoked a sense of humiliation on which the country preferred to turn its back. The *Sabras,* native-born Israelis, were raised as the better, proud Jew who could fight back, unlike the European Jews who went without resistance. That kind of thinking was a terrible blow to us survivors. The Six Day War changed this kind of attitude and baseless humiliating thinking. Then came the Yom Kippur War of October 1973 that brought about a tremendous change in the attitude of the Israeli Sabra towards the Holocaust survivors. Suddenly they discovered that the enemies of Israel were prepared to bring another calamity on our people. They realized that the Biblical injunction that, "The Jews are a people that shall dwell alone and shall not be reckoned among the nations," (Numbers 23:9) is a part of Jewish existence, because no nation came to Israel's aid in this war in order to stand firm against the new evil forces.

More than any other time, there was a complete turnaround in the attitude of Jews in the Diaspora and in Israel, when the Yom Kippur War broke out. This war put Israel in great danger by the Arab sneak attack on the holiest day of the year. Even the most severe critics of the Jews of Europe for their subdued behavior in the Holocaust, now realized that European Jews were by no means cowards or weaklings. They actually found out that the Holocaust victims were great heroes, but even great fighters cannot always stand up to overwhelming satanic forces.

There is another kind of heroism that European Jewry discovered during those hellish years. The Nazi enemy did not declare open war against our people. The Germans acted in stages and through deceit. They used all kinds of cruel tricks to fool the Jews and mislead them. European Jewry did not know what was in store for them. They could not believe that a very developed country in the heart of Europe was capable of committing the murder of innocent men, women, and children. They also thought that the free world would not stand for such treatment. However, as soon as they realized the bitter truth, individuals, and organized groups prepared for a revolt and self defense.

Without weapons, without any allies, they fought in the ghettos and some concentration camps like lions and fell like heroes. Their great and daring heroism was not sufficient to save themselves and their brethren. They caused tremendous casualties to the enemy, but the few could not overpower the millions and millions of well armed Germans and their collaborators. When the tragic terrorist attack in Israel at the school of *Maaloth* happened, where 80 high school students and their teachers were taken captive by P.L.O. terrorists, they were also helpless against a few well armed terrorists. However, there was no comparison between the Jews of Europe during the Shoah and the Maaloth captives because Maaloth was situated inside Israel. Therefore, if the teachers and students would have attacked the P.L.O. murderers, the survivors had a place to escape. This is what was different for European Jewry, because even those who put up armed resistance and tried to escape, had no place to find shelter. Since most of the nations in Europe collaborated with the Germans, many times the escapees were returned to the Germans to be put to death. There is an ancient Jewish *klal*, a rule, that a prisoner cannot cause his own freedom. (Babylonian Talmud Tractate *Berachot* 5B)

These tragic incidents, and the like, should once and for all open the eyes of every Jew to see the Holocaust in its proper perspective. Those of us survivors who were refined in the hellish fire of the Shoah can testify that the German policy during the Holocaust was to weaken and crumble the physical, ethical, and spiritual resistance of the millions of Jews who were led into the crematorium. Daily acts of the highest heroism in the concentration camps were recorded against the deceit of the Germans and the collaborators, and their methodical organized annihilation plan. Manifestations of numerous instances of passive heroism, mutual help and human dignity, and actual daily existence is enough to see the great strength exhibited by the Holocaust victims.

The Holocaust survivors accumulated great anger and desire for revenge. They hoped that after the war came to an end, they would be able to unload some of the anger and rage they harbored in their hearts. The question was where to take revenge and against whom. Do we take revenge only against the Germans or also on other European nations who helped the Germans every step of the way?

As one of the survivors, two voices struggled within me. One voice demanded all the time, to take revenge for our tragedy, for the children who were completely innocent. The struggle within me was very powerful. The other reminded me that Jews are a peaceful people. There were moments when this rage and the struggle subsided. However, until this very day when I am alone, or at night when I lie in bed and cannot fall asleep and the bitter memories of the Shoah come to my mind, I am overtaken by these memories. I still see their faces. I recall images of the Jews of Bilke, my community, gone after 300 years. I am doing this to save memory from oblivion. I write about my father, mother, sisters, brothers, aunts, uncles, neighbors, friends and our Jews of Bilke, who were lost with no trace in the horrible Shoah. Many times I see in my dreams the horrors which I experienced in the camps when I was there. Sometimes I wake up in the middle of these dreams and I see that I am free and alive, but my dear ones remain there.

The survivors waited in vain for the free, enlightened world to punish the Nazi war criminals who committed these terrible atrocities. The political situation, which was created right after the war among the former allies, caused each side to quickly forgive the murderous nations. The entire world was waiting to bring about a new dawn, a new era for humanity, that the evil forces would be wiped out for their heinous crimes, and brotherly love would be the new reign in the new world.

The question arises, "Is there a punishment that can fit the crimes committed by the Germans and other racists?" G-d has not yet created such a punishment that should be meted out for these cruel and criminal acts.

In the past, the Jewish people excommunicated nations (such as Spain after the expulsion of the Jews in 1492) for far lesser crimes. The excommunication placed an *Ot Kayin*, a sign of Cain, (Genesis 4:15) upon murderers of Jews. And what is even more important is that the Jews observed this excommunication, and passed it on from generation to the coming generations. This gave the Jewish people great moral and spiritual strength to continue their struggle against satanic forces.

The contacts with the Germans and other cruel nations after the Shoah put a great sin on us. The official and almost friendly relations between the Jewish State and official officers of other Jewish organizations in the Diaspora with the Germans, burns and scorches the souls of the Holocaust survivors like white hot irons. Perhaps this is the reason that anti-Semitism has become fashionable again in the East, West, and especially in the Arab and Muslim countries, because the enemies of the Jews realize that for *A Soup of Lentils*, (Genesis 25:34), meaning for a small price, they were ready to forgive the murderers.

There have been arguments pro and con. It was pointed out that Israel needed the money and the Germans were willing to pay for the absorption of the new immigrants. However, if the Israeli leadership at that time would have appealed to the Diaspora Jewry, especially American Jewry, with the choice to increase their financial support for Israel or tarnish the name of the Jewish people and desecrate the memory of the Holocaust victims by taking a pittance from the Germans, I am confident that world Jewry at the time would have chosen to preserve the memory of the victims. At least if Israel would have received from the Germans half of the Jewish property which they confiscated and stole, one could have said that Israel would have received a decent settlement. But this way, in the eyes of the world, the Germans appeared as a different people than the Nazis. In reality, German prosperity and the ability to rebuild their ruined country after World War II came about from the vast resources, equipment, gold, silver, currencies, art, and many other properties which they forcefully took from the Jews. There is not enough money in Germany to be able to compensate the Jews for the suffering, the humiliation, degradation, and the loss of life.

The Torah tells us, "No expiation can be made for the land, for the blood, that is shed therein, but by the blood of him that shed it." (Numbers 35:33) No money or reparations can be permitted, because human life would be cheapened, and the land would become wholly corrupt. If honor and dignity cannot be bought and sold, can the Jewish loss of life in the Holocaust be compensated with money? Such events have no price. Loss of life cannot be undone by money. There is no adequate restitution for these horrible crimes. After the Holocaust, many survivors wanted to spurn restitution altogether. Protesters outside the *Knesset*, the Israeli parliament, denounced compensation as blood money. To this day, there are survivors who feel that accepting restitution is a betrayal of the dead. Others bring the Biblical statement which states: "Hast thou killed and also taken possession?" (First Kings 21:19)

Paying restitution gives Germany a new identity since it enables her to become an accepted people among the nations. But this is a very small price that Germany is paying for her heinous crimes. By giving restitution, the Germans want to wash away the stain, but the survivors want the stain to remain forever. The Germans hope that reparations will atone for the guilt and want to emerge cleansed. There has to be a reckoning with those who profited from the evil. Financial restitution can serve to acknowledge and recognize suffering, but what it cannot buy is either forgiveness or forgetting.

Until now, no revenge has been taken against the Germans. I believe that there will yet come a day, perhaps not in our generation, that the day of reckoning will descend upon the German people. The Jewish blood of our brethren does not rest and still cries out to heaven and reaches up to the throne of Glory. G-d's justice will someday avenge the blood of our dear ones. We don't know G-d's ways or how and when He will bring His wrath upon those nations who have afflicted our people, because it is not possible that G-d's world shall be built on evil. There can't be complete peace and tranquility in the world until the horrible wrong is corrected. Only then will people and nations live in peace side by side, and human beings will be able to enjoy the goodness and prosperity that the Almighty will provide.

Why The Horrible Holocaust?

In the late 1930s and in the beginning of the 1940s when the Germans and other Fascists created political upheaval and began persecution and systematic destruction of European Jewry, Rabbis, Talmudic scholars, and others were searching for reasons why this was happening. Throughout history, Jews have been persecuted, but never before to such an extent and of such magnitude. Kabbalists and other *Mechashvey Kitzin*, men who calculate the date of the Messianic era and redemption from some indication in the Bible and other holy books, are searching the various sources to try to understand why such a calamity befell the Jewish people.

Jewish sources tell us that before the Messiah comes, there will be very difficult times, that terrible ordeals and suffering will precede the redemption. Some great Rabbis in Europe, such as Rabbi Elchanan Wasserman, leader of the Baranowiczer Yeshivah Academy in Poland, who perished in the Holocaust, spoke about the reasons for the hard times which befell the Jews during the Holocaust. In his book, *Ikvata D'Mshicha*, In the Foot Steps of the Messiah, he says he thought the persecution heralded the coming of the Messiah and redemption.

In the Babylonian Talmud, Tractate *Sanhedrin* (page 98A), there is a discussion about the Messianic age. Rabbi Yochanan states, "If you see a generation upon which numerous troubles come like a river, expect the Messiah." The Talmudic commentator, the *Maharsha*, Rabbi Shmuel Eliezer Halevy Edelish explains, "If the troubles constantly grow like a river which constantly flows without stopping." As it says, "For distress will come like a flood which the breath of the Lord driveth." (Isaiah 59:19) And next to that verse it is written, "A redeemer shall come to Zion." (Isaiah 59:20) This would be a sign of the Messianic Age.

We all know that, unfortunately, the Messiah did not come and the Holocaust decimated European Jewry. Since then, until this day, many have wondered, especially Holocaust survivors, why this calamity happened to us. I have searched for an answer far and wide. Theologically and intellectually, it is a deeply perplexing subject. How can one explain effectively the most traumatic Jewish experience in history? Simplistic statements about the Holocaust are probably easier to deliver to people who have not suffered the trauma, or to someone who has not read basic works of literature about this subject, and it is very perplexing, especially to people whose families have been decimated by the Nazis.

To some survivors, the enormity of the tragedy forced them to abandon faith in G-d and become complete Atheists. Jews who survived the Nazi death machine were so traumatized by the experience that it completely eliminated their belief in G-d. Some survivors say that if good people, like my parents, could have been murdered for no reason at all, then there cannot be a G-d. At the same time, there are Holocaust survivors who became more religious. We have to admit that no one has the key to understanding the framework of providence of each case or happening. The Torah encourages us to ask difficult questions about faith. We may question the way G-d conducts his world. Within this framework one can delve into questions of nature and substance which deal with life and death, about reward and punishment, about Israel and the other nations, about good and evil in the world, and about suffering and death. We can see this in the book of Job, who was a righteous person, but suddenly was afflicted with terrible loss and suffering, and he does not understand why. Job says to G-d: "Let me know what you charge me with." (Job 10:2) In the midst of the travails, three of his friends come to see him and tell him that G-d is always right, so his suffering must mean that he sinned. At the end of the book, however, G-d tells Job that his friends were utterly wrong, that Job was not being punished for his sins (because he had none). As he states: "Let G-d ascertain my integrity." (Job 31:6) He was being tested by G-d for His own reasons.

The extreme *Charedim*, very religious Orthodox Jews, personified by Rabbi Joel Tietelbaum of Satmar and the Neturei Karta, who reject the idea of Jewish statehood which the Zionist movement brought about, claim that the Shoah was a punishment, since we Jews violated three prohibitions of G-d. We have been foresworn by G-d Almighty: Firstly, "Not to enter the Holy Land as a group before the predestined time." Secondly, "Not to use human force to bring about the establishment of a state. Not to rebel against the nations but to remain loyal citizens." Thirdly, "Not to leave exile ahead of time." (Babylonian Talmud, Tractate *Ketuboth*, page 111A)

It is explained that the Almighty alone, without any human effort or intervention, will redeem the Jewish people from exile when the true Messiah will come. Contrary to this kind of thinking, the religious Zionists who base their idea on the same Biblical and Talmudic tradition, believe that the Shoah was a part of the beginning of the redemption of the Jewish people. The religious Zionists say that the best proof of this theory is the establishment of the State of Israel just three years after the Holocaust, which is a confirmation of their thinking.

One theory says that during the Holocaust years, G-d hid His face from the Jewish people for reasons we don't know. In the Book of Isaiah, we find some insight into this problem. It says, "For a small moment have I forsaken thee; but with great mercies will I gather you. In the overflowing of wrath I hid My face from thee; but with everlasting compassion I will take you back in love, said the Lord your redeemer." (Isaiah 54:7-8). Here we can see that the religious Zionists may have a point about their theory.

From the Book of Job, one can derive a conclusion about the Shoah, that the moral of Job's story is that there is indeed divine reason behind every disaster, but it is not always the reason that appears at first to be self evident.

Some Charedim also attribute the Shoah to the sins of rapid assimilation by the reform movement which originated in Germany and the fact that the Nazi butchers also came from that country.

Professor Avi Ravitzky, of the Hebrew University in Jerusalem, says: "There is an extreme, small group of Zionists," whom he calls *Hyper-Zionists*, "that saw the Holocaust as a punishment for our betrayal of the Holy Land since the 19th century and the Balfour Declaration, and for the fact that most of the Jewish people did not respond to the divine call to go to the Holy Land."

The Lubavitcher Rebbe, Menachem Mendel Schneerson, compared the Holocaust to a surgical amputation resulting from the sins of the Jews, past and present.

The former Sephardic Chief Rabbi of Israel, Ovadyah Yosef, caused great uproar, resentment, and much pain to the Holocaust survivors when he explained the Holocaust tragedy as a mystical happening. He said that the 6,000,000 *Kedoshim*, martyrs and Holocaust victims, were *Gilgul Neshamoth*, the reincarnate sinners of previous generations whose purpose on earth was to atone for mistakes in past lives.

Gilgul Neshamoth is a known Kabbalistic doctrine of reincarnation of souls, which is found in the book *Sefer Habahir*. This doctrine is a very marginal idea in Judaism. It has been denounced by many great Jewish Sages.

A rational person cannot accept the idea that innocent people including 1,500,000 children lost their lives in such a brutal way because of the Gilgul Neshamoth idea.

It has to be stated that the Holocaust was a demonic idea, a terrible tragedy and catastrophe and nothing else. What punishment for sins can explain the murder of 6,000,000 Jews? What justification can there be in the case of the horrible Shoah that was out of proportion for any kind of transgression. No one has a right to come up with these kinds of unbelievable ideas.

The Shoah was too big and too tragic that this generation should attempt to analyze the meaning of the Holocaust when there are still Shoah survivors alive. We survivors, who still live with the open wounds of the Shoah and the tragic memories engraved in our soul and our flesh, reject these simplistic and superstitious ideas. It must be emphasized that all Jewish souls who perished in the Shoah were innocent human beings. Like everyone else, mothers, fathers, and children were led by evil forces to their slaughter because they happened to be born Jewish. On Yom Kippur at the morning and concluding *Neilah* service, we pray, "Give hope to the Jewish people and restore again our nation's home in the land You promised to our forefathers. For wicked people have devoured the Jewish people. But despite all this, we are G-d's and our eyes look to G-d. Do not delay freedom. Only He is the hope of Israel."

The Holocaust is one of those tragic events that is impossible to understand. A thousand years will pass and no answer will be found. It is one of the great unsolvable riddles of humanity. How can a normal and decent person, if he is a human being and not a beast, take a small child and smash his head in front of his mother? Also, why was the entire world dead-silent? These are the personal questions that continue to eat away at us survivors. Why were my father and mother the victims? Why the small children of my sisters? Why did I survive and not them? Many questions remain unanswered, and many wounds remain open.

It is extremely difficult for us survivors to reconcile the fact that the evil Germans enjoy prosperity after the heinous crimes they committed during the Holocaust. The Prophet Jeremiah asks that question, "You will win, O Lord, if I make claim against You, yet I shall present charges against You. Why does the way of the wicked prosper? Why are the workers of treachery at ease?" (Jeremiah 12:1) In other words, I know that in any argument You must be right because You are a righteous G-d. It is very hard to accept the sight of wicked men triumphing and flourishing. All seems to be well with them; their defiance of G-d brought them no setback, yet the righteous suffered. Can one blame the survivors by doubting G-d's judgment!

The ways of G-d in conducting the world are an eternal mystery. Any explanation does not remove the veil of the secret of his judgment. On the contrary, it envelops it with additional veils in our human thinking, because nobody knows for sure the ways of G-d's judgment. Despite appearances to the contrary, G-d does differentiate between good and evil, deciding their ultimate fate.

The question of why the Holocaust happened will have to remain until the end of days to find the real answer. When there is no answer to a dispute, the Talmud uses the term *Taiku, Tishbi Yetaretz Kushiyoth Veaboyoth*, the *Tishbite* will answer all the questions and solve all the problems. Elijah the Prophet, the Tishbite, who will come with the Messiah, the son of David, will resolve all difficulties and will probably have the answer to the question of why the Shoah happened.

The prevailing wisdom among many intellectuals has been that evil has nothing to do with human nature and must be attributed to a higher power. They claim that it is scientifically incorrect to say that war or other violent behavior is genetically programmed into our human nature. One sees that when given the right environment, it does happen. When it comes, however, to the German people, they were brainwashed to believe that they were *Ober Menchen*, Superman, a superior race. This brutality became a basic ingredient of German behavior.

We need not look too hard to see the monsters the Nazi regime bred. In the beginning of the Bible, we find that human nature encompasses evil inclinations and destructive impulses. The Bible states, "And the Lord saw that wickedness of man was great on the earth, and that imagination of the thoughts of his heart was only evil continually. And it repented the Lord that He had made man on earth, and it grieved Him at His heart." (Genesis 6:5-6) G-d does not cause evil. It is man who causes it. A human being has freedom of will and can choose to do good. In another passage in Genesis, it states, "For the imagination of man's heart is evil from his youth." (Genesis 8:21) This is the *Yetzer Hara*, the evil inclination in man, which sometimes gains the mastery over the *Yetzer Hatov*, the good inclination.

Much of the 20th century has been filled with barbarism. It was the century of the German Final Solution; the killing of 6,000,000 innocent Jews, among them 1,500,000 children. The suffering of the Jewish people during the Holocaust is beyond comprehension. Technological progress became a destructive tool in the hands of the old fashioned evildoers. No matter how bad one thinks the Holocaust was, it was even worse than one can imagine.

The Nazi political movement was bent on obliterating all morals, human decency, and value of life. These monsters and sadists waged an uncompromising war of genocide against the Jewish nation. Their atrocities were accompanied by tactics of humiliation and dehumanization. The Germans flipped a mental switch and saw the Jewish *person* as a *non person*, making it easy for them to torture or kill him. All human sympathy was turned off. This allowed the Nazi guards to commit their inhuman acts, since their indoctrination made them believe they served a higher purpose. In committing their horrible crimes, they drifted downwards to a beastly level. When the average German soldier saw that the entire army was involved in the mass killings, he functioned like a robot.

The Germans did not loathe in documenting their worst atrocities, even when they committed the most despicable acts of brutality; executions and gassing of Jews. The photographers were clicking away with their cameras and movies.

Professor Robert Glaytlee of Canada established in his research that 80% of the information the *Gestapo*, the German Secret State Police, collected for the Reich about the enemies of the state was supplied to them by ordinary German citizens. This information was supplied voluntarily. The majority of the German people were very satisfied with the Nazi regime during the second world war. Daniel Goldhagen, in his book *Hitler's willing executioners: Ordinary Germans and the Holocaust*, states that there is a murderous streak in the character of the German people. He says that ordinary citizens were Hitler's silent partners for which they bear responsibility. Hitler gave a free hand to his subordinates Henrich Himmler, Hermann Goering, Joaichim Ribbentrop, Josef Goebbels, and others to commit atrocities. The Nazis formed a mental consciousness and readiness to annihilate an entire people in the concentration camps, which they established especially for that purpose. The Holocaust became a German national project among ordinary citizens, not just Nazi leaders, driven by a particularly virulent anti-Semitism.

Brutality is deeply rooted in the German people. Even the German women took part in the annihilation of the Jews. Ten percent of the concentration camp staff was women. Ten thousand women served in the S.S. units. They were responsible for the selection of the Jews to be sent to be gassed or executed. Some of these women like Ilse Koch committed horrible atrocities. The German women greatly admired Hitler. There were, and still are other anti-Semitic nations in Europe, but only the Germans led the annihilation of

6,000,000 Jews.

After all this, whoever says the Holocaust happened just like that denies that there was a Shoah. It is a sad commentary on those who come out with unacceptable ideas, because with these kinds of ideas one crosses all lines. One must state unequivocally that the Shoah was not an act of G-d. It was a well planned, diabolic idea by the German people and their collaborators, the most willing partners in the murder of 6,000,000 Jews, because they were Jews. Only they have to be held responsible and accountable for the atrocities. Only they should be branded and carry an *Ot Kayin*, a sign of Cain, as murderers of 6,000,000 innocent people until the end of time. I do believe that a time will come when the Almighty will severely punish all those murderers and their nations at the right time, in His own way, because the world cannot co-exist with wickedness.

As The World Stood By In Silence

The Holocaust was not an act of G-d and not an act of Satan. It was a well organized and well prepared plan by the German State that utilized modern techniques.

In the time of the Holocaust, the Jews lived in a *society* where mass murder was routine, mechanized for economy and efficiency. This society was Hitler's inferno. All this industry was planned and executed by a highly developed *civilized* nation in the very heartland of Europe. It obliterated all religious, moral, legal, and ethical considerations and values which gave reason to human existence. It successfully eliminated mercy, pity, conscience, guilt, and recognition of common humanity.

In this incredible society, a new technology was created, a new vocation of killing was cultivated. Professionals were scientifically trained how to dupe their victims skillfully, to lessen their resistance; how to transport expeditiously the millions of human cargo to their death; how to select the strong to work as slaves; how to depersonalize, terrorize and dehumanize their victims; to kill at the lowest per capita cost; to process the corpses and extract the maximum money's worth from them.

The German government appealed to the basic human instincts to compel the ordinary German to act violently against the Jews. The German government used its various communications media to label violence against the Jews as a manifestation of strength and courage. To the dismay and disbelief of the Jewish people, the message found receptive ears in many European countries. The Holocaust was the ultimate consequence. The Shoah left an indelible stain on humanity.

History has recorded mass murders before. Jews lived through persecution and suffering in the Crusades (1096-1330), the Inquisition (1483-1650), the Chmelnitsky Pogroms (1648-1658) and the Czarist Pogroms (1882-1906). In our own times, we read of tens of thousands dying of starvation, of thousands wiped out by the ravages of war. However, the 6,000,000 Jews killed during the Nazi Holocaust exceeds the combined total of all these catastrophes.

So what makes the Holocaust, the slaying of 6,000,000 Jews a special tragedy? It is true that precious human beings of different nationalities, faiths, and ideologies were annihilated in the millions, but it was the Jews who were singled out for total destruction, for no earthly reason. There is no parallel in history for what occurred to the Jews during the years of World War II.

The organized, systematic slaughter of 6,000,000 people cannot be understood in any rational way. Jewish children were special targets in order to insure the extermination of future generations, and so were women, the bearers of children. No frame of logical and understandable pattern of human behavior into which we can place these events exists, so that they become comprehensible in terms of our own experience.

How did the enlightened world react to the Jewish tragedy, while the axe of the executioner was hanging over them? The indifference and passivity of the Gentile world will never be understood nor ever forgiven.

We should not forget that there were many European nationalities that watched with satisfaction and refused to help the Jews as they were doomed to die. There were also those that helped to kill Jews with great zeal.

The Germans knew in advance that they could slaughter the Jews without punishment. They knew the world would watch silently and in many instances even help them to accomplish their goal. Goebbels wrote in his diary: "I believe that deep in their hearts, the British and Americans are pleased that we are annihilating the Jewish rabble."

The nation that gave the world the Magna Carta was in a position to help rescue Jews, but it refused. The British Government refused to allow Jewish refugees who were lucky enough to escape Hitler's inferno to enter the Land of Israel, the land that always belonged to the Jews.

The United States of America, the great humane power, was not any better during those tragic years. It was inconceivable that President Roosevelt refused permission to give temporary asylum to a few hundred refugees whose ship, the St. Louis, cruised the shores of the United States near the Statue of Liberty. The many appeals remained unanswered, thus forcing the ship to go back to Germany where the refugees were seized and put into concentration camps. Most of them died.

I shall never forget, as my family and I were herded into the freight train to be taken to Auschwitz, the people in the boxcar saying: "As soon as America finds out what is going on, she will surely stop this." That's the kind of faith the Jews of Europe had in America, who was known until then to be the protector of the downtrodden. But America did not act to save Jews during the Holocaust years. President Roosevelt and his government were bystanders. Roosevelt, who was careful not to confront the British because of the White Paper, was very interested in the idea of settling the Jews of Europe in a remote place like Madagascar, in the Indian Ocean, or in the Amazon Forest, since this would have served the British well.

How naive we Jews were then! Jewish leaders in the free world pleaded with the Allies to bomb the rails leading to Auschwitz and the crematoriums and thus interrupt the process of annihilation, but to no avail. There were Jewish pilots in the United States Air Force who volunteered for such missions, but they were refused. Even though the Jews in the free world contributed much to the war effort, the Allies refused to consider rescuing Jews. It is a known fact that 1,500,000 Jews were fighting in all the Allied Forces.

We should not forget that the powerful Catholic Church and it spiritual leader, Pope Pious XII with his moral authority, remained silent all those years, although he received many appeals from non-Jewish and Jewish leaders like the Chief Rabbi of Eretz Yisrael, Rabbi Hertzog. They appealed to him to speak out against the atrocities. One remark from the Pope to his followers would have saved countless Jews. Even some Nazis might have reconsidered their actions, but he remained silent.

The International Red Cross knew about the conditions in the labor camps, concentration camps, and death camps, however, their official policy was to not reveal the horrors and crimes the Germans and their collaborators were committing during the second world war. The International Red Cross did not attempt to arouse public opinion against the daily crimes that were committed against the Jews. The International Red Cross admitted a few years ago that they could have done more and could have been more aggressive in their responsibilities, but they have not changed. Until this day, the International Red Cross refuses to recognize *The Red Star of David* in Israel as a legitimate health organization, while they do recognize the *Red Crescent* of the Arabs. The outright rejection of the Red Star of David is a deliberate and blatantly hostile act of anti-Jewish and anti-Israeli discrimination.

A study of the International Red Cross records during the Holocaust proves that this organization was far from impartial or dedicated where Jewish victims were concerned. As a survivor, I cannot help but recall the agony of the starving Jewish prisoners in the concentration camps who witnessed the distribution of life saving food parcels to all camp inmates, except Jews. The parcels were clearly marked in bold letters, "to prisoners in Bolkenheim from the International Red Cross." We Jews were told that the International Red Cross followed German orders to exclude Jews as recipients.

We know that in response to numerous appeals by rescue groups and Jewish leaders from the International Red Cross to visit the known extermination sites, or to grant the Jews in death camps the protected status of civilian internees, the organization's explanation was that the Nazi treatment of Jews constituted a *German internal matter.*

There is definite evidence showing that during the Shoah, the International Red Cross, very much like the Vatican and western governments, lacked positive humane will and courage to help in efforts to rescue Jews. The total indifference to Jewish suffering, as well as the timidity and weakness of wartime leaders, and the open anti-Semitism of the International Red Cross staff has tarnished the image of the organization whose lofty ideals turned out to be a myth. The organization's standard reply to Jewish agencies was that helping Jews in the concentration camps was inconsistent with Red Cross traditional functions.

The International Red Cross has condemned the violence in Israel against Arabs, citing the fourth Geneva Convention to respect and protect civilians. Only when the victims are non-Jews does the International Red Cross get involved. Then it is not an internal matter. However, when Jews are massacred, the International Red Cross keeps quiet. All gates were hermetically shut except the gates to the gas chamber.

We should indeed remember that the Church in Europe did save a few thousand Jewish children... but with a purpose in mind. Those children were forcefully converted to Christianity. After the war, when surviving relatives wanted these Jewish children back, the Church refused to return them. The conversions created many tragedies, which exist to this day. Who knows how many Jewish children have been lost in this way to the Jewish people, especially those children who remained without survivor parents. They are lost forever.

Even the Swiss were in collusion with the Germans, as it was revealed after the war.

However, we must also remember the decent human beings, which we call, the *Righteous Among The Nations*, who saved Jews from Nazi persecution, often at the price of their own lives. The Scandinavian people in general and the Danes in particular, rescued many thousands of Jews. This proves that with a little bit of good will and human decency, much could have been done to save innocent people. We Jews will always remember and be thankful to them for their courageous and righteous acts.

The Holocaust of European Jewry was the most traumatic event of the 20th century. The Holocaust kingdom was the most inhumane system ever known to man. The German atrocities robbed the innocent Jews of Europe of their humanity without any distinction. The entire world however, was silent, as if it was happening on another planet.

Even after the war was over and the unbelievable atrocities discovered, the nations did not punish the Germans. The International Tribunal at Nuremberg in 1946 dealt with the Jewish Holocaust only as a marginal event. The German plan of the Final Solution to annihilate the Jews of Europe and the destruction of European Jewry was discussed in the category of crimes against humanity and not as a crime of the genocide of the Jewish people.

Only the Adolf Eichmann trial in Jerusalem Israel in 1961 presented to the world a broader picture of the tragedy of the great losses to the Jewish people and the severity of the crime that has no parallel in the history of humankind, which was, and is, and will be forever, the responsibility of the Germans, the Hungarians and other collaborators. The German murderers were not a bunch of robots. They were men and women who were forged into a killing machine, and indoctrinated with the ideas of Nazi spirit.

The loss of the Jewish people was not only loss of life, but it was also the destruction of the demographic and cultural center of World Jewry, which had existed in central and eastern Europe. A highly developed culture based on the Yiddish language was obliterated in a single blow. The combination of Nazi ideology, modern bureaucracy, and advanced technology to carry out the genocide of European Jewry characterizes the Holocaust and marks it unique in the annals of history. The Jewish Holocaust must serve as a warning to all mankind regarding the danger, which stems from hatred, based on ideology, and the abrogation of human values and morality.

Hard Lessons I Learned From The Holocaust

Deep in my soul, I absorbed the suffering and the persecution of the victims of my family and 6,000,000 of my brethren. The cruelty and the horror of the non-Jewish world to our people during the Holocaust years is deeply embedded in my mind, and because it is such a powerful event, it overshadows everything else. It will remain there forever. I took upon myself, or obligated myself deep in my soul, to remember and remind the world of those tragic years when the Germans conducted a systematic annihilation of our people; to live in the present a simple, humble, and modest life, and to believe in the future of the Jewish people, especially after the establishment of the State of Israel in our homeland. I pray to the Almighty that in His conducting of the world, in His own time, and in His own way, He will doubly punish the nations who participated in the persecution of the Jewish people.

During those fateful years, when Hitler and his cohorts were running wild, world Jewry was caught unprepared. There were no Jewish organizations in America, in Europe, or in Palestine, or any place that had any plans to save European Jewry. Only Vladimir Zev Zabotinsky, in the late 1930s, was calling for evacuation of East European Jewry to Eretz Yisrael, even if they would have to fight their way into the land. Nobody listened to him. On the contrary, certain Jewish leaders denounced him as a person who would endanger the Jews.

There was no plan to encourage young Jews in Eastern Europe to resist the evil forces or to try to hinder the German plan of the destruction of European Jewry. At that time there was no Jewish State or Jewish Army who could have rushed to the rescue, as the Israeli Army did in 1976 to rescue the Jews who were taken hostage by the P.L.O. terrorists in Entebbe, Uganda.

During those hellish years, the Jews were isolated, neglected, and despised. The verse in the Bible, which says, "It is a people that shall dwell alone and shall not be reckoned among the nations," (Numbers 23:9) came to pass.

No nation or group of nations on this planet came to their rescue. Instead they were treated as if they were subhuman.

At that time there were four categories of people: The victims – mostly Jews; The murderers who killed with zeal; The bystanders, who looked on with indifference; The leaders of the great powers who did not lift a finger to save Jews.

Leaders like Franklin Roosevelt, Winston Churchill, Joseph Stalin, and others did not even warn the murderers that after their defeat, they would be tried as war criminals, and that they would pay for committing atrocities. On the contrary, Britain made a great effort to hinder and stop, at all costs, the immigration of Jews to Palestine who miraculously saved themselves. The United States also closed its doors to Jewish immigration.

The Pope, more than anyone else, could have saved countless lives, yet he was silent. Pope Pious XII did not raise his moral voice even when the Germans rounded up thousands of Jews in Rome who were deported to the death camps. He did not intercede on behalf of the victims, or protest to the Germans, nor did he ask mercy for them. He watched with satisfaction that finally the Germans were doing the job for the Church, because in this way, the Church would get rid of the problem it had with the continuous existence of the Jewish people. The entire non-Jewish world ganged up on the Jewish people, some by actual murder, others by an unprecedented silence.

There were only a few, the Righteous Among The Nations, who saved some Jews. This proved that if there was a will, there was a way to save Jews. One can only imagine how many more could have been saved if there would have been more Righteous Gentiles.

The Talmud, in Tractate Sanhedrin (37:1), states, "Whoever destroys a single life is as guilty as though he had destroyed the entire world, and whoever saves a single life, he is thought of as if he had saved the entire world." There were 6,000,000 lives destroyed. That means that 6,000,000 worlds were eradicated. The Jewish people had suffered the greatest loss in its 4,000 year history.

It is a known fact that the Germans were the ones who planned the Final Solution, the annihilation of our people. They said, "Come and let us wipe them out as a nation, that the name of Israel will be remembered no more." (Psalm 83:4) But to be true to history, it should be pointed out that many European and other governments and millions of their people were in on the plan by actively collaborating with the Germans on various levels, in the murder of European Jewry. The majority of the murderers were Christians with the silent consent of the Vatican and the Church. There were many Christians who actively participated in the persecution of our people. There were high percentages of Catholics among the S.S. beasts, the Latvians, Lithuanians, Estonians, Ukrainians, Hungarians, Slovaks, and Polacks. Many of them served as Wachman guards in the various concentration camps, such as John Demanyuk, who was a guard at Treblinka. I myself encountered them in the camps in which I was interred.

There were a number of well known Christian clergy who were in the forefront of the Jewish persecution. To mention but a few: Bishop Jozef Tiso, President of Slovakia, was instrumental during the war in deporting 135,000 Slovakian Jews. He paid the Germans 500 marks for every Jew the Germans shipped to the death camps, since the Germans promised that the Jews would never return. Rabbi Samuel David Ungar, of the City of Neitra in Slovakia, turned for help to Bishop Ketemka, and begged him to intercede on behalf of the Jews of Neitra. This Jew hater said to Rabbi Ungar that this was not an ordinary deportation, "All of you will be slaughtered there in one day, and you deserve it because you killed our Lord."

Bishop Valerian Trifa was the leader of the *Iron Guard Militia*, a Fascist organization in Rumania. He led a pogrom in Bucharest in 1941 where 1,200 Jews were killed and thousands wounded. After the war, he escaped to the United States and practiced his ministry until a few years ago, where he evaded justice. Rabbi Michael Dov Weismandel of Slovakia in his book, *From the Depth of My Affliction*, writes, "I sent a number of telegrams to Pope Pious XII and appealed to him to save the Jews of Slovakia, especially since Bishop Jozef Tiso was the head of the government. I received no answer. There was dead silence."

After the war, the Vatican and the Churches helped hundreds, perhaps thousands of Nazi war criminals to escape from the Allies, to South America, Canada, Australia and other countries. These countries became a haven for the Nazis, as well as for Holocaust survivors. It was a place where children of people with Auschwitz tattoos could find themselves in school besides the children of guards who had manned the concentration camps. These Nazis built a whole network in South America and had important contacts all over the continent, instead of being brought to justice for their horrible crimes.

In March 2000, we witnessed through the media, the Pope's journey to the Land of Israel. It was a very well planned journey. It had all the trimmings of a good Hollywood show. I would call it a real carnival. Maybe this Pope is a humanist. But let's not get carried away. Let's not walk on the clouds; let's be down to earth about this whole thing. It was this Pope who a few years ago received the Nazi, Kurt Waldheim, against the appeals of Jewish and other leaders not to do so. Let us not be blinded by the diplomatic expressions the Pope uses, such as: "Our older brother," or a visit to a Synagogue in Rome.

One cannot bridge oceans of Jewish blood by small gestures. The magnitude of the Shoah caused by the Christian world is such that no one can be forgiven in the name of the 6,000,000 martyrs. The Jewish hearts still bleed, and the blood of our brethren still cries out to heaven, about the enormous tragedy of the Shoah.

We survivors were hoping that after the enormous Jewish losses and our sufferings, the world would try to make it up to the Jewish people by admitting their crimes, by compensating for the losses, by fully supporting the just rights of the Jewish people to a state in the land of their fathers, and once and for all, to let us live in peace. But our hopes did not materialize. In the last few years we have witnessed that very little has changed.

As a survivor who lost most of his family; parents, brothers, sisters and their children and an extended family of over 200 martyrs, I cannot and will not forgive the Vatican and the Church for their part in the Shoah until at least the following conditions are rectified:

1 - To admit openly that the Church hierarchy in many countries was involved in collaborating with the Germans and other Fascists in the Shoah.

2 - Until the Vatican opens all their archives including Pope Pious XII's private archives during the years of the Shoah.

3 - Until they reveal the details of what happened to the 10,000 Jewish children who were forcefully baptized by the Church all over Europe during the Shoah, and their whereabouts.

4 - Until the Holy See opens for inspection the tunnel under Vatican City and returns to the Jewish people the spoils of the Holy Temple of Jerusalem and many other religious ceremonial objects, books, and manuscripts which they forcefully took from the Jewish people over the last 2,000 years.

5 - Until the Vatican and the Church fully support the rights of the Jewish people to greater Jerusalem, which was united in the 1967 Six Day War, and stops conspiring with the Arabs and other enemies of Israel to take it away from us.

Even on the Pope's current trip to Israel, the Vatican's actions were not a sign of change or repentance. Every place the Pope traveled in Israel, an ambulance accompanied him. The Vatican demanded that the Jewish symbol of the Red Star of David be removed from this ambulance, which Israel foolishly did. But no such demand was made by the Vatican from the Jordanians or Palestinians to remove the Red Crescent, which is a Muslim religious symbol. While there, the Pope visited an Arab refugee camp. Did any one of us ever hear of Pope Pious XII visiting any concentration camp of Jews? Did anyone of us hear that the Vatican protested to the British when their navy hunted down Jewish refugee ships trying to reach a safe haven on the shores of Eretz Yisrael?

It took the Vatican 2,000 years to recognize that there was a Jewish people, but this Pope was in a hurry to recognize the need for a Palestinian homeland. It is only a question of time before the Vatican makes Pope Pious XII into a saint, even though they know how much pain it will cause the Jewish people.

The Pope, in his speech at Yad Vashem, the Holocaust Museum in Jerusalem, mentioned the word "silence" a number of times. This is the entire problem. The silence of the Vatican and the Church during those trying years when they were supposed to raise their moral voice, they were silent. There was a reason for that silence. The continued existence of the Jewish people, even in the face of various attempts to destroy us, was a theological problem for the Church. Their entire theology is based on the premise of the degradation and scorn of the Jew. They claimed that they have replaced the Jewish people, that the Holy One, blessed be He, broke His *brith*, His covenant, with the Jewish people. When Hitler rose to power, the Church saw a perfect opportunity to get rid of the Jews once and for all, by collaborating with the Germans and other anti-Semites in the Final Solution.

We should know that the late recognition of the State of Israel by the Vatican, and the carnival put on by the Pope on his trip to the Holy Land, was not done because they suddenly loved us. It came for practical and pragmatic reasons. The Church has a great deal of property and many holdings in Israel. Since Israel is now the power in the Holy Land, they need her good will. We Jews have a tendency to get excited when a Gentile says a few nice words about us. Let us not be fooled; there cannot be reconciliation or forgiveness until the wrongs are corrected.

Two miracles happened to us after the Shoah. The establishment of the State of Israel, and the revival of the survivors. Many of us who did not die in the Shoah or shortly after the liberation, gathered strength, little by little, but with this, our tragedy did not come to an end. The tragedy only deepened, because only then did we realize the enormity of our losses. Since the liberation, we survivors applied ourselves to the revitalization of our dry bones. We rebuilt our lives, established new families, and forged new links in the golden chain of the Jewish people.

I learned an enormous amount about human nature, about loyalty, about treachery. It was a very condensed education in coping with living and in sorting out a sense of our values. One had to decide what was important in life. Was it money and possessions, people, family and friendship, and plain survival? One had to develop extraordinary survival skills. When one looks at historic heroes, they all lose their stature when one compares them to the Holocaust survivors. They are the real heroes, the living ones because they outsmarted death.

The children and grandchildren of survivors, every one of them, are miracle children. None of them were supposed to have been born. They are not just ordinary children. Many of them have been named after relatives who were murdered in the Shoah. Many of these children are highly intelligent, are extremely well educated, and quite sophisticated. Their parent's past has been a dominant influence on the basic choices the children have made in their lives. The second generation, children of Holocaust survivors, tend to choose a profession which involves helping other people. They also have decided to have larger families as a small token of compensation to their parents for their great loss of family during the Holocaust.

The lifestyle of many of the Shoah survivors is relatively modest. Work and family are the center of their lives. It is a duty and a passion and a source of satisfaction. The survivors shy away from leisure time. They want to keep busy; it gives them no time to think of what happened during those horrible years. They are extremely giving and generous with their children, their families, and to Jewish causes.

The survivors try to cover up their pain by not talking about it. Whatever pain they go through, they do it alone. Their looks, their mannerisms tell it all. They have known the taste of inhumanity that others don't know about, and will never be able to understand. They are very suspicious people. They teach their children not to expect much from the world because they learned the hard way that even the best of Gentile friends and neighbors in their native land turned against them and took everything they had. Actually nothing has changed since then.

There exists a variety of upbringing that is characteristic of children of survivors. Some parents kept their Holocaust experiences a secret from their young children. Some told their unpleasant experiences gradually so as not to overwhelm their children. Some never wanted to talk about those terrible years. Most children of Holocaust survivors say that they have absorbed their parent's attitudes towards the Germans and other countries, and their Holocaust experiences, through a kind of wordless osmosis. They were not explicitly instructed to feel one way or another, but they have identified with their parents so closely that parental attitudes that were forged during the war have become their own.

The children and grandchildren of the survivors represent the links of a chain of the Jewish people that Hitler failed to break completely. They represent a victory over the evil forces.

But as far as our families in Europe, our homes, and 1,000 years of countless Jewish rich creativity, nothing was left. Just the silence of one huge cemetery. One has to picture the great multitude that was put to death on the hellish continent. What if we again lose for one moment our alertness, our vigilance? Will it, G-d forbid, happen again? There is always a danger for the Jewish people to be caught again. The danger hovers somewhere all the time. The enemies of the Jews and the State of Israel are still many. They are just waiting for the right moment.

We Were Not Sheep To The Slaughter

Many times one hears the question, "How come Jews did not resist the Nazis?" Most people think that there was no resistance at all. Totally unprepared for the unparalleled assault and deceived by cunning and wily Nazi tactics, Jews began physical resistance late, however, the Jews used other kinds of resistance very early in the war.

People have a tendency to think of resistance only as armed resistance. This is unfair and untrue. There are many different kinds of resistance. There was massive Jewish psychological and spiritual resistance from the very beginning of German occupation of Poland in 1939.

The Jews immediately organized their own self help organization. House committees were formed; public kitchens were set up for the poor. Under the German rule, Jews were not permitted to have cultural events, so Jews organized illegal lectures on Jewish subjects. People were starving, yet many tried to buy books with their last few pennies.

The Nazis had forbidden Jewish schools, but those existing before the Nazi occupation went underground and even expanded. Ultimately there was a broad chain of illegal schools; there were *Yeshivoth*, *Chadarim*, and others.

When the deportations started, it was not announced. The Germans were very clever. They concealed the horrors until the last moment. They said the Jews were to be relocated to other cities far away from the frontline. Realization came slowly. Can one ever imagine one's own death? The Jew had been conditioned to almost everything in his 4,000 year history; to slavery, dispersion, torture, pogroms, expulsions, cultural repression, ghettoization, but not to total destruction.

So how does one resist the unknown?

The ghetto philosophy was first to survive physically, and then to survive with dignity as a human being. The Jews, under Nazi rule, knew of course that the Nazis wanted to crush their spiritual, cultural, and political life, but they never assumed that the destruction would be total.

However, once the German plan to totally destroy the Jews became clear, they decided to fight, even though there was no hope of winning. And so it began, uprising after uprising, in the ghettos and in the concentration camps. Those who had a chance to escape into the forests organized themselves into partisan units, others fought in various European undergrounds.

In the history of man, guns and fighting seems to be the only type of resistance that is respected, but there are other kinds, so many other kinds. We, who were in deep trouble cried out for help, but the world was silent and indifferent.

Jewish armed resistance took three forms: armed rebellion in the ghettos and death camps; the formation of partisan units; and by joining the resistance movements in occupied Europe. The most dramatic and widely known resistance was that of the fighting organization in the Warsaw Ghetto, which was the first armed revolt in occupied Europe. A handful of Jews fought for 42 days against the elite Nazi troops and against overwhelming odds they caused many casualties.

On October 14, 1943, 600 inmates of Sobibor Concentration Camp in Poland made a break for freedom during a savage revolt. Jewish camp tailors and shoemakers hid hatchets under their clothes and invited their Nazi *clients* in for a final fitting. The Jewish rebels killed ten S.S. men and wounded one. Four hundred prisoners actually succeeded in breaking out of the camp. Almost half fell, casualties to land mines. The S.S., police, German troops, and East European *Wachman,* numbering in the thousands, killed most of the others by pursuing aircraft and other means. Only 60 men and women succeeded in making contact with Soviet partisans.

In and around Paris, during the Nazi occupation, a well organized resistance operated and in the French underground the proportion of Jews was far above the percentage of the French population.

In Berlin, a Jewish underground group known as the *Baum Group*, operated in the very heart of the Nazi fortress. They succeeded in setting fire to Joseph Goebbels' prize propaganda show, *Das Soviet Paradis*, the Soviet Paradise, an anti-Russian exhibit.

We were not sheep to the slaughter. The German people were the sheep, because they followed their dictator blindly. When the Jews went quietly to their deaths, without physical resistance, you could feel in their silence a moral resistance to the Germans. There was a resistance of dignity, something they had within them.

Kiddush Hachayim, the sanctification of life, is a form of *Kiddush Hashem*, the sanctification of G-d, which is a kind of resistance, a refusal to be brutalized.

When Jews put on *Talit* and *Tefillin*, and sang *Ani Ma'amin*, "I believe with complete faith in the coming of the Messiah," on the way to their death, was this not resistance? They could sing of their belief because they deeply believed in humanity. They wrongly believed that the world would not know what was happening to them.

In 1944, a group of Jews in the *Sonder Commando*, Jews who were chosen by the Nazis to help them in the gas chambers at Auschwitz, rebelled and killed many Nazis. This was the first time prisoners of the Sonder Commando in Auschwitz did that and finally a few of them escaped to tell the world of the killings. They also revolted in Treblinka.

There were Jewish resistance movements in Belgium, Italy, Bulgaria, in the ghettos of Minsk, Vilna, Bialystok, and many others.

The chief reason why so little is known of the Jewish valiant struggles is that writers and historians have relied primarily on German sources. It is natural that the Nazis would deliberately hide the fact that there was a network of Jewish resistance.

The death of 6,000,000 people is so overwhelming, so vast a tragedy that the resistance of so many is understandably overshadowed. Whether with arms or moral stamina, the ways of resistance were as varied as the ways of death. Jews were not willing accomplices to their own slaughter.

There is indeed proof beyond any doubt that Jews resisted the overwhelming might of the German Army, to which a whole continent had capitulated. Weaponless, they stood up to the might of the German *panzer* divisions in many places, under conditions of starvation and deprivation, in which their own doom was almost a foregone conclusion.

In both the ghettos and the death camps, they resisted, as much for self esteem and self respect as for self defense, imbuing themselves and their people with heroism, honor, humanity, and dignity.

Who Was Responsible For The Murder Of The Jews?

Most people don't know who, besides the Germans, was responsible for the mass murder of 6,000,000 Jews during the Holocaust. It is a known fact that the Germans were the initiators and the leaders, but to be truthful to history, it should be pointed out that many nationalities collaborated with the Germans in the extermination of European Jewry. We should also point out, that in addition to some Arabs and Moslems, the majority of the murderers of European Jewry were Christians.

Today, studies show that most Christians in Europe continue their lives as before, as if nothing happened, without much concern about what they did to the Jews. The majority of Christians in the world view the Holocaust as merely one of the general tragedies of the second world war. Some divest themselves of responsibility for it arguing that the Nazi movement was anti-Christian. Some claim that the Jews brought the Holocaust on themselves, since they were agents of modernization; they destroyed traditions and thus caused the Nazi movement to come to power. Some claim there was no Holocaust; that only some 300,000 Jews died during the war. Others say openly that the Jews deserved it, since they didn't accept Jesus as the Messiah. Even in the year 2000, a woman was overheard saying to her daughter as she was visiting the U.S. Holocaust Museum in Washington, D.C., "Don't be so upset. This never really happened."

There is a small minority who regard the Holocaust as a test of their Christianity, and for the last 50 years or so, have been seeking a fitting Christian response. Many scholars say that there is no doubt that Christianity played a decisive role in the spread of anti-Semitism into the roots of Western civilization. For many centuries, the Christian Church taught contempt for the Jews, which prepared the soil for the Holocaust.

The Nazi death camps were not built and operated by ignorant, superstitious savages, somewhere off in the bush. They were planned, built and operated by well trained individuals from one of the best university systems in the world. Himmler was proud of the large number of Ph.D's in the officer corps of the S.S..

Many Christians, theologians, and agencies are still bothered by the reality of Jewish survival. Jewish survival proves the contradiction of the perpetuating dogma of the Gentile church fathers. The founding of Israel and the reunification of Jerusalem are hard for some Christians to come to terms with, precisely because this is positive proof that Jewry will survive.

Professor Roy Eckardt, of the Lehigh University, said that one can divide the Christian world into three main groups with regard to responses to the Holocaust:

1 - The Liberals recognize the justice of the Jewish cause, but see it simply as one of many causes. Thus, the Liberal Christian threatens to overwhelm his concern for the Jews with his universalism. For example, in any discussion touching upon the Holocaust, he quickly wants to talk about Biafra, Cambodia, Vietnam, and the like.

2 - Christians who are willing to accept the Jews and the reality of the Holocaust, but only on Christian terms. Such individuals are willing to rethink their Christian predisposition, but do not go far enough. In discussing the Holocaust, they immediately turn to the crucifixion as their model and compare the hanging of a small Jewish boy during the Holocaust, described by Elie Wiesel near the end of his book *Night* to the crucifixion. The Holocaust, in comparison to Jesus' triumph over death and suffering, is reduced to secondary importance. Accordingly, Christianity's triumph as a religion and as a message of redemption remains absolute. This implies that Christianity was right and Judaism was wrong. But in light of the murder of 6,000,000 human beings, among them 1,500,000 children during the Holocaust, the crucifixion is a very minor event. We must say that Christian Jewish rapprochement will lead nowhere unless this is realized, unless the Christian world rethinks its attitude to Judaism in light of the Holocaust.

3 - Right wing, fundamentalist Christians say that the Jewish cause is a lost cause and the Holocaust is seen as the continuation of the Jew's suffering for their rejection of Jesus. Instead of recognizing the grave flaws of Christianity exposed in the Holocaust, the group continues the old Christian triumphal, claiming to have superseded Judaism. In this connection, Evangelical missionaries who still attempt to convert the Jews attempt what some German thinkers call a *Geistlich endlosung*, a spiritual final solution. This only continues the Holocaust and presents Christianity as unrepentant, having learned nothing from this awesome event.

One cannot avoid mentioning that the Allies had a great share in the Holocaust. Franklin Roosevelt, Winston Churchill and Joseph Stalin were accomplices of Hitler in the murder of 6,000,000 Jews. The Stalin Hitler Pact, the British White Paper, closing the ports of Palestine to Jewish immigration, Roosevelt's refusal to lift immigration quotas and the ignoring of Jewish pleas to bomb the railway to Auschwitz, all this sealed the fate of the Jews of Europe.

One might ask if there has been a change in attitude towards the Jews. Of special interest we find the reaction of the non-Jews to a 1978 Holocaust telecast. The following are some Gentile reactions to that telecast:

"I was shocked that so many perished while millions of us remained ignorant about the entire tragedy."

"I don't know why they have to bring up something that happened years ago. Who needs it?"

"It is a lot of propaganda to create sympathy for Jews, because of what's going on now with Israel."

"Someone is making a lot of money on us, just like *Roots*. I didn't think much of that either."

"Why do they have to keep showing this? I think the Jews got what they deserved."

"The acting was so realistic, it almost seemed like it was true."

"I didn't allow my family to watch the Holocaust telecast because I am sick and tired of this crap being jammed down my throat. I am in perfect sympathy with the P.L.O. I think we should use the cluster bomb on the Israelis and get rid of them all at once."

"I think it would be very easy for a similar situation to explode here. Personally, I think things are going to get so bad in this country that Jews are going to be blamed again. They will become scapegoats."

Dr. G. Douglas Young, founder of the Institute of Holy Land Studies, a Christian clergyman, maintains that Jewish groups are only wasting their time trying to re-educate top leaders of the Christian Church because the World Council of Churches is a predominantly pro-Arab group that tends to side with the Arab world on all issues. Dr. Young said that the average clergyman takes his lead from the higher echelons, and so the masses of Christianity are being taught a philosophy of contempt for Jews that fosters anti-Semitism.

In February of 1978, the Vatican sharply criticized the Italian-Jewish community for refusing to forgive Nazi war criminal Herbert Kapler who died in West Germany after his wife and secret agents smuggled him out of an Italian prison hospital. He was serving a life sentence for wartime reprisals, having killed 335 Italians, 70 of them Jews. According to the Vatican, the survivors seem to have lacked moral strength to overcome their past and forgive. "As Christians, and citizens, we feel we cannot praise that final inflexibility."

I must say that it is ironic that the Vatican is asking the survivors to forget what happened to them some 50 years ago, but the Christian world doesn't want to forget what happened 2,000 years ago. As a survivor myself, I cannot forget or forgive the atrocities perpetrated on my family and my people.

It should be noted that the most important precondition for saving the Jews of a country in Europe during the Holocaust period was the willingness of the Gentile populace to speak up for its Jewish members. Before instituting anti-Jewish measures in occupied Europe, the Germans tried to ascertain to what extent the non-Jewish population of these countries would support their actions.

In most of the countries under their domination, the Germans reached the conclusion that arrest and torment of the Jews would meet with little or no opposition. Their research revealed only one outstanding exception, Denmark.

The Gestapo was constantly searching for Jews who succeeded in hiding. The Gestapo received a great deal of help in finding the hiding places through collaborators, professional informers, anti-Semites and chronic Jew-haters. To anyone turning in a Jew, the Gestapo usually paid one quart of brandy, four pounds of sugar, a carton of cigarettes and a sum of money. The prices varied at different places and times.

When one reads in the Foreign Affairs magazine (April 1977) that the former Assistant Secretary of State George Ball, would have the United States, "save Israel in spite of herself," one wonders about his real intentions. Does one read or hear that America has to *save* other countries in the world in spite of themselves.

The sorry truth is that Christian conscience has been trying to *save* the Jews despite themselves for 2,000 years. To be both protective and condescending of the Jew or the Jewish State fits nicely into this anti-Semitic frame of reference. The old prejudices remain and invariably assert themselves even in foreign policy, especially when the Jew *presumes* to be successful, and self assertive, as any other free individual. Little value is given to the proposition that Hebrew civilization is at least as worthy of national expression as any other culture.

Like a contagious virus swept along by the currents of historic change in Europe, the former Soviet Union, the United States, and especially in the Middle East, the forces of bigotry and hatred are growing. And once again Israel and Jews the world over are threatened.

The new Freedoms have also unleashed the dark side of humanity. Jews in the Former Soviet Union live in daily fear of new anti-Jewish pogroms. New and resurgent nationalism in Rumania, Hungary, Germany, and other central and Eastern European countries has taken on frightening anti-Semitic proportions.

And the outward signs are back again: Swastikas painted on Synagogues; School children taunted in class; Graves vandalized and even bodies disinterred; Neo-Nazi political rallies; New anti-Semitic books and articles; and now, even video games that give children the chance to run Nazi concentration camps.

There are numerous examples of attempts to stir up hatred for the Jews. Unfortunately the world has not changed in regard to Jewish survival. However, one basic fact has changed. Since the Holocaust, the Jews consider themselves to be one people. There is greater solidarity among Jews. There isn't one Jew who was left untouched by the events of the Holocaust.

We have to be on guard at all times so such a tragedy should not befall our people again. We must learn from the past and thus secure our future. We must learn from the past and also from recent events that the world remained apathetic toward the plight of the Jew. Thank G-d we now have a State of our own. Had there been an Israel at the time of the Holocaust, thousands of Jews, perhaps millions, could have been saved. The *Entebbe* rescue operation is a good example of what could have been done.

We see what is happening to the Jews in totalitarian countries, in Arab countries, and especially when it comes to the politics of the United States concerning Israel. We see it time and again. The fate of the Jewish people is universally linked. In conclusion, I must point out that the Holocaust must be portrayed for what it really was... an attempt to annihilate the Jews as a people.

Theological Issues In The Holocaust

I describe here only a trifle about the holy martyrs, the dead and beloved souls who were cut down during the young and early years of their lives. The Talmud says: "*Harugey Malchut*, the martyrs, executed by an (evil) government, enjoy such an exalted level that no other person can stand in their enclosure." (Babylonian Talmud, Tractate *Pesachim* page 50A)

Until this day, I cannot divert my attention and mind from my dear family, all the holy Jewish martyrs of our town, Bilke, and all the Jewish martyrs who in their lives and deaths did not part. As a survivor of the Holocaust, a great deal of anger, rage, and desire for revenge still fills my soul. Rabbi Saadyah Gaon, the great Jewish sage wrote, "Revenge is desirable as a tool for enforcing justice, which brings about the remedy of the ills of society." (*Emunoth V'deot*, chapter 10.)

One may ask the question, is there at all an appropriate punishment for the crimes perpetrated against the Jews by the Germans, the Hungarians, and all the other collaborators, wherever they are? Even the devil has not yet invented a proper punishment for the horror and crimes the German and Hungarian beasts perpetrated against the Jewish people.

Peace and tranquility cannot exist in the world as long as the Gentile world will not confess publicly to the sins and crimes they have committed against the Jews. Otherwise, it appears as if the victims died twice; once when they were murdered, and again when the criminals denied their deaths altogether. The nations of the world are to ask forgiveness of the Jewish people in general, and in particular of the State of Israel, the embodiment of the Jewish people. Only then may the blood of our brethren cease to cry out to Heaven: "Why? Why?"

I have been searching for answers regarding the Shoah, the greatest Jewish tragedy, and asking how such a calamity could have happened to our people. I want to find the truth, but I have been led nowhere. The more I search in the Jewish sources, the more the imperfection of the world order is revealed, which increases my frustration. This search brought to mind King Solomon's statement in Ecclesiastes, "He that increases knowledge, increases sorrow." (Ecclesiastes 1:18)

After the Shoah, my soul was in crisis. There was a fracture in my soul that still remains. The survivors established families, had children, and they traveled the world, but there was a black thread through their lives which they could not forget. A pail of sadness stays with them all their lives.

The survivors are a very special species, the most endangered species in history. The destruction of 6,000,000 Jews during the Shoah posed the most radical philosophical and theological problems ever faced by our people. Perhaps our ancestors were confronted with a similar dilemma after the destruction of both Temples in Jerusalem, and the end of Jewish sovereignty in their own land. The question of G-d's involvement in the history of the Jewish people becomes a problem when one cannot find an explanation as to how such a calamity could have happened. Some Jewish thinkers call for an overhauling of Jewish theology because the traditional answers to problems of evil cannot explain the enormity of the suffering during the Holocaust.

Our forefathers, especially Abraham, as he encountered suffering and evil, debated and argued with G-d and said, "Wilt Thou indeed sweep away the righteous with the wicked? That be far from Thee to do after this manner, to slay the righteous with the wicked; that be far from Thee; shall not the Judge of all earth do justly?" (Genesis 18:23-25)

There were other great Jewish leaders and Prophets such as Moses, Jeremiah, and Job who asked questions regarding the anguish and evil in the world. Since those famous and unique dialogues between G-d and man, despite the lapse of thousands of years, mankind has not fully grasped the lofty conception of the justice of G-d and its ethical consequences in human society.

The Jewish people believe that theirs is a G-d who conducts the affairs of the world. The Prophet Isaiah states about the powers of G-d in the following verse: "I make the light, and create darkness; and create evil, I am the Lord that doeth all these things." (Isaiah 45:7) The term *evil* in this verse denoted calamity and suffering. Moral evil however, does not proceed from G-d, but is the result of man's action.

At times, a person reacts to tragedy with total and utter nihility. In the face of tragedy, one's faith in G-d is tested. When the righteous (seemingly) suffer and when evil (seemingly) prospers, how does one react? In truth this test of faith, when faced by adversity, is difficult to pass. How a just G-d can allow the reign of evil, or why bad things happen to good people, is not a question that can easily be answered. In fact, our tradition tells us that the struggle to understand G-d's ways goes back to Job and indeed to Moses. When Moses asked G-d, "Show me your Glory," (Exodus 33:18), it refers to, according to Maimonides, exactly this problem of theodicy, justifying G-d's inscrutable ways to man.

The enormity of the sufferings during the Holocaust raises even more difficult questions. Some scholars contend that while, psychologically, the enormity of the evil involved in the Holocaust creates unique difficulties, logically, the theological questions are not different than if one confronts evil on a smaller scale. The ancient problem of how an omnipotent and benevolent G-d can tolerate evil is not affected by the quantity of evil that is involved. The possibility of faith in a benevolent G-d is in no way diminished by the unspeakable tragedy of the Holocaust. We still can maintain that, for reasons beyond our comprehension, G-d's plan for the world includes such colossal evil. What is the meaning of the terrible Shoah that befell our people during the second world war? Is it possible that the G-d of judgment and justice kept silent? And in the words of Abraham: "Shall not the judge of all the earth do justly?" (Genesis 18:25) And in the words of Moses, "Lord wherefore hast Thou dealt ill with this people." (Exodus 5:22)

One can raise very critical questions such as: Are the other nations more worthy than the Jewish people? Aren't we the Chosen People? Or have we been selected to suffer?

In the late 1930s and beginning 1940s, among the Yeshivah students in Eastern Europe, there was a popular song that combined Hebrew and Yiddish in the form of a monologue of the Jewish people with G-d. It is a long song but the first lines will suffice. It questions the established notion that the Jewish people are the chosen people.

Habet Mishamayim Ur'eh, Gib a kook arup fun himel und zeh: Look down from heaven and perceive.

Ki hayinu laag, Und du machst a shwag: For we have become an object of scorn and ridicule and You G-d are silent.

Madua ashamnu mikol am: Why are we guiltier than the other nations?

Woo bist du di shofeth bain dam ledam: Where are You, the Judge who distinguishes between blood and blood?

Es haist atah bechartanu mikol haamim: It is stated that You have chosen us from among all the nations.

Veahavtah Otanu: And You loved us.

Veratzita Banu: And You found favor in us.

Ober heint az mir zenen tzushpreit oif shivah yamim: But since we are scattered on the seven seas,

Fregen mir dir goteneu bameh ahavtanu: We are asking You, G-d, in what way do You love us?

Dr. David Roskies, Professor of Jewish Literature at the Jewish Theological Seminary in New York, wrote a Midrash on the Shoah. In it, he discusses the silence of G-d during the Holocaust. He writes that after the destruction of the Second Temple in Jerusalem, the Rabbis were trying to deal with the calamity which befell the Jewish nation in those days. The Rabbis tried to channel Jewish rage back toward the wellsprings of great sanctity.

Dr. Roskies says, "The oldest and most celebrated instance of sacred parody is from the Talmud (Tractate *Gittin* 56:8) which says: Who is like unto Thee among the mighty (*Elim*) O Lord?" (Psalm 89:9) In the school of Rabbi Ishmael, this same passage was taught: "Who is like unto Thee among the silent (*Illemim*) O Lord?" since G-d sees the suffering of G-d's children and remains silent.

Jacob Zilberberg, a former Yeshivah student from the town Zakrochis near Warsaw, Poland, who was forced to work in the Sonder Commando, the unit of Jewish prisoners in Auschwitz who removed the dead in the concentration camp, lost his faith because of what he endured. He questioned where was G-d during the Holocaust. He quotes Rabbi Yitzchak Bar Shalom who lived in the Time of the Crusades. He wrote a *Kinah*, an elegy, in which he cries out to heaven, "Who is like unto Thee among the *illemim, domem v'shotek*, speechless, silent, and still." Thus, he expressed his disappointment that his outcry was not answered in his days. A word game? Hardly. These words of the Rabbis border on blasphemy. They give license to argue with G-d, using G-d's own words. Such arguing with G-d, what the Rabbis called *chutzpah klapei sh'mayah*, impudence toward Heaven, is nowhere more radically expressed than in the Book of Job.

The self confrontations of the Jews in the ghettos and concentration camps regarding their suffering recreates the dialogue of our brethren with G-d. Our later day Job, however, does not conclude with a voice that answers from the whirlwind. The whirlwind alone is the answer. One must come to the conclusion that the Holocaust signals a rupture in the divine order and in Jewish self understanding. However, the fact that the Jewish people continue to exist in spite of the persecution by the nations is a unique and irrational phenomenon. This cannot be explained as usual and normal historical happenings. On the contrary, because of the unusual phenomenon, the Jewish people exist forever, in spite of the persecutions and in spite of the hatred by most of the nations.

The traditionalists say that the Holocaust can only be explained as a *Hastarat Panim*, a temporary eclipse, where G-d hid his countenance as it says: "I will keep my countenance hidden." (Deuteronomy 31:18) G-d removed his protection from the Jewish people during the Holocaust.

Like the parable of the vineyard in Isaiah, (Isaiah 5:1-7) when the animals, (the Nazis) got into the vineyard, (the Jewish people who are compared by Isaiah to a vineyard) they did not distinguish between the good vine and the wild one. They destroyed everything because once permission is given to the evil forces to destroy, they do it indiscriminately.

Therefore what happened during the Holocaust was Hastarat Panim. G-d hid his countenance and the evil forces did whatever they wanted.

Rabbi Avigdor Neventzal of Yeshivat Hakotel in Jerusalem discussed the Shoah in 2001 during one of his weekly Torah lectures. He asked the question, "Was the Shoah a *Kiddush Hashem* or a *Chillul Hashem*?" A sanctification of the divine name or a desecration of the divine name? He continued and said, "When one discusses the Shoah, which befell our people in our generation, one can say that on the one hand, it was a terrible Chillul Hashem, a desecration of the divine name, the likes of which was never seen before. Until this day, the Gentiles and some Jews ask where was G-d in Auschwitz? It is like what is written in the verse, Why should the nations say, Where is their G-d?" (Psalm 79:10)

The Germans and their partners did as they pleased with the Jews, they persecuted them for years by degrading and murdering them. Six Million Jews were murdered and many remained orphans, widows and bereaved parents, and so they ask: "Where was their G-d?" Whenever the enemies of Israel have the upper hand, and no one sees G-d's strong hand, that causes Chillul Hashem, if, as it were, that G-d can't help the Jewish people. As we saw Jews were dying on Kiddush Hashem, the sanctification of the divine name, there was only sanctification on the Jewish side, because the Gentiles saw this as a Chillul Hashem, a desecration of the divine name, because they say they are powerful.

The question about the Shoah actually has to be divided into two parts: The first one, Why did such a terrible Shoah befall the Jewish people? The second one, which is composed of millions of individuals, invokes personal questions. Why did certain people perish in the Shoah, among them great Rabbis, leaders, and righteous people, when others survived? On this question, which is actually the question, "Why do the righteous suffer and the wicked prosper?" (Babylonian Talmud Tractate *Berachot* 7A) we have no answer. Only at the end of days will we be able to see the justice of G-d's deeds.

The Rambam, Maimonides, said that there are three states of *Hashgacha*, Divine Providence. There are laws that govern the world that G-d made at the time of creation.

The normal state, the positive one where G-d, because of his kindness, steps in when one of these natural laws will lead to disaster.

Then there is the *neutral state*, where G-d will not intervene even when a disaster is imminent. The Rambam refers to that as *Hastarat Panim*, hiding His countenance.

Finally there is the *negative state*, where G-d will intervene directly in order to punish man. The Prophet Jeremiah expresses a similar idea when he says, "My soul shall weep in secret for Your pride; and mine eye shall weep sore, and run down with tears, because the Lord's flock is carried away captive." (Jeremiah 13:17) The Talmud interprets this verse to mean that G-d is the speaker, as a loving father sorrowing over his son's suffering. He weeps in a secret place over Israel's glory that has been taken away from him and is being persecuted. (Tractate *Chagigah* 5B) The Psalmist expresses a similar idea: "Thou hidest Thy face and they are panic stricken... Thou sendest forth Thy spirit and they are reborn anew." (Psalm 104:29-30)

It was in our generation the Psalmist described, that G-d hid His presence from the world, and mankind plunged into the Holocaust. Then wondrously and inexplicably, his spirit came forth and defeated the evil forces and Israel was reborn. We understand neither the terror of his absence nor the warmth and miracle of his presence. However, we are witnesses to his hand that guides history. There is definitely a hidden meaning between the Shoah and the establishment of the State of Israel immediately afterward. These two historic events have a mystical connection somewhere.

Therefore the question arises, Is there any hope for the Jewish people? The answer to this question lays in the fact that the Jewish people still exist, in spite of all the problems they constantly encounter.

One is reminded of the Midrash that tells us once Rabbi Akiva and some of his colleagues passed by the ruins of the *Beit Hamikdash*, the Holy Temple in Jerusalem and saw foxes running around in the ruins. They lamented because the passage in Lamentations (5:18) came to pass: "For the mountain of Zion, which is desolate, the foxes walk upon it." To the astonishment of his colleagues, Rabbi Akiva smiled. They asked him why he was happy when the Temple was in ruins. Rabbi Akiva answered, "Just now we saw that one part of the prophecy came to pass, therefore, I am happy because there is hope that the second part of the prophecy will also come true which says that the children of Israel will return to their land." (Jeremiah 31:16)

We can arrive at the same conclusion in regard to the Holocaust and what happened thereafter. We saw in our generation that G-d kept His promise, since the State of Israel was established. We see that two very important events took place in our generation, which did not happen for thousands of years, the Holocaust with its cruel destruction of European Jewry and immediately after the Holocaust, the establishment of the Jewish state and the beginning of the ingathering of the exiles.

Eliezer Berkowitz in his book, *Faith After The Holocaust*, explains the events of the Shoah as a temporary eclipse. According to his philosophy, G-d watches over the world and metes out rewards and punishments. However, at times he removes his protection of his faithful, and thus we can have a Holocaust. Some say that cruelty and the killing raise the question whether even those who believe in G-d after such an event, dare talk about G-d who loves and cares, without making a mockery of those who suffered.

Emil Fackenheim in his book, *God's Presence in History*, says, "Although we cannot understand how G-d permitted the Holocaust to occur, He was present in Auschwitz." As the Psalmist says (91:15) "I am with him in his distress." He says that this was a new revelation, and that the Jews learned that G-d was there and he demanded of them to overcome Hitler and his evils, by sanctifying life and declaring faith in life. The Talmud states: "Every place the Children of Israel were exiled to, the *Shechinah*, the Divine Presence, is with them." (Tractate *Megilah* 29A)

The true believer in G-d does not base his faith in G-d on any condition. Rightfully, we can question His deeds, but the mystery will remain. We can only suggest that we approach the suffering of our people during the Holocaust as a disclosure of the mystery of Jewish existence. It is in this respect that one can refer to the establishment of the State of Israel, not as an explanation of the suffering, but as an indication that certain events in Jewish history disclose the mysteriousness of our existence. In following this approach, when teaching the Holocaust, we can also stress the pathological hatred of the Jew, which *Amalek* displays, is not a natural phenomenon, but a facet of the mystery of Jewish existence. It did not make sense for Hitler to divert attention from the war effort in order to execute his Final Solution. It did not make sense that he regarded the extinction of the Jews as more important than winning the war. It similarly did not make sense for Jews, after enduring the most brutal fate on account of their survival as Jews, to create the State of Israel. The phenomena cannot be explained. All we can do is confront the mystery, which should be our goal in teaching the Holocaust and for that matter, in teaching Jewish history.

The Shoah and the establishment of the State of Israel immediately after will forever dominate Jewish history, by the fantastic transition from tragedy to triumph, from the depths of misery and suffering, to new heights of sovereign pride. The emergence of the State of Israel is G-d's answer to the German design of Jewish extinction. Within a few years of that unprecedented disaster, the Jewish people had established itself in the family of nations. There is a definite connection between Kishinev, Auschwitz and the sands of Sinai, the Golan Heights and the Temple Mount in Jerusalem. This is the only explanation we have.

But no matter how one tries to explain where G-d was during the destruction of European Jewry, the lives of most survivors remain fractured forever, without finding peace and tranquility for their souls. This dilemma will live with us as long as we live. It is futile to further seek an answer to the tragedy of the Shoah. How can one reconcile what happened in the Holocaust, and the Jews being the Chosen People? I assume we will continue to be vacillating between these two questions.

In Every Generation, They Rise Up Against Us, To Destroy Us

Passover Haggadah

Passover is a joyous time for the Jewish people, but it also marks the beginning of a sad season of the *Sefirah*, the counting of the *Omer*, and the days of mourning of the bitter days in the time of the Second Temple era. It also ushers in the sad season of the remembrance of the Holocaust. The second day of Passover is the anniversary of the Warsaw Ghetto uprising. *Yom Hashoah*, Holocaust Memorial Day, falls less than two weeks later.

We are reminded not to forget the horrific events that took place earlier in the 20th century. We also are reminded not to feel too secure as the rumblings of hatred once again are in bloom in many countries and continents, including the Arab and Muslim world. The level of intolerance of the Jewish people is also evident in the established Christian religion in the various churches. They consider the Jewish people to have an unworthy religion, therefore it should not be allowed to exist.

The theme is *Zachor*, remember and do not forget what the modern *Amalek* did to the Jewish people. The death of millions of martyred brothers and sisters has charged us to live, to tell what happened, to tell the surviving Jews in other countries and the world. To forget, is to make Hitler the victor.

The Bible states numerous times not to forget the cowardly attack by Amalek on the weak and faint Israelites who lagged behind during the exodus from Egypt.

"Remember what Amalek did to you. You shall blot out Amalek from the very memory of men; do not forget." (Deuteronomy 25:17) And in Exodus (17:16) it states: "Because the Lord hath sworn that the Lord will have war with Amalek from generation to generation."

To *remember* is a moral imperative upon every Jew and to pass it on to the coming generations. The last words of the dying victims to us were: "If you are spared, we want you to tell the whole world about our destruction, and do not let the world ever forget the Holocaust."

We dare not forget the 6,000,000 martyrs who perished and the Jewish communities that were destroyed. We need to remember how they lived, what they stood for, and how they died. We are told that, "Those who were murdered by an evil power enjoy such an exalted level that no other person can stand in their enclosure." (Babylonian Talmud, Tractate Pesachim, 50A) The martyrs who were slaughtered during the Shoah have a reserved place in Heaven.

The Jewish people have endured much suffering and anguish. History's bloody pen has recorded countless atrocities against our people; as Jews we were singled out as perennial scapegoats. However, during the second world war, our people encountered the gravest period of their existence. The Nazi Holocaust was the greatest challenge to our existence, an attempt to totally annihilate the Jewish people. What happened to our people during the years of the Shoah has no parallel in the history of mankind.

We feel that by transmitting, not only the bitter facts of the Shoah, but also the emotions of our brethren, we contribute to a better understanding of this most tragic period in the history of our people. We also want to show that even in the tragic days of the Shoah, our people continued to create cultural pearls, and that there was heroism even in the face of a most brutal enemy.

Some of the victims tried to communicate their pain. The children expressed their puzzlement about a cruel world. Even in the face of death, music and poetry were a part of Jewish life, thus expressing defiance to inhumanity. The songs and poems written during the Holocaust are only small proof of the tremendous spiritual strength the Jews of Europe showed during the years of the Shoah. The poetry related to the Holocaust expresses various moods; softness and bitterness, tenderness and determination, history and fate. The poets described sorrow. They eulogized, lamented, protested against G-d and man, rebelled against society, and asked questions. A special sense of mission unites them all, mainly the desire that the tragedy should not be forgotten.

Yitzhak Katzenelson, the best known Shoah poet, cried out in a poem, *I Dreamed a Dream*, the poet had a nightmare. This poem sets the tone and describes a dreadful reality. Katzenelson was sent to Auschwitz from a concentration camp in France where he perished.

Children wrote some of the poems. They too wanted to know why G-d was hiding his face and what happened to man. Among them, Pavel Friedman, wrote in Theresienstadt an unforgettable poem, *The Butterfly*. These poems tell us to remember the most gruesome tragedy of our history and it is only right that we do not forget them. By reading their poetry, or singing their songs, we prove that we have not forgotten our brethren in the Shoah, and that the eternity of Israel has prevailed.

These songs, readings, and poetry of the Shoah were composed and sung by the Jewish people in the ghettos and death camps. They originated in the depths of the human soul. Our people sang these songs on their journey of suffering and death; these songs traveled with them wherever they went. These are songs and prayers of the tormented. These songs are the true genuine expressions of suffering as well as hope for a better future. They also tell us of various kinds of heroism, passive as well as active heroism. These songs are supposed to remind us of the grimmest catastrophe in our long history. We hope that the words of our heroes from the Shoah will inspire our youth to dedicate themselves to remember the 6,000,000 *kedoshim*, martyrs of our people, and never to forget.

The persecuted and oppressed Jews created a vast body of music during the Holocaust years. More than any other means of expression, the songs can convey to us the suffering of the men, women, and children who were part of the terrible tragedy described. They scale down the almost incomprehensible horror of the Holocaust to human dimensions. Books recording their suffering may perhaps be forgotten, but the songs and poems transcend the limits of memory.

The inmates in the ghettos and concentration camps realized they were faced with certain death. Dreams of freedom, the passionate desire to break out from the barbed wire encirclement past the walls, the brutality, the suffering filled the hearts and minds of many. The helplessness, the demoralization and physical degradation were turning to desperate struggles. Simultaneously, the hopes of the victims were being raised by rumors of the advancing Allied Forces, from the East and the West, and also by the actions encountered by partisans in some parts of Europe. Underground committees worked tirelessly to raise the fallen spirits, bolster the hopes of the remaining survivors, and organize them for resistance.

The number of satirical songs increased along with songs expressing hatred, desire for revenge, hope in victory, and determination to fight on until liberation. Some of the songs became a powerful weapon in building the morale of the Jewish inmates. One of the songs written in Yiddish, *Zog nit keynmol az du geyst dem letsten veg*, Never say that you are treading the final path, became the official hymn of all Eastern European partisan brigades and was subsequently translated to Hebrew and many other languages.

We survivors are most directly involved in guarding the memory of our martyrs. They cry out in deadly silence: *Remember us.* We ask the Jewish people to fully comprehend the magnitude of the suffering inflicted upon our brethren, of the 6,000,000 degraded, murdered, gassed, burned and buried alive, sisters and brothers, parents and children, and friends.

We, the haunted, ask how is it the world could not see the enormity of the mass murder and the greatest robbery in the history of mankind? How could so many people become accomplices to the inexplicable cruelty by not averting this crime, standing unaffected with impunity on the soil soaked with blood of the innocent? We, survivors, as long as we live, and our children and all the coming generations, will not forget and will remind the cruel world of their horrible deeds. The kedoshim, the martyrs, command us and all future generations, not merely to remember passively, but to perpetuate the memory of those who perished in the Shoah as a warning to humanity.

There will never be a final moral accounting, for that will enable the murderers of many nations to relegate the mass graves to oblivion.

The Active Role Of The European Nations In The Holocaust Crimes

In the Jewish calendar, we have a number of national days when we remember our past. On Passover we recall the cruel slavery of the Israelites in Egypt and the exodus from slavery to freedom. On *Tisha B'Av,* we recall the destruction of both Temples in Jerusalem and the loss of our statehood. On Chanukah, we remember the struggle of the Maccabees against religious oppression. On Purim, we remember the great danger the Jews of Persia experienced and the triumph over Haman. On *Yom Hashoah*, we recall the tragedy that befell our people in Europe during the Holocaust and the cruel, most inhuman and powerful regimes the Jewish people ever encountered. On Yom Hashoah we express our grief, our rage, and our pain over the enormous losses our people suffered during the tragic years of the destruction of European Jewry, while the free world watched in silence.

One thousand years of rich and great Jewish creation on the European continent was wiped out in a few years by cruel murderers. All that was left of European Jewish life were ashes and one huge cemetery. Europe is a continent that devoured its Jewish inhabitants. Every inch of ground on the European continent is cursed, because it is soaked with Jewish blood. Every silent barrack in the hundreds of concentration camps over Europe is crying out the pain of the victims. The air and wind blowing over Europe will forever carry the smoke and the ashes of the Jews murdered in the death camps. Facing loneliness, degradation, humiliation, hunger, cold, torture, and abandoned by all, they faced their fate with Jewish dignity and courage.

A half a century after the Shoah, our ears still hear their cries and agony. As long as one Holocaust survivor remains alive, we will never forget and never forgive. I feel compelled to represent our victims, as if I am a living Holocaust museum.

"O earth, cover not thou their blood, and have their cry no resting place." (Job 16:18)

From time to time, every nation has to make a *cheshbon nefesh*, a soul searching, or taking stock or call it a historical evaluation about the other nations who were considered a friend and who were the enemy. Those who were with the Jewish people, and those who were against us. As far as the Jewish people are concerned, we have a long account with a number of nations. With some of them from earliest times, with others in this century, and still with others, the account is still open and perhaps will never be settled.

During the Holocaust years, most of the nations betrayed our people. Quite a number of them were active participants in the murder of 6,000,000 of our brethren. Others collaborated in many ways. Some by barring Jews from finding a haven in their countries, among them the United States. Remember the St. Louis ship whose Jewish passengers begged President Roosevelt to allow them to land on United States soil. The State and Defense Departments ignored desperate appeals of Jewish leaders in this country and the world over to bomb the rails leading to Auschwitz.

The British Empire also stood by and prevented Jews from rescuing themselves by preventing them from entering British territory; especially their prevention of Jewish immigration into the land of Israel, their own historic homeland. The British published the *White Paper*, forbidding Jews from entering Israel. The British navy was busy hunting down Jewish refugee boats when they should have been fighting Nazis. All the rescue roads were blocked everywhere. The song *We Ahin Zol Ich Gehn*, "Tell Me Where Shall I Go," which was composed during the Holocaust years, tells it all. Only a handful of Jews were saved through miraculous ways and deeds.

We have all heard of a few *Righteous Among The Nations*, the Gentiles who saved Jews, which proves that a single person or a few people can make a difference. People such as the Swedish diplomat, Raoul Wallenberg distributed Swedish documents to thousands of Jews to stay in safe houses under Swedish protection that he set up in Budapest, Hungary.

Oscar Schindler, the German industrialist, saved over 1,000 Jewish prisoners by employing them in his factories near the concentration camp, Plaszow, in Cracow. (This story was made into the movie, *Schindler's List*.)

The Danish people rescued 8,000 Danish Jews who were about to be deported to death camps, by shipping them off secretly on fishing boats to a sanctuary in neutral Sweden.

There was a lesser known dramatic rescue of Jews from the Nazis as they planned to deport 50,000 Jews from Bulgaria to Auschwitz. This small Balkan nation refused to let them go. The Bulgarians considered their Jewish neighbors' deportation as a stain on Bulgaria's honor. In open defiance of the

Estimated Number Of Jews Killed In The "Final Solution."

Germans, Bulgaria refused to hand over its Jews. King Boris of Bulgaria died mysteriously a few days after the deadline. Later it became known that German agents poisoned the king.

There were hundreds of other individuals who saved groups or individual Jews because they were decent human beings. The Jewish people showed their gratitude after the war in many ways to those individuals and their descendants. Their righteous deeds will be remembered for generations to come. The rescue of the thousands of Jews by the few Gentiles, or the Righteous Among The Nations, proves that if the people of Europe wouldn't have cooperated with the Germans, either actively or passively in the murder of Jews, perhaps millions could have been saved from the clutches of the German beasts and their helpers.

The question arises, Has this passive cruel world learned anything from the Holocaust? Can we, as Jews, say with confidence that in the new millennium such a tragedy can never happen again to our people?

Let's glance at the media and see what has happened during the last few years. The following are a few news items about the Holocaust and its consequences which have been reported in the press in the United States and abroad. Let's see from these news items whether anything has changed for the better or if the same could be repeated; the good people will continue to do good deeds and the wicked will remain wicked.

The people of Denmark celebrated the 50th anniversary of the rescue of their country's Jewish population from being annihilated.

The United States Holocaust Memorial Museum was opened in Washington, which tells the story of the murder of the 6,000,000 Jews of Europe. It graphically shows what human beings are capable of doing to other human beings.

Rabbi Israel Meir Lau, who was liberated in Buchenwald by the American Army at the age of eight, was elected Chief *Ashkenazic* Rabbi of Israel.

We are told in the book *Aleh Tomer*, that Rabbi Abraham Jacob Friedman, the grand Rebbe of Sadigora, who lived in Vienna and was forced by the Nazis to sweep the streets of Vienna during the war and to raise the Nazi flag over a building in Vienna, made a *neder*, a vow, that if he survived and arrived in Israel, he would sweep the streets in Israel and raise the Jewish flag. Miraculously he survived and made aliyah to Israel. Every year on *Yom Haatzmaut*, Israel Independence Day, the surviving Rabbi of Sadigora sweeps the street he lives on in Tel Aviv. After the services, he goes out in dance and song with his congregants.

Chanah Senesh, a young Jewish Hungarian woman made aliyah to the land of Israel in the late 1930s, at the time the British ruled Israel. She volunteered to parachute into Hungary in 1944 to help in the rescue of Jews. The Hungarians captured her, accused her of treason, tortured her, and sentenced her to death and executed her.

After 50 years, the Hungarian government cleared Chanah Senesh from any guilt of treason against Hungary. The clemency, which the Hungarians gave Chanah Senesh retroactively, was done for the purpose of attracting Jewish investment in that country, and not because they regretted their actions. This reversal has no real meaning to her family, to the Jewish people, and surely not to the heroine Chanah Senesh, who became a legendary heroine to Jewish youth. She endangered her life to save other Jewish lives. She left a great legacy of courage and boldness. Perhaps it corrects a historic wrong, but it does not minimize the inhuman treatment by the Hungarians. This act can never be forgiven.

Chanah Senesh wrote poetry in her youth. The last poem she wrote is called *Blessed Is The Match.*

Blessed is the match that is consumed in kindling flames.
Blessed is the flame that burns in the secret fastness of the heart.
Blessed is the heart with strength to stop beating for honor's sake.
Blessed is the match that is consumed in kindling flame.

The same Hungarian government recently reburied the remains of the despot, Admiral Miklos Horty, the Hungarian leader during the Holocaust who was an ally of Hitler. Admiral Horty was going to be put on trial after the war. He ended up in Portugal where he died in 1957. During Horty's reign, 700,000 Jews were deported to labor camps, to Auschwitz and other death camps, where most of them perished. Many thousands of Hungarians participated in the reburial. They said that he was a great man and patriot. The small surviving Jewish community in Hungary protested this royal ceremony by the current Hungarian government, as a disgrace, stating that Horty was an evil man who conducted a state of terror and inhuman treatment of the Hungarian Jews. To the Fascists of Hungary today and all over the world, it is a signal that one may commit war crimes, that one can go scott-free, and will even be honored.

Recently, the Rumanians, in a suburb of Bucharest, erected a statue to Ion Antonescu. He was the Rumanian dictator directly responsible for the deaths of 300,000 Rumanian Jews.

In Slovakia, a statue was erected recently to the Fascist Catholic Bishop Jozef Tiso, President of Slovakia, a puppet German state during the Holocaust. He was responsible for the inhuman treatment of the Jews of Slovakia and the deportation of 135,000 Jews to Treblinka and Auschwitz.

These ceremonies by European governments honoring the second world war dictators and war criminals has become, of late, a brazen campaign to rehabilitate notorious mass murderers. This revival of Fascism in Europe and the upsurge of anti-Semitism in the United States and all over the world should be cause for great alarm for all Jews wherever they may be.

The reality is that the forces of evil still exist and the Gentile world has not changed.

Recently a register of 50,000 Jewish names was discovered in Vienna. This material was compiled in 1938 after Austria's *Anschlus*, union with Germany. The Nazi government of Austria forced the Jews on that list to hand over their properties to the Austrian Nazis. The Jewish property in Austria was worth millions of dollars. To date, the Austrians have not paid any reparations to the Jewish victims. This discovered list should help to press the Austrians to finally accept their responsibility for the crimes they committed against the Jews in Austria.

During the Holocaust, the French police rounded up the Jews and imprisoned them in concentration camps in France, such as Drancy and others which were guarded by French police. From these camps the French Jews were transported to Auschwitz and other death camps.

A French newspaper recently discovered that during the Holocaust, a group of Frenchmen would lure well-to-do French Jews by promising them protection and hiding them in return for their wealth. However, as soon as they robbed them of their possessions, the Frenchmen turned in the Jews to the authorities, which meant ending up in concentration camps. The man who was the head of this group was none other than Renee Boska, who was later the French police commissioner of the Vichy government. These criminals took billions of francs from these wealthy Jews.

After the war, the French government received hundreds of millions of dollars from Germany as reparations for the suffering and loss the French Jews endured. The French government took the money, but never gave a penny of reparation to the few French Jewish survivors. This was a double cynical and cruel behavior. We find in the Bible in the Book of Kings, a most appropriate protest in a situation like this. (First Kings 21:19) "Hast thou killed and also taken possession?" Eighty-six thousand French Jews were murdered during the Holocaust, among them thousands of children!

The quiet and respectable people of Switzerland on the surface make an impression of a pleasant and decent people, however, when one looks closer at their record in treating Jews during the war, one is in for a surprise and shock. During World War II, there were 40 Nazi groups in Switzerland. The most well known was the National Front, a French-speaking Nazi organization. After the war, it was discovered that 800 Swiss Nazis volunteered to serve in the German S.S. units who ran the concentration camps. During the War and after, the Germans used Switzerland to transfer Jewish money and valuables, which they robbed from the Jews. Some of the money was later used by German war criminals to escape to various countries. As of 1938, the Swiss government closed its borders to Jews. They called this policy, *The boat is full.* Many Jews tried to enter Switzerland, but were refused.

There was one Swiss gentleman by the name of Paul Gruninger, who was the chief of police of the Saint Gall Canton near the Austrian-German border, who over a period of time secretly helped over 1,000 Jewish refugees enter Switzerland on their way to seek a haven elsewhere. When the Swiss authorities found out, Paul Gruninger was fired from his post, put on trial, paid a fine, and lost his pension. Before he died a few years ago, he received a letter from the Swiss government stating that they were aware of his humanitarian act, however, they could not rescind his sentence. Israel and the Jewish organizations took steps to memorialize his name. They also demanded from the Swiss government that they clear his name. They called the campaign, Justice for Paul Gruninger. Only now, after 50 years, have the Swiss authorities informed Paul Gruninger's daughter that his name has been cleared of any wrongdoing.

We all know that German doctors under Hitler were a driving force in the destruction of European Jewry. Their cruel medical treatment and experiments on the victims in various concentration camps was a horror in itself. Such a doctor was Joseph Mengele, the angel of death, in Auschwitz. He and many others like him have never been punished for the atrocities. Mengele was captured in 1945 by the American forces in Germany and was held as a prisoner of war, but for some reason was released.

One other such doctor, who served during the Holocaust in Dachau Concentration Camp, was Professor Sabring. For many years after the war, he served on the board of the World Medical Organization. A few years ago, he was proposed by his German colleagues to be the President of this World Medical Organization. The Israel Medical Organization finally succeeded in removing this murderer from the World Medical Organization. He was still not punished for his war crimes.

In December of 1993, a movie was made in Germany with the financial assistance of the German authorities. The name of the movie was, *Profession Neo-Nazi.* In the movie, the hero calls upon Germans to once again establish a new Nazi regime. This German hero is standing on the grounds of Auschwitz today, and claims that no Jews were killed in Auschwitz. He claims that all survived, emigrated to other countries, and now are demanding reparations from Germany.

Recently, an addition was added to Yad Vashem in Jerusalem, called *The Valley of the Destroyed Jewish Communities in Europe.* It is placed on a hillside area, containing tombstones with the names of 5,000 cities, towns, and villages where Jewish communities were destroyed.

After eight years of holding John Demanjuk in Israel, who was on trial for committing war crimes against the Jews in Poland, he was released. This unfortunate act of the Israeli Supreme Court caused great pain to many Jews all over the world, especially to survivors of the Holocaust. It is hard to believe that Jewish judges could come to such a conclusion, when it was proven beyond any doubt that John Demanjuk was a Nazi guard at Sobibor and other concentration camps. Maybe he wasn't Ivan the Terrible, but he was a Nazi guard at the death camps. He was trained in Travinki, where guards were trained how to handle the Jews. Personally, I encountered the Ukraine *Wachman* guards in three of the camps in which I was imprisoned.

Aba Kovner, a poet and writer who survived the Holocaust demanded of the Jewish people who were fortunate not to have been victims of the Holocaust, that they should understand the feelings of the survivors.

He wrote, "From the murdered Jewish people, to the living Jewish people. You, who could not help us, listen to us with your heart, and understand us, and do not forget the murder of 6,000,000 Jewish victims."

He had a feeling that Jews would forget quickly and forgive these murderers. With all due respect to these honorable Israeli judges, they were wrong, and had no right to play politics with the memory of our martyrs and the emotions of the survivors. They should have known that the Holocaust touches the core of the Jewish people. The Jewish State also belongs to the Holocaust victims and martyrs, and it is the duty of the state to protect them and their interests. An undertaking, which David Ben Gurion, the first Prime Minister of Israel, began by bringing Adolf Eichman to Israel for trial, should be continued.

In Israel, there are two primary points of electricity pulsing with spiritual, emotional, psychological, and national current. They are the *Kotel*, the western wall of The Holy Temple in Jerusalem and Yad Vashem, the Holocaust Memorial Museum for the Holocaust Martyrs. Both sites mark terrible tragedies and defeats of the Jewish people. This is in marked contrast to the practice of other nations – The *Arch de Triumph* in Paris and the *Arch of Titus*, in Rome. These are tributes to proud accomplishments. While other nations mark gains, the Jews focus on losses. This tells us something about the Jewish people. Strange as it may seem, it is profoundly optimistic. Judaism's view of man says that good times don't need reminders, bad times, says Judaism, must be remembered and not swept under the rug of forgetfulness.

Jewish remembering is much more than paying ancestral respect. It is a conscious statement to those we lost, that their hopes will not become orphans. We affirm our commitment to further their resolve and continue their legacy.

The Vatican And The Illusions Of The Jews

The visit of Cardinal John O'Connor of New York to Israel at the end of 1986 evoked great hopes and expectations in many Jews. It turned into a great disappointment and despair. During his visit, Cardinal John O'Connor deliberately avoided meeting with the Prime Minister and Foreign Minister of Israel in their official offices and with the Mayor and other officials of Jerusalem, with the reasoning that he followed the policy of the Vatican, which forbids high ranking clergy from official meetings in Jerusalem.

During his stay in Israel, he visited an Arab refugee camp and he later declared that he supported the establishment of a Palestinian State. His behavior and his statements during his visit to Israel brought a wave of protest by Israeli and Jewish American leaders. This experience should serve as a lesson and a reminder to our Jewish leaders, both here in the United States, and in Israel, that very little has changed, if anything, in the policy of the Catholic Church towards the Jewish people. For many years, numerous attempts have been made by Jewish leaders to bring about better relations and understanding between the Jewish people, the State of Israel and the Catholic Church. Each time such a meeting has taken place between representatives of the Church and Jewish leaders, we heard that, on the one hand, progress was made, and on the other hand we heard there was regression in the relations with the Church. Actually, the interpretation of the Vatican's smoke signals have been fraud, because they all contained meaningless statements. However, since the Jews are by nature believers and optimists, we believed that perhaps there would be a change for the better in the near future. We Jews always interpreted gestures and hints by the Vatican as positive developments. It is high time to draw some hard conclusions. The visit of the New York Cardinal in the Middle East must certainly shake us up and awake us from these illusions. We Jews must remember and not forget a number of basic moves and acts which were committed over the years by the Catholic Church against the Jewish people, and which had important consequences for the Jews. All the beautiful stories, which our Jewish leaders fed to us, that we could shortly expect changes in the attitude of the Church towards the Jewish people and the State of Israel, were false rumors; a good will gesture here and there was only an optical deception. The visit of Pope John II in the Synagogue of Rome was also an optical deception.

We must remember that the existence of the Catholic Church and its continuous reign over hundreds of millions of Catholic believers has priority above all. Morality, fair play, justice and righteousness towards the Jewish people are not important factors in the eyes and minds of the policy makers and leadership of the Catholic Church.

Historically, the facts are clear. Jewish independence in our own historic land creates a tremendous problem for the Catholic Church, because the essence of our existence undermines the foundations of the Catholic Church. From the ideal and ideological points of view, the Jewish return to Zion and the reestablishment of Israel in this historic land, and especially Jerusalem as its capital, is a tremendous blow to the Christian world.

The Jewish people have a long and bitter account with the Church. Let us not forget for a moment what Christianity has done to the Jewish people over the generations. Persecutions, the inquisitions, the pogroms, the crusades, and above all, the terrible and tragic Holocaust, occurred in a climate of opinion conditioned by centuries of Christian hostility to the Jewish people which was basically rooted in the Christian dogma. Also let us not forget the active participation of devout Catholics, Priests, Cardinals, and others in the annihilation of the Jews of Europe during the 12 years of destruction of European Jewry. As a matter of fact, there is symbolic and optical kinship between the cross and the swastika. Over thousands of years, the Church denigrated and demonized the Jews. Christianity used its power to persecute, banish, and murder Jews throughout history. There was unrelenting Christian persecution of Jews all over Europe. Under the Inquisition, the Church instituted expulsions and demarcated Jewish ghettos. After creating the ghetto in the mid 16th century, the Church made special laws for the Jews detailing what they could do or not do, or what kind of living they could earn, and how they could live. These special Jewish laws were the forerunners of the Nuremberg laws decreed by the Germans.

One can see the continuous link between the Church's hatred of the Jews and the final act of vengeance during the Holocaust. The Nazi evil, the eliminationist anti-Semitism found fertile ground in Christian Europe which came to fruition between 1933 and 1945. It was a direct outcome of Martin

Luther's vicious rhetoric about *the pest in the midst of our lands,* referring to the Jews. The road from Martin Luther's Church led to Auschwitz.

The early pact of Pope Pious XII with Adolf Hitler was a foundation stone of the Shoah. Pious the XII's elevation of Catholic self interest over Catholic conscience was the lowest point in the Church's moral stand. No honest Catholic can look objectively at what Pious XII did and did not do during the Holocaust without simple shame.

In Jewish tradition, *Edom* which is mentioned many times in the Bible, is considered to be the Christian world. In the book of Ovadiah the Prophet, there is a single theme, an imprecation against Edom the Christian world of our time, the bitter brother of Israel. Throughout their common history there existed an implacable enmity against Israel. The Christian world showed themselves particularly treacherous and hostile during the Holocaust. The Prophet Ovadiah states, "For the violence done to thy brother, Jacob, disgrace shall engulf thee. On the day when you stood aloof, as evil doers carried away his goods, you stood and watched. How could you betray those who fled? Nor should thou have delivered those of Jacob that did remain on the day of his anguish." (Ovadiah 1:10-14)

The Prophet Ovadiah emphasizes the heinous character of Edom's (the Church's) guilt because the Church stood aloof, allowing others to do the evil acts but sharing in the outcome. Such callous aloofness is harder to forgive especially when the Church is claiming high moral ground. Pope Pious XII and the entire Christian Church in Europe were onlookers on the day the Jews, their brothers, met their doom.

The Prophet Ovadiah ends his prophecy with this future vision, "The day of the Lord is at hand. The final reckoning with the nations which have oppressed Israel will come." (Ovadiah 1:15)

The official leadership of the Church was silent. It closed its eyes and refused to listen to the pleas and appeals, which were presented to them by Jewish leaders in occupied Europe, and in the free world including the Chief Rabbi of the Land of Israel. Also the dramatic appeal by the well known Rabbi Michael Dov Weismandel from Slovakia (see his book in Hebrew, *Min Hameitzar*, From the Depth of Affliction,) to Pope Pacelli Pious the XII remained unanswered. Pious the XII was a *Germano-Phile*, unemotional and impassionate. All the appeals met with a stone wall, with dead silence. The silence was a loud signal to all Christians that the Holy See did not interfere. In addressing the College of Cardinals in June 1943, the Pontiff told the assembled of his duty to be impartial. If the Catholic Church would have raised its voice, or at least asked its followers to help rescue Jews, or even told them not to collaborate with the Nazis, hundreds of thousands of Jews, maybe even millions, could have been saved.

We should also not forget what the Church did with the thousands of Jewish children, which the Church agreed to *save,* meaning that they saved the children from physical annihilations, but *rescued* their souls from Judaism by converting them secretly to Catholicism.

When the second world war was over, parents or the surviving relatives tried to retrieve their dear ones, but were turned away empty-handed by the Church. The Church tried through various means to hide these unfortunate children from their relatives, so that they wouldn't be able to find them. Who does not remember the tragic and heartbreaking case of the Finnaly Brothers, two young Jewish children from France, who were entrusted by their parents to the Church in order to save them from the Germans? After the war, when the only surviving aunt came to claim the two boys from the Church, the nuns refused to return them since they had been converted to Christianity. The nuns moved the children from convent to convent, and from one Church to another, in order to prevent their return to the Jewish fold.

Then there were heartbreaking emotional scenes when parents or surviving relatives went to claim their children who were placed with non-Jewish families. The Christian families refused to return the children. In many cases these children became so much attached to these new parents and families that they refused to return to their Jewish families or to the Jewish religion. These children were indoctrinated to think that they were Christians and not Jewish. Some were also afraid that their lives would be in danger if they returned to Judaism since they had seen what happened to Jews during the Holocaust. Some of those who did return to Judaism and to their families were still living in two worlds, since they were not sure which was the real one.

Rabbi Isaac Herzog made great efforts to retrieve the Jewish children who were kidnapped by the Church and bring them back to their parent's religion. He was successful only in small measure. Thousands upon thousands of Jewish children were forcefully converted to Christianity. One of them is now a Cardinal in France. No one will ever know the exact number of Jewish families who became extinct because the chain of Jewishness was cut off by annihilation, and by forced conversion. Thus the Jewish people forever lost a large segment.

The children who were entrusted in the hands of the Christians or Church institutions suffered a great deal from the anti-Semitic environment into which they were placed. They had to adjust to a new life, language, culture, religion, food, work, insensitive treatment, loss of parents, loss of family, loss of community, friends, and to a complete change. Some of them also resented the fact that their parents had left them, even though it was to save their lives. Some of the Christian families who took these children in, exploited them by demanding hard labor from them. Many of these families received pay or valuables for agreeing to take a child.

The Pope's policy of neutrality encountered its crucial test when the Nazis began rounding up 8,000 Jews in Rome in October of 1943. Two thousand of those Jews, more than two thirds of whom were women and children, were sent to Auschwitz. This was done under the wall of the Vatican. Almost all of them perished in Auschwitz and Pope Pious the XII remained silent.

A few years ago, it was announced that the Catholic Church was establishing a monastery on the grounds of the infamous Auschwitz Concentration Camp. Thus will the Church spread its wings over a place which is soaked with Jewish holy blood. In the last few years there has been a tendency in Catholic circles to eradicate from memory the fact that the death camps were mainly intended for the Jewish people. This is a chutzpah of the first degree. This kind of attitude helps minimize the horrendous tragedy the Jews endured and it strives to emphasize that non-Jews were also annihilated in Auschwitz. The Church wants to turn the place into a symbol of Polish Catholic suffering. These kinds of attempts are very similar to the efforts being made by neo-Nazis who are spreading venom and lies by saying that only a few thousand Jews actually died in the Holocaust.

We had hoped that the Honorable Cardinal John O'Connor, after his visit to Yad Vashem, Israel's Holocaust Museum in Jerusalem, would better understand the connection between the tragic events of the Holocaust and the rebirth of the Jewish people in its homeland. It seemed the visit did not cause him much pain, nor did it stir his feelings. However, we find a different person when he visited Arab refugee camps in Jordan, Judea, and Samaria. There he showed great anxiety and compassion for the refugees. They are held in these camps because of the intransigence of their brethren. The Arabs keep them in camps for two reasons: the Arab countries do not want to integrate them as citizens; and the Arabs use these poor people as a political weapon against Israel.

The Jewish state, on the other hand, took in almost 1,000,000 Jews who fled with their lives from the Arab countries, and accepted them with open arms, and turned them into respected and productive citizens. If the

Arab countries had pity on their own flesh and blood, with the trillions of dollars they possess, these people could have been a blessing to the absorbing country, to themselves, and to the entire Middle East. The Cardinal expressed himself during the visit: "This is a very sad picture, it stirs in you great emotions." And when his Honor was asked by Israeli correspondents if he sees the connection between the Holocaust and the recognition by the Vatican of the State of Israel, his answer was, "I think it is totally irrelevant."

To John O'Connor this was a theological problem, not a political one. We deal here with people who use a double standard of justice because when it came to Arab refugees, he shed crocodile tears about the lot of the Palestinians who did not have a homeland of their own. (There is already one Palestinian state on the east side of Jordan River called Jordan, where 60 percent of the population is Palestinian.) Cardinal O'Connor told Zevulun Hammer, the former Israeli Minister of Religion, that, "It might well be that the Holocaust may have been an enormous gift that Judaism has given to the world." This shows a great insensitivity to the Jewish people. Is the honorable Cardinal ready to sacrifice a third of his followers in order to present a gift on the altar of his theology?

When the Israeli reporters asked him why the Vatican kept silent during the terrible destruction of the European Jewry, his answer was: "I do not know." This is a real evasive answer because as a Cardinal, it behooves him to know the history of the actions and inactions of his Church, the background of his theology and what happened during the Holocaust years. If he claims not to know them, then something is rotten in the Church.

Thank G-d that there are still righteous people among the nations and decent Christians to whom the attitude of the Vatican towards Israel causes great pain. The spokesmen of the International Christian Embassy, which is located in Jerusalem, (against the wishes of the Pope), accused the Catholic Church leadership at the Vatican of having turned the Cardinal's visit to Israel into a means of throwing insults at the State of Israel. This spokesman added: "It is sad to see that the heads of the Church refuse to recognize the rebirth of the Jewish people in their land with Jerusalem as its capital."

In 1904, Theodor Herzl went through considerable pains to get Vatican approval for the return of the Jewish people to Zion. In his famous audience with Pope Pious the X, the Pontiff then, (as now) emphatically opposed Zionism and the idea of Jews ever being allowed to return to Zion. The Pope said to Herzl, "The Jewish people have not recognized our Lord, therefore we cannot recognize the Jewish people and if you, sir," continued the Pope, "bring

Jews to the Holy Land and Jerusalem, we will send all our Priests and missionaries to convert you to Christianity." One can see that centuries of history, antipathy towards Judaism, and spilled Jewish blood are implicated in the above statement.

The hostile attitude of the Catholic Church toward the Jewish people stems from the ongoing ideological clashes between Judaism and Christianity. It is based on the following facts: the continued existence of the Jewish people for whom exile, degradation, persecution was supposed to be a deserving punishment. Because the Jews refuse to recognize Jesus as their savior, the Jews according to this theory, were supposed to disappear and the Catholic Church came to replace Judaism. Therefore, the Church can't easily digest the return of the Jews to their ancient land, especially to Jerusalem. The reestablishment of Israel in its historic land is a clear contradiction to the entire Catholic theology and ideology.

It is interesting to note that since the crusades, when the Christians lost their last foothold in the Holy Land, they never tried to oppose the various conquerors who captured the land of Israel and Jerusalem, and they never demanded to hand over the authority over the Holy City to the monotheistic religions. Only when the Jews were privileged, through the beginning of the redemption, to liberate Jerusalem did they suddenly remind themselves that they wanted a foothold in Jerusalem. This is an unheard of chutzpah. After what the Christian world inflicted upon the Jewish people, the Holy See comes and wants to have the right to decide which city will be Israel's capital!

The enemies of Israel created the Palestinian monster in order to cause problems for Israel. It's regrettable that the Vatican, too, fully supports the P.L.O. The Pope, at the Vatican, received Arafat with full honors. Some clergy actively support the P.L.O. with weapons as in the case of Bishop Helarian Capucci who was caught smuggling arms for Arab terrorists from Jordan into Israel.

The government of Israel, more than any other government in the history of the Holy Land and Jerusalem, treats all Churches and religions located there with more respect and understanding and compassion than ever before. There has never been such a liberal policy and freedom for all religions to practice. However, it is incumbent upon the government of Israel not to allow international organizations, or Churches, to dictate to Israel her rights, or give up historical religious sites and interests in Jerusalem, or any other parts of the historical land of Israel.

If the Vatican sometimes shows a positive attitude towards Jews and

Israel, it does not stem from great love of justice, only practicality. Israel rules over the entire western section of the Holy Land comprising only 22% (Jordan rules over the eastern section, comprising 78% of the Holy Land). The Catholic Church has many important interests in Israel and they know how to value local power. Therefore, they have no choice but to sometimes show a decent human face towards the Jewish people.

Certain Christian individuals have taken some small steps by admitting some of the wrongs which were perpetrated against the Jewish people. There still is a reluctance, however, to confront the horror inflicted upon the Jews in the name of the Christian faith. The Church has to confront its relationship to the Holocaust with honesty and repentance for the evil that was done in its name.

Arab And Muslim Involvement In The Holocaust

The Arab propaganda machine has spread the myth that throughout history Jews and Arabs lived in peace, one beside the other. They claimed they value and admire Judaism and that they were only combating the racist Zionist entity. They argued that how could they be anti-Semites when they themselves were descendents of *Shem* and why did they have to suffer and foot the bill, so to speak, of the European Nations who were responsible for the Holocaust crimes.

This idyllic relationship that the Arabs are trying to sell to the world has no foundation or truth. Their real attitude toward the Jewish people throughout our long history that our Sephardim brethren lived in Muslim countries is proof to the contrary. The Jews suffered from persecution, degradation, discrimination and pogroms inflicted by the Arabs. Throughout history there was no era when the Jews enjoyed equal rights under Muslim rule. Most of the time Jews were required to live in designated ghettos. Their professional rights were restricted to certain professions. They were limited in buying and holding property. They were required to pay heavy taxes and their lives were in danger many times. From time to time, Jews were accused of false charges and blood libel. The blood libel of 1840 in Damascus is one of those known examples of the Arab persecution of the Jews.

Even less is known to our people and the world at large of the involvement of the Arabs and Muslims in the annihilation of European Jewry during the Holocaust. Immediately after the Shoah, it became known that the Germans received a great deal of cooperation from Arabs in the Final Solution during the Holocaust years. Also very little is known by the public of the great help given to Nazi war criminals after the second world war, to escape judgment in Europe, by granting them asylum in various Arab countries.

In the Nazi archives, which were found by the Allies in Europe, they found many documents which attest to the close cooperation between the German, Arab, and Muslim leaders. This cooperation began as early as 1933 when the Nazis took power in Germany. As a part of the Arab cooperation with Germany and Fascist Italy, they organized riots in Palestine against the British during period of 1936 to 1939, at which time Arab terrorist gangs attacked their Jewish neighbors in Eretz Yisrael. More than 600 Jews were killed in these attacks and thousands were wounded. There was much looting and destruction of Jewish property. The Nazis financed these terrorist activities and provided the Arabs with many weapons and ammunition.

A revolt broke out in April 1941, in Iraq against the British with the help of the Nazis. The leader of the rebels was Rashid Ali, a Nazi agent who received from them weapons and political backing. There was also an attempt in Egypt to overthrow the government through Arab Nazi agents. Among those Nazi agents was a young officer in the Egyptian Army by the name of Anwar Sadat, who later became the president of Egypt.

The British discovered the plot; they arrested many of these Arab Nazi agents, among them Sadat. He had direct contact with the military headquarters of Field Marshall Romel, The German African Corps. At that time when Romel was at El Allamain, there were pro Nazi demonstrations in Cairo, Alexandria, and other Egyptian cities.

The Jewish community in Eretz Yisrael (Palestine) made preparations for guerrilla warfare on the Carmel Ridge Mountain and in the Galilee in the event Romel and his army would reach Israel. The closest cooperation with these highest Nazi officials was with Chaj Amin El Husseny, the Mufti of Jerusalem. His activities were supported financially and diplomatically, directly from Germany and Italy. This Jew hater dedicated the best years of his life to a war of annihilation of the Jewish people wherever they happened to be. He became known as "Satan in the Black Robe."

On November 10, 1941, the Mufti met Hitler. The meeting lasted an hour and a half. Hitler was very impressed with the Jerusalem Mufti. Hitler instructed his aides to give the Mufti two villas on the outskirts of Berlin and five million marks monthly for his Nazi propaganda. He had a special office in Berlin, which became known as the office of the Great Mufti. The Mufti's agents were active in the Arab countries, Muslim countries, and in the Balkans where there was a Muslim population.

He was provided with two powerful radio stations. He spread his venom against the Jews to the Arab and Muslim world. He urged the Arabs to rebel against the Allies. His motto was, "Kill the Jews wherever you can, because it causes pleasure to Allah, to our prophet and our religion." This Mufti organized a special legion of Muslims fashioned after the S.S.. They participated in the atrocities against the Jews and other minorities in Croatia and in Yugoslavia. They also participated in the murder of Jews in Kovno, Vilna, and other east European countries. Some 2,000 of them were captured by the Allies at the end of the war and were imprisoned in P.O.W. camps in Alabama. The Mufti followers composed Nazi songs in Arabic. They had a popular song, which they sang, *In heaven is Allah, on earth is Hitler*, thus Hitler became the most beloved hero of the Arabs and Muslims.

The Mufti corresponded frequently with important Nazi Leaders. In one of the letters he received from Hitler, it said, "Germany recognized the right to full Arab independence. The Arabs and Germans have the same enemy, the English and the Jews. We will stand together in your struggle against them." (From documents of the German Foreign Ministry, Berlin, April 8, 1941.) In one of those letters it says in return for the help which the Arab world would give the German Reich, Germany pledged to recognize the independence of the Arab States and the liquidation of the Jewish National home in the Land of Israel. (A copy of those statements can be seen in Yad Vashem in Jerusalem.)

According to a report of the *Luftwaffe*, the German Air Force, the Jerusalem Mufti demanded in March 1944 to bomb Tel Aviv, the Haifa Port, the Israeli electric power installations and the Jewish Agency headquarters in Jerusalem. In those days it was not of strategic importance for the Germans to fulfill the Mufti's request to bomb Palestine, but to the Mufti it was an urgent matter.

Each time a German official was ready to make a deal with Jews in Europe to free a number of them from concentration camps for a bribe, the Mufti intervened and the deal was off. He was responsible for ruining the possibility of exchanging 1,200 Jewish children from a concentration camp for German prisoners of war who were being held by the Allies. The Mufti sent a telegram to Hitler protesting and demanding that Jewish children be treated like adult Jews. These children were then sent to Auschwitz where they were gassed.

In May of 1944, Boris, the King of Bulgaria, agreed to allow 4,000 Jewish children to leave for Palestine. As soon as the Mufti heard about it, he protested and the plan was cancelled. At the Nuremberg trial of the Nazi war criminals after the war, the high Nazi officials testified that the Jerusalem Mufti was the moving force behind the annihilation of European Jewry. He was in close contact with Adolf Eichmann, from whom he received regular reports about the speed of the annihilation. The Mufti and Adolf Eichmann became close friends. The genocide of European Jewry deprived the Jewish people of the human reserves needed to fortify the future of the Jewish state. In this sense, the Holocaust served Arab interests, for it greatly reduced the threat of mass immigration to the Jewish homeland.

The Mufti once said to Heinrich Himmler, "I hope that after Germany's victory, you will lend me Mr. Adolf Eichmann, who would be of great help to us in bringing the Final Solution to the Jews of Palestine also." Simon Wiesenthal, the Nazi hunter, claimed that the Mufti visited Auschwitz, Majdanek and other death camps during the Holocaust, and inspected the gas chambers, and even was present during the gassing of Jews in those camps. In the German archives which the Allies confiscated, they found proof of the preparations that the Mufti and his aides made for the annihilation of the Jewish community of Palestine, by planning to use the same techniques as the Germans used to annihilate European Jewry.

Hundreds and maybe thousands of high level Nazi war criminals were received with open arms by the Arab countries where they found a haven. These Nazis changed their names to Arabic names. The Arabs utilized the experience and talents of these Germans in many fields in their wars against the Jews and Israel. These Nazis served their Arab masters well and with devotion. They were involved in counseling the Arabs in their intelligence services and in military advice. Some of them became bodyguards to Arab Leaders. German scientists worked diligently in producing sophisticated weapons including missiles that would reach the heart of the Jewish state.

The Arab propaganda machine adopted the Nazi style of disseminating information about Israel. These Nazi war criminals found in the Arab countries a very fertile ground in spreading the hatred and venom against the Jews. The Arabs, with the help of these Nazis, put out publications in various languages including Arabic, English, French, Spanish, and many more. In these publications, they spread lies and libels against the Jewish people, stating that the religious and ethical requirements of the Jew is to rob the other nations and subjugate them. Hitler's book *Mein Kampf*, and *The Protocols of the Elders of Zion*, were printed by the Arabs by the millions in many languages. The Arabic leaders distributed these books to their foreign dignitary visitors. In 1974, King Faisal of Saudi Arabia gave these publications to Michele Jobert, the French Foreign Minister, during his visit to Saudi Arabia. The King's advisors noted to the guests that these were the most admired books by King Faisal. During the Sinai War in 1956 and the Six Day War in 1967, the Israeli Army found on the Arab soldiers Hitler's book, *Mein Kampf*, in which he wrote with venom of the Jews and *The Protocols of the Elders of Zion*, in Arabic translation.

The Arabs also had close relations with Nazi and Fascist organizations in various countries in order to enlist them in their war against the Jews. Saad Eldin Shazali, the former Egyptian Army chief of staff, had close ties to the Nazi party in England. He made an agreement with the British Nazi leadership about joint activities against Zionism and Judaism with the goal of destroying the State of Israel and returning Arab rights to the Palestinian Territory.

Abdul Nasser, the President of Egypt, gave an interview to a German neo-Nazi paper, May 1964, *The German National Paper and Soldiers Paper*, in which he stated: "The lie about the murder of 6,000,000 Jews is not believed by any serious person." The Arabs claim, "What Hitler did to the Jews, he did as revenge for what they did to Jesus." They claim that the Jews of today have no right whatsoever to the land of Israel, because they are not the descendents of the ancient Hebrews, but rather the descendents of the Russian Kazars.

A few years ago, an Israeli delegation visited the Dachau Concentration Camp in Germany to pay homage to the Jewish martyrs. As they signed their names in the visitor's book, they saw a shocking inscription which read: "By chance I came to Dachau. I am an Arab, and was happy with what I saw that Hitler did to the Jews. They are the kind of people who do not deserve to live. I am confident that their day will come and another Hitler will arise."

In 1953, after Anwar Sadat read in the newspaper that there were rumors that Hitler was still alive, he wrote to the daily newspaper in Cairo the following poem of praise, "Dear Hitler, I would like to bless you from the depths of my heart. You should be proud that you became the immortal leader of Germany. We will not be surprised if you will appear again in Germany or if a new Hitler will rise in your stead. Germany will rise and be revived again in spite of the scorn of the great powers of East and West." (El Musavar, Daily Newspaper, No.1510, Cairo, September 18, 1953.)

On January 13, 1978, in the popular Egyptian paper *Al Ahbar*, the columnist Ahmed Hasin threatened American Jewry with a Holocaust such as that which befell European Jewry. "The Jews of the world, who do not lack cunning and intelligence, understand the danger that Prime Minister Begin places them in when he again stirs up the attitude that nations once had toward them. I warn the Jews of America of a similar fate to that of the Jews of Germany."

Even with the peace process, as Israel has been relinquishing historic areas of territory, and making all kinds of concessions, the Arabs continue with their deep hatred of Israel and the Jewish people. The book, *The School of*

Ba'athusim, a Study of Syrian Schoolbooks, by Dr. Meyrav Wurmser (A MEMRI monograph, the Middle East Research Institute Washington, DC, 2000), deals with the curriculum of the Syrian school system. The author examined 40 school text books which were an integral part of the official Syrian school system. In it there were references to the Jews, Zionism, and Israel. They claimed there was no Holocaust, that Zionism was a dangerous cancer. They described the Zionist movement as a Nazi racist organization. They quoted a great deal from German Nazi literature or other anti-Semitic sources. In one of the books it states that the Holocaust took place as a reaction to the Jewish economic control over Germany, the exploitation of the Germans, and the Jewish betrayal. In this book there was a question defaming the Jewish people, it said: What is the difference between Nazi and Zionist ideology? The Nazis claimed that they were the master race, and the Zionists claim they are the chosen people by G-d, and the other nations have to be subservient to them.

The spirit of the Jerusalem Mufti lives on even after his demise and his influence in the Arab world continues to poison the hearts and minds of the New Arab generations against the Jewish people. It is very important that all Jews understand the Arab mentality and hatred so that we can be on guard.

Hast Thou Murdered And Also Taken Possession

Kings 1; 21:19

Among all the Fascists in Europe during the second world war who took part in the murder of its Jews, Hungary is the country that benefited more than any other country. The Hungarians were opportunists who joined the German camp in order to gain territory. They expanded in three directions, north into Carpathia, east into Transylvania, and south into Yugoslavia. With the help of the Germans, this expansion was accomplished in a short time.

The Hungarian measures against its Jews were enacted without much German prodding and without any German help. At its peak, 130,000 Jews were inducted into Munko Tabor, forced labor battalions. Almost half the Jews of all forced labor battalions died on the Russian front.

Hungary originated the idea of the Munko Tabor in 1940. Hungary was the one that brutally deported 50,000 Jews from Carpathia in 1941 because they could not prove their citizenship, even though they had lived there for generations. The Hungarians drove them across the Polish border to Kamenets-Podolsk in the Ukraine. There these Jews were machine-gunned on August 27 and 28, 1941. Entire families were buried in mass graves. Then came the final deportation of 600,000 Jews; elderly, women, and children to Auschwitz, the largest slaughterhouse in all of Europe.

Unlike other European countries, the Germans did not conquer Hungary during World War II; she was a willing ally of the Nazis. The Hungarian authorities instituted racial laws against the Jews of Hungary, which also included the Jews of Carpathia, parts of Rumania and parts of Yugoslavia, which were annexed by the Hungarians.

With the blessing of the Germans, the Hungarians confiscated Jewish property of the deportees. They took their dwellings, businesses, factories, their silver, gold and all valuables. Before the Jews were shipped from the ghettos to the concentration camps, where they were annihilated, they were ordered to remove their gold, silver, jewelry, and precious stones from their possession. I personally witnessed these brutal acts in Ghetto Berehovo when we were ordered to deposit all of our valuables in the big baskets and buckets which were placed in front of each barrack just before we were deported to Auschwitz. The Hungarian authorities took everything; of course no one gave us receipts.

Throughout history, no nation was ever as lucky as Hungary. In a very short time they acquired a huge windfall of billions of dollars of property and valuables. Hungary was the first country in Europe in 1947, which succeeded in stabilizing her currency, the *Forint*, with the backing of stolen Jewish gold, silver, and properties. Until this day, Hungary has not returned Jewish property or valuables that was accumulated by the Jews over hundreds of years to the handful of survivors that remain.

The Hungarians might agree to stand up for a moment of silence in memory of the Holocaust victims, but that is all. They are not willing or ready, however, to return the valuables and properties, which is estimated to run in the billions. They also are not willing to compensate the survivors for their suffering and for the loss of their families. The Hungarians have tried to evade their responsibility and have even refused to repent for these great crimes and injustices.

It is important to remember the *Train Full of Gold*, which was described in the press in October 1999. According to reliable eyewitnesses in the last weeks of World War II, as Soviet troops advanced from the east, Nazi officials in Hungary ordered a train with looted Jewish riches be sent west towards Germany, with the collected wealth of Hungary's decimated Jews. Wedding bands alone filled crate after crate.

American troops intercepted the train in Austria, in May 1945. Soldiers of the United States Third Infantry Division found the train hidden in the Tauren Tunnel, 60 miles south of Salzburg. Hungarian officials and guards who were interrogated after the train's capture, told the Americans that the property had been taken from the Jews. The train also contained more than 1,100 paintings taken from Hungarian Jews according to documents. The Gold Train set out from Budapest on December 15, 1944 on orders from Adolf Eichmann. Eichmann had supervised the extermination of most of the 750,000 Jews who lived in Hungary at the beginning of the war, after they had been forced to turn over their gold, jewels, and other valuables to the Hungarian puppet Fascist Government. There were several other trains sent from Hungary by the Germans into Germany, but no one knows where their contents disappeared. The Gold Train was returned to Hungary by the Allies in 1946. Some claim that with this gold, Hungary paid war reparations, which were

An American soldier guards the "Gold Train" after it was intercepted by the Allies.

imposed on her by the Allies. There are other witnesses who claim that the gold cargo from that train is kept in the treasury of the Hungarian National Bank in Budapest. These valuables are now an integral part of Hungary's gold stock.

To add insult to injury, after the war, Hungary received reparations from Germany, which were designated as reparations for the Jewish Hungarian Holocaust survivors. It was also stipulated that if there were no survivors, the reparations would be passed on to the lawful heirs, and to the Jewish community. However, Hungary never paid a penny to any survivor.

After great efforts by individuals and Jewish Organizations in Hungary and the world over in December 1998, the Hungarian Government enacted a law which was supposed to express the regret of the Hungarian people for totally collaborating with the Germans. This collaboration brought about the annihilation of 600,000 Hungarian Jews together with the other Jews from the Hungarian occupied territories, in less than two months.

The survivors of Hungarian Jewry were shocked to hear the amounts the Hungarians offered as reparations. For losing a parent, they offered $140. For losing a sister, brother, son, daughter, husband, or wife, they offered $70. If there was more than one sibling among the survivors, the $140 would have to be divided among them. The immediate reaction of the survivors was anger, rage, and scorn. They said they were not ready to accept such an insulting offer, because it was an outrage and a shame to the memory of the Holocaust victims and their families, who were murdered in such a brutal and cruel way. This kind of offer does not represent even a symbolic compensation. As a mockery to the poor, the survivors who did apply to the Hungarian Government had to pay $40 from their own pocket... a fee for the bureaucratic procedure. This kind of treatment of the survivors is not asking forgiveness. It is pure degradation. They think that we are still in the 1940s.

Can anybody accept such an insulting offer of $70 for the life of a human being? Perhaps the Hungarians came up with such a ridiculous offer as a public relations stunt, and also to disgust the survivors, so in reality they would not have to pay any compensation. With such a gesture they would be able to claim to the world that they were righteous people who were willing to repent, because they were doing a noble thing for the poor surviving Jews.

In the peace treaty that Hungary signed in Paris in 1947 as a satellite of Germany, she promised to pay reparations to the Holocaust victims who suffered because of the Hungarian collaboration with the Germans. The communist regime, which existed in Hungary for 45 years, did not fulfill this obligation. After the communist regime collapsed however, the Hungarians did pay non-Jewish Hungarian families who were executed by the communist regime $12,000 for each person executed. It was not much, but still a big difference from what they offered the Jews. It proves that the current Hungarian government discriminates between Jewish and non-Jewish blood.

Even if they paid $100,000 for every Jewish person murdered during the Holocaust, we Jews could not close this chapter with the Hungarians. It should be clear that the historic account between the Hungarian people and the Jewish people remains open.

Even the few survivors who did apply for reparations for their properties that were confiscated by the Hungarians, have had scanty and meager results. The procedure is long and complicated, only causing grief and frustration. The Hungarian government estimates the value of Jewish properties at a ridiculous sum and they only award that small amount by dividing it among all the descendents, including those who perished in the Shoah, since they have the records of all Jewish families from before the war. That means that if there were 10 children in the family, and the parents together with 9 children perished, the survivors would get only one tenth of the amount the government assessed that the property was worth. After all this, the survivor can receive that amount in Hungarian Government Bonds spread out over years. These bonds can only be redeemed in Hungary in Hungarian currency.

Until this day, the Hungarian people hate Jews and there are a number of extreme right wing parties who are fomenting this hatred. In the Hungarian Parliament, there are Fascist parties disguised with names such as *The Party of Life and Truth*, which is an extreme right wing party headed by the known anti-Semite, Eshtwan Tchorka. The current Minister of Agriculture who is a member of the Government Coalition is the Chairman of the popular Hungarian soccer team known as *Francewarosh*, who are known to be a group of hooligans. In one of the derby games against the group known by its initials as M.T.K. (which is considered to be a Jewish group) the fans of the Francewarosh group cheered on their players and shouted, "The train is leaving for Auschwitz, the train is leaving for Auschwitz." The chairman of the organization of former political prisoners, under the communist rule, declared, "Whoever condemns Fascism is a despicable and low Bolshevik agent."

From what has been described above, one can see that Hungarians have not changed their attitude and hatred of the Jewish people. Whoever visits that country can feel at every step, how much their hatred for the Jews burns in them. It is difficult to believe, but it is a fact that thousands of Jews from the Diaspora and Israel are rushing to Hungary to spend their vacations, celebrate the holiday of Passover, other holidays, to get medical treatments and dental work. There are also Jews from the Diaspora and from Israel who found bargains for investment in real estate in this blood-soaked country. Some think they will become rich overnight.

The Hungarians welcome this kind of tourist industry and investments of hundreds of millions in foreign currency since they discovered the great economic potential which these Jewish activities would bring them. It is a sad commentary on our people that even after such a tragic Holocaust caused by the Hungarians, they see fit to engage in these activities in a Fascist country. It is late, but not too late, to use international pressure on the Hungarian Government to return what they have confiscated and looted and that they should compensate the survivors for their dear ones whom they murdered. The Jewish organizations such as The World Jewish Congress, B'nai Brith, Holocaust Survivors Organizations, and the Government of Israel should make an effort to block Hungarian entry into the European Union and NATO and also bring up the Hungarian crimes at all international gatherings until Hungary repents and corrects the great injustice that the Hungarians perpetrated. Regarding the Hungarians, our relations to them must consider their horrible deeds as a yardstick of what is acceptable and what is not. Otherwise, they and other evil forces will think that you can persecute the Jews with impunity.

The Distorters Of The Holocaust

I beg forgiveness from the reader for evoking the horrible acts of the Germans and other evil forces in Europe during the Holocaust. I have used restraint in telling the most inhuman sufferings and also shortened many of the details of the horrors so as not to burden the reader too much.

However, it has to be told about this Hell on Earth; about this Kingdom of Evil, even though human language cannot describe the Holocaust period. This is why I have written this book, not only to serve as a memorial for my family, my friends, my hometown, and all the Jews who perished in the Holocaust, but also as an eyewitness to clarify what really happened in the concentration camps.

In the world of the concentration camps, the prisoner felt the horrible reality at all hours, day and night. One could not escape it even for one moment. Nowhere in the world was reality so realistic as in the camps. The constant torture, the degrading, the weakening, the attrition and death around you. In the concentration camps, reality ruled without boundaries. The S.S. was the S.S., the beatings were painful, the torture was unbelievable.

It is incumbent on me to tell about this brutal system, which made me into a victim due to *sinat chinam*, hatred without cause. This experience sunk into my being and was engraved in my heart and mind, which it does not let up and appears constantly before my eyes. It never gets lost; my body and mind have a hold on it. The experiences my body and soul had to endure will be carried with me all my life until my last days.

For many years after the Holocaust, I kept everything to myself. I kept silent, not because I forgot what happened there. I simply did not know how to tell about such a horror. How do you tell normal people, who, by G-d's grace, did not experience it? How do you tell decent human beings what the German beasts did... a nation that was once the most cultured and advanced on the entire European continent? But as soon as I began to write, my pen flowed by itself. There were times that I could not stop, but I had to go on.

There was an inner force that encouraged me to go on and tell it all.

To be a victim in a concentration camp meant that you were *hefker*, an abandoned object of complete helplessness, of loneliness, of complete loss of trust in the world. It was a situation which all Jews felt in the concentration camps during the Holocaust years. The torture remains with you forever; it can never be erased because whoever was persecuted does not forget it.

Many books have been written about the Holocaust by survivors, historians, writers, and others. Those written by the survivors are the most authentic and real. Also many movies and films have been produced dealing with the subject of the Holocaust. History must be understood even when it is dramatized. We, the Holocaust survivors, are very sensitive as to how the Holocaust is portrayed in books or films. That is why so many of us react with rage to the Holocaust deniers.

There was a time when memory was sacred, that words like Hitler, Nazi, Gestapo, and S.S., may their memory be eradicated, were reserved to describe one of the most horrific events in the history of mankind. The uniqueness of the Shoah endowed its language with a singular shock value, and its words stirred outrage at the systematic slaughter of 6,000,000 Jews. There was no way that the words and images of the Nazi period could be understood or taken lightly.

Unfortunately there is much trivialization of Holocaust imagery. The mass media are the vehicles for teaching new generations about the Shoah. But it is necessary to be very careful how one approaches this sacred subject, to know what the words and images mean and how they were used. Steven Spielberg, in his film *Schindler's List*, succeeded in portraying the Plaszow Concentration Camp (in which I was a prisoner) with great accuracy. This film should and could be used as a teaching tool. However, Roberto Benigni's film, *Life is Beautiful*, makes a mockery out of the great suffering and the memory of the victims.

Creative works such as *Life is Beautiful* gives the new generations the wrong idea about what it was like to be in Auschwitz. To treat the whole idea as an elaborate game is very sad. Reports of moviegoers who came out from the theater with tears in their eyes cannot forgive the distortion of the truth. In Auschwitz, it was impossible to lie to the children because they were sent immediately after their arrival into the gas chambers.

It should also be emphasized that this kind of story is not credible, is not realistic, and therefore suspicious in forgery and commercialism of the Holocaust, because a child successfully hidden in a barrack of a concentration camp was a rarity, maybe one in a million. A child of eight was hidden with us in Buchenwald. This was Israel (Lulek) Lau, who was hidden by his brother Naftali, who was 10 years older than he, by bribing certain officials in camp. But as I said, this was a great rarity.

The attempt to connect between Auschwitz and *Life is Beautiful*, no matter how clever or sophisticated it might be, crosses all boundaries. This breaks the taboo and opens another way, which makes it easier to deny the Shoah. Whoever visits Auschwitz or Buchenwald, even today, knows that this represents different worlds. The movie can leave in the minds of the viewers an impression that during the Shoah it was like that, very bad, but bearable. This impression makes it easier to deny the horrors.

Whoever tries to describe the Holocaust today as a background for Jewish cleverness, whether it is a comedy, or in the form of romantic love, or fiction, takes the risk of blurring the line between the truth and legend. These kinds of films minimize the uniqueness of the catastrophe, reduce it, distort it, limit its implications and create a situation where it is placed on the same level with other stories.

In 1940, Charles Chaplin, the talented actor portrayed Hitler in the movie, *The Great Dictator*, which was also a comedy. After the war, he confessed and said, "Had I known of the actual horrors of the German concentration camps, I would not have made the movie." In the death camps, life was not beautiful. It was Hell on earth. It was an inferno administrated by evil people.

If the language and images of the Holocaust become debased, we will lose the ability to identify and grapple with crucial issues and *Tikun Olam*, the correction or improvement of the world and society.

Indeed, today in more than one country, there are still open Nazis, hidden Nazis, neo-Nazis, Fascists, and all kinds of Jew haters. Their hatred of the Jewish people does not lessen and they have now taken a new twist and a new turn. They use slogans such as, *Gas the Jews, Finish Hitler's Job; Oil Yes, Jews No; Hitler's and Goebbels', Destroy the Jews.* Not only do they hate the living, they are even desecrating the memory of our fathers, mothers, brothers, and sisters by denying that there was a Holocaust. They deny that 6,000,000 Jews died at all.

The deniers have published books in Europe, in Latin America, in the Middle East, even in the United States disclaiming the Holocaust. (It is quite a puzzle why the American soldiers who liberated the concentration camps in Europe have not spoken up forcefully to refute the claims that the camps never existed, that 6,000,000 were never killed.)

We recently witnessed the libel suit of the author David Irving in London, England, against Deborah Lipstadt. Irving denies that Jews were murdered during the Holocaust.

An anti-Semitic pamphlet appeared in London, which was titled, *Did Six Million Really Die?* It describes the death of 6,000,000 Jews as, "the most colossal piece of fiction and the most successful of deceptions." The pamphlet also claims that the enormous fraud was committed with the deliberate intention of blackmailing the world into accepting the establishment of the State of Israel. The Arab League propagandists say that the entire Holocaust story is a *Zionist conspiracy*. The Liberty Lobby, the Christian Nationalist, the K.K.K., and other Jew haters distribute this kind of propaganda in the United States.

In Frankfurt, Germany, there appeared an anti-Semitic booklet entitled, *die Auschwitzluege*, the Lie of Auschwitz, in which the author tries to whitewash the atrocities perpetrated in the notorious concentration camp. A third book with similar objectives, *It Never Happened After All* was published in Europe for English-speaking countries. Another Holocaust-denial book is *The Truth At Last.*

The evil that is inherent in man and that was released by Hitler, can, given certain conditions, break out again. Today, with the words of the Holocaust deniers getting stronger, we must not be lulled into a mood that it can never happen again. The Shoah teaches us to be ever on the alert, lest the twisted road that led from Auschwitz to the Yom Kippur War, lead to another Holocaust.

Part 6

Educating Today's Generation About The Holocaust

Forgetfulness leads to exile, while remembrance is the secret of redemption.

The Baal Shem Tov,
Founder of the Chassidic movement

Lessons To Be Learned From The Holocaust

One of the saddest phenomenons of our time is the tragedy of the ignorance of what actually happened in the years of the Holocaust. Now that more than two generations have passed, it becomes possible for sensitive people to talk about the event and to reflect upon what lessons are to be learned from it.

New generations have grown up since the fires at Auschwitz have gone out, generations who have no knowledge of the tremendous spiritual and physical resistance the Jews put up in 22 European countries under Nazi occupation. It is not that we are callous, not that we have forgiven or even that we never knew, but over 50 years have passed since the defeat of the Nazi armies and half of the Jews alive today were not yet born when the remnants of the survivors were freed from bondage. Even for those of us to whom the Holocaust, through personal experience or vicariously, is a searing component of our Jewish consciousness, it was such a dreadful period in Jewish history that we tend to force the memories into the backs of our minds. Normal people do not dwell on death, pain, torture, and misery if they can avoid it.

A commanding voice speaks to us from Auschwitz; it commands us to remember the Jewish victims of the Holocaust, lest their memory perish. Jews now know that they must forever remember Auschwitz, and be its witnesses to the world. Not to be a witness would be a betrayal. In the slaughter camps, the victims often rebelled with no other hope than that one of them might escape to tell the tale. For Jews to refrain now from telling the story would be unthinkable.

There is a tendency to forget the entire subject. Possibly, because it is a very unpleasant topic for adults and surely for young people. Therefore, some of us follow the example of the Gentile world that is trying very hard to forget those incriminating years. However, by not teaching and remembering the Holocaust, we are doing a grave injustice to the 6,000,000 Jews who perished as well as our own future. Unfortunately, a number of the Hebrew and

Jewish schools do not teach about the Holocaust. Only a small number of schools observe a memorial day for the 6,000,000 Jewish martyrs. The school that does observe such a day usually has an insignificant ceremony.

You will not read much, if anything, about this tragedy in the textbooks used in public schools. In fact, historians generally neglect to write about Gentile-Jewish relations in textbooks. To most historians, Jews, as such, do not exist. They are viewed as nationals of countries, or as members of any economic class, not as members of an ethnic religious group. With a few notable exceptions, historians have not made known to the world the great tragedy of the extermination of Jews... as Jews. Where mention is made, it is capsulated into a kind of statistical abstract, giving the number killed, mentioning the names of a few death camps and concluding with a few moral phrases. No graphic documentation of the Holocaust, such as pictures, maps, charts, or quotes from primary sources is included to impress the facts on the mind of the reader.

Not only is the Holocaust minimized, but also efforts are being made to obliterate the Jewish tragedy as such. In Russia, in Poland, and other East European countries, the official governmental policy is to wipe out any mention that the Jews were mostly the victims. Instead, they are described as victims of Fascism and Nazism. Thus the Warsaw Ghetto Uprising became an uprising of the Poles.

The Shoah cries out for some kind of rational explanation, but there is none. It is incomprehensible; it defies all parallels. No fitting words have yet been created to describe how 6,000,000 worlds have been destroyed forever.

Teachers must teach how society could lose its mind. Understanding the Nazi years is a matter of survival, not just for Jews, but for all people. I would venture to say that anyone who doesn't engage actively today in keeping the truth of the Holocaust alive is an accomplice to the killers.

Never has the teaching of any subject been more urgent. With so few survivors left, and their number is decreasing daily, it is the last chance for our generation to study and communicate, explore and analyze this event that will forever remain a challenge in history and perhaps to history.

Holocaust study should become an integral part of our school curriculum. Our youth must be aware of the tragedy of the Holocaust and the capacity of human beings to be violent and destructive. If they explore and take ethical positions on this issue, they will be more mindful of their moral obligations to all people everywhere whose destiny and lives are jeopardized.

The lessons to be learned from the Nazi era are a challenge to humanity.

The Holocaust is a compelling case. It reveals the human potential for extremes of both good and evil. In an interview that I read with Nazi hunter, Simon Wiesenthal, he declared, "People must be aware of what happened, for if we forget this genocide, we open the doors for the next." He explained that now, more than 50 years after the war, many people know nothing of what happened, referring to a survey that was conducted in Germany amongst school children. One of the questions asked was, "Who was Hitler?" Wiesenthal said answers ranged from, "Hitler was a Socialist killed by the Jews, to Hitler was a Jew killed by the Nazis."

When asked why it was necessary to "keep old wounds open," Wiesenthal replied, "We are living in a world which has seen other genocides since the Nazi Holocaust. I believe that only by learning about the Holocaust, by education through books or through lectures, will the term "genocide" be fully understood before it has a chance of disappearing." He explained that several U.S. Congressmen had told him that today was a new world, where issues such as pollution were now top priority. "But we have different pollution. We are living amongst murderers and we must first clean up this pollution."

Wiesenthal recalled that in 1944 an S.S. officer told him, "He could tell the truth about the death camps to the people of America, and you know what would happen? They wouldn't believe you. They'd say you were crazy. They might even put you in a madhouse. How could anyone believe this terrible crime unless he has lived through it?"

When Wiesenthal was asked why he still continues to hunt Nazis, his answer was a simple one. "I believe in life after death." He said, "When we come to the next world and meet the 6,000,000 Jews who perished in the concentration camps and they ask, "What have you done?", there will be many answers. Some will say, I became a jeweler or I built houses, but I will say I did not forget you.

Although the Nazi era affected many nationalities, it mostly affected the Jewish people. Therefore it is a subject of utmost importance for Jewish survival. Recently it was revealed that international organizations like Interpol were involved in serving the Nazi machine during World War II by informing the Nazi police of Jews who were using alias identities.

For the Nazis, the extermination of the Jews was a fundamental urge and a sacred mission, not a means to other objectives. The Nazi exterminatory drive against the Jews remains unmistakably singular. Our knowledge of what happened at Auschwitz has vastly increased, but not our understanding. To this dilemma, one may tentatively answer that the Holocaust indeed does not fall within the framework of explanatory categories of a generalizing kind.

Our martyrs died because they were Jews. They were not murdered as members of a wartime enemy or because they posed a threat to any nation. They were killed simply by virtue of being members of a unique nation whose prime characteristics are kindness and holiness. In the final analysis, it was this aspect of the Jewish people that the Germans and their collaborators worked so hard to eradicate. Our enemies correctly perceived that our existence represented the greatest possible threat to their own world view. Our challenge today is to articulate to our children this uniquely Jewish aspect of martyrdom. If we allow the echo of the voices of the Holocaust martyrs to weaken, we will not survive as well.

The structural link between the behavior of the exterminators and that of the onlookers in the context of the destruction of European Jewry is obvious. The extermination of 6,000,000 Jews did not take more than a few years to accomplish. It emerged and developed virtually unchecked, and therefore could reach such proportions in a very short time. Any important countervailing forces, by their massive attempts at hiding, constant protests and demonstrations, or violent intervention from outside occupied Europe, would have made the course of extermination much less radical and more difficult. Whatever the motivation of the passivity of the Gentiles, not to speak of the collaboration with the Nazis, it always resulted from a choice in which the Jew was considered less of a priority. Several explanatory frameworks could contribute to our understanding of these attitudes: A general trend of indifference to mass death in modern society, mostly in the midst of war. The intensity of the traditional anti-Semitism of Eastern and Southeastern Europe is another reason. The tacit or explicit admiration of many Gentiles of the national Socialist Revolution. This includes not only European Fascists; it includes some so-called Liberals and even groups, who could be considered as tending towards the Left. All these were not immune to such temptation.

Until the middle of the second world war, the Nazi Reich was considered an acceptable partner to many. The New Order was not only the aspiration of a small minority of extreme collaborationists, but rather collaboration was accepted, if not actively sought, by important sectors of the society in the occupied or neutral countries of Europe.

Until 1943, there was deep admiration for their reign as representing the true values of Western civilization in this fight against Bolshevism. In general, it seems that regarding European public opinion, the tide turned against the Reich only some time in 1943, when Germany's defeat became a certainty. It appears, therefore, that the more or less explicit revolt of an important part of the Western middle classes against the Liberal tradition contributed a great deal to the isolation of the Jews. Therefore, the Jew had no chance of being massively helped, be it for this fundamental reason alone, until it was too late for a great many of them.

The identification of Jews with world and Communist revolution made the task of Nazi propaganda easier and reinforced the pre existing tendency of Western society to consider the Jews undesirable elements who had to be excluded, whatever the consequences this would entail for the victims of exclusion. A famous sentence from Kafka's novel, *The Castle*, in which the hero, the symbol of the Jew, is told: "You are not of the castle, you are not of the village, you are nothing at all." The hero of the castle, the Jew, is a foreigner who believes that he has been allowed to enter the social system represented by the castle and the village. Indeed, he has been formally asked to join, although I personally am not certain of that, but when he tried to fit himself into the system he discovered that no one was really ready to accept him.

There has been no serious attempt yet at a general outline, not even at a general conception of how to address oneself to the history of the life and death of the Jews of Europe in the Nazi era! We have to turn to the victims and ask, "Did anything in the behavior of the Jews either play into the hands of the exterminators or hamper them? Did anything in that behavior contribute to the passivity of the onlookers?"

The question immediately evokes the rumors about the behavior of the Jewish leadership in occupied Europe, specifically the *Judenraete*, the Jewish Councils. I shall not deal with this aspect at any length, since the facts are more or less known, although the polemics about their significance go on unabated. Raul Hilberg, the well known Holocaust scholar, states: "The Councils were not the willful accomplices of the Germans. The Jewish Councils may have facilitated the task of the Nazis in the majority of the instances; subjectively, the intention of the Jewish leadership was obviously the very opposite of this." (The ghetto as a form of government: An analysis of Isaiah Trunk's *Judenrat*; Paper presented at the Conference on the Holocaust, N.Y. March 1975.)

The Jewish people have a number of customs, symbols, and practices for remembering its past, both its happy occasions and its sad occasions. When we make *Kiddush* on Friday and Holiday evenings, we say *Zecher Leyetziat Mitzrayim*, recalling our liberation from Egypt. In the Ten Commandments, it says, "Remember the Sabbath day, to keep it holy." (Exodus 20:8) We were commanded to recall what Amalek did to us: "Remember what Amalek did to you as you came out of Egypt." (Deuteronomy 25:17)

When our people were driven from the Land of Israel and lost their independence, our sages created many customs and observances to commemorate this tragic event. The question arises: How does one remember the Holocaust? Some people think that only survivors can and should remember. If so, then the memory of the terrible event will die with them, and this must not happen.

All Jews must know and remember the unique crime of the Nazi Holocaust. It should never be forgotten. The preservation of the Jewish people depends a great deal on the memories of the events that happened to our people. If the memory of the Holocaust is preserved, and our children know the history of our martyrs, about those who died *Al Kiddush Hashem*, for the sanctification of the Divine Name and the sanctification of the Jewish people, then we have a good chance to survive all the attempts to destroy us.

We have to be very careful not to compare the Holocaust to other tragedies in our own history, or to tragic events that befell other nations. Let's make it clear that there can be no comparison and no analogies to the uniqueness of the Holocaust. Some circles are trying to minimize the Holocaust by making comparisons to other horrible events in history. Even Hiroshima, Biafra, or Vietnam cannot be compared to the Shoah. Each of these tragic events should be viewed on its own terms and merits. In an article widely reprinted in the North American Student Press, a lecturer, incidentally Jewish himself, has seen fit to compare the situation of the student on the American campus with that of the victims of Auschwitz. Some Jews criticize those of us who talk about Auschwitz and don't lament other tragedies. They say: "Auschwitz was only half the story, and that the other half was Vietnam." These self-hating Jews do not understand that Auschwitz is a story in itself. This type of Jew, though safe in the United States, is running away from the Holocaust.

Some say, "Why bother with ancient history?" It is true that this history cannot be as alive to them as to those of us who lived through it. Is the Holocaust really ancient history to them? Or is it just an excuse and an escape? To our regret we even have Jews now supporting the Palestinian cause, even the P.L.O. terrorists. Escapism into *Universalism* is very fashionable among our Liberals. Maybe they don't know or maybe they have forgotten that at Auschwitz Jews were singled out as Jews. In the camps our people were tortured and murdered as Jews, but since then they have been honored and memorialized as

Frenchmen, Dutchmen, Russians, Poles, and the like. We should emphasize that escapism into Universalism induces Jews to fight for all sorts of causes, except Jewish ones and it is detrimental to Jewish existence.

As I mentioned before, we should never compare the Holocaust to prior tragedies in Jewish history. There is a radical, fundamental, shattering difference. Prior to the Shoah, Jews died for their faith, believing that G-d needed martyrs. The 1,500,000 Jewish children murdered by the Nazis died, not because of their faith, nor for reasons unrelated to the Jewish faith, but rather on account of their Jewish grandparents. Even if a Jew wanted to denounce his Jewishness, even if he wanted to convert and accept another religion, be it even the Nazi ideology, he could not have saved himself. As long as there was a drop of Jewish blood in his veins, he was marked for destruction. Our people were killed not for what they did or did not do, what they thought or did not think, but only for their being what they were by birth.

For 12 long years, the world had been divided into those bent on the murder of every Jewish man, woman, and child on earth, and those lukewarm or indifferent. For 12 long years, the world had conspired to make every Jew wish to flee from his predicament in every way he could. Yet to this unprecedented threat to Jewish survival and sanity, the Jewish people have responded by a reaffirmation of their Jewishness. Where in the world do we find a comparison that out of darkness and despair arises a reaffirmation of faith as in the case of the Jewish people? The Jewish people have reaffirmed their Jewishness after the Holocaust with greater zeal and devotion. Where do we find witnesses comparable to the Jew who stayed committed to his Jewishness, that said "No" to the demons of Auschwitz. Now the Jew has a second *Shema Yisrael* – Never again a Belsen or an Auschwitz.

The Jew of today faces the forces that denied the Jew the right to existence itself, and who, thus, by the simple act of reaffirming his Jewishness, defies the devil himself. The words *Am Yisrael Chai*, the Jewish people live on, have always signified joy and defiance. Today they signify radical surprise as well. The words have become sacred. For the Jewish nation collectively is what each survivor is individually; a testimony on behalf of all mankind to life against the demons of death, a hope and a determination that there must not be, shall not be, and never will be, a second Auschwitz. And with this hope, this determination, every man, woman, and child of the Jewish people stakes his life. In an age in which Auschwitz has happened and Israel is reborn and Old Jerusalem has become Jewish again, no self respecting Jew outside Israel can remain outside, unless he has detached himself from the Jewish people.

Jewish Psychological Factors In Teaching The Holocaust

There is a good reason why we must study the Shoah. To put it bluntly, it is self preservation, for we always face the unthinkable possibility that it may happen again.

The overwhelming cataclysm of the Holocaust has presented the Jewish people with an enormous pedagogical challenge. Today one cannot understand Jewish life without a thorough knowledge and understanding of what took place during the European Jewish catastrophe. It is therefore essential that Jewish educators contemplate how to transmit the account and significance of the Holocaust experience to the present and future generations, and incorporate the study of the Shoah into the very core of the Jewish educational program.

In teaching the Shoah to Jewish pupils, the teacher has a dual obligation; first, to teach what happened and explain why it happened; second, to transmit that knowledge in such a manner that it will reinforce the self esteem of the pupils. In teaching the Shoah, one can impart to our young people not only factual knowledge, but also moral meaning. The value of history is that we learn from the past and how we have arrived at the present and how we should face the future.

The teacher has to decide how to approach the subject matter; whether he examines the origins, development, and execution of the German program to destroy the Jews (the Final Solution), or whether he concentrates on the Jewish response to that destruction, (the Holocaust), or how he can combine both aspects. The historical truth should be a guiding principle. With enough knowledge and understanding about the subject, for example, the *Judenraete*, the Jewish Councils established by the Germans, the teacher could make fair, honest, and balanced presentations. There is no need to apologize for, or whitewash the behavior of Jews who merit critical historical judgment. Since there is so much that is noble in the Jewish history of the Holocaust, such as courage, nobility of spirit, sense of community responsibility with which young people can identify, it is easier to accept the fact that there was also ugliness and evil among some Jews too.

In his preparations for teaching the Shoah, the instructor needs to take into account his ultimate goal, the essence which he wants to transmit to his students about the Holocaust, besides the specific information. We must try to instill in our students a sense of empathy with the victims, but it is also our obligation to teach *hope*, not *despair*. For at the base of Jewish tradition stands redemption at the center, and not the destructive force of evil let loose in the world.

A good Jewish history course, and a course in *Hashkafa*, Jewish philosophy, must incorporate the painful lesson of the Shoah, our contemporary national disaster. The grim reality that G d's action in history, good or bad, is but another manifestation of his covenant with Israel that zigzags throughout Jewish existence, with all its painful seeming contradictions must be presented to our youth. We have a right to question his actions like many generations before us did: "Why does the way of the wicked prosper?" (Jeremiah 12:1) and why should the nations say, "Where is their G-d?" (Psalm 79:10) The inability to explain the divine design is certainly no ground for disbelief, not as long as the sense of G-d persists in man.

The Jewish student should be presented with the lessons of this painful multi-faceted Holocaust event which relates to mass psychology, of the abnormal behavior of the satanic forces in man.

The Bible instructor, as he teaches the lesson in *Shemot*, Exodus, about the *Sneh*, the Burning Bush, "Behold the bush burned with fire, and the bush was not consumed," (Exodus 3:2), can teach a great moral lesson by comparing our people to the Sneh, the Bush that burned but was not consumed. Here we find the transcending enigma of *Netzach Yisrael*, the eternity of Israel, and the tragedy of the Shoah, our Shtetl, consumed by fire.

But like the Sinaitic bush, G-d revealed himself and did not entirely consume the burning bush of Israel, and so in our own time, a remnant was saved and our people reestablished itself in our own old new land.

We can say, "The Lord's steadfast love has not ceased, and His compassions do not fail." (Lamentations 3:22)

Some of us do not dare ask the difficult questions about the Shoah. But there are many survivors who harbor these difficult questions in their minds and in their hearts, but cannot articulate them. Many question G-d's role in the Holocaust. It is not simple to absorb the frightening and horrifying truths of the Shoah. The widespread theory among traditional Jews is that G-d hid His face during the Shoah, for reasons we do not know.

In the book of Isaiah, we find some insight into this problem. There it says: "In the overflowing of wrath, I hid My face from thee for a moment; but with everlasting compassion I will take you back in love, said the Lord your redeemer." (Isaiah 54:7-8)

In another passage in Isaiah, we find that G-d also suffers when the Jewish people are persecuted. "In all their affliction, He was troubled, and the angel of His presence saved them; in His love and His pity, He himself redeemed them, and bore them, and carried them all the days." (Isaiah 63:9)

G-d himself, so to speak, participates in the suffering of His people. We find in the book of Judges: "And His soul was grieved for the misery of Israel." (Judges 10:16) In the book of Psalms, we find a similar idea: "I will be with him in trouble." (Psalm 91:15) G-d suffers when the Jewish people are afflicted. The cause of the Divine is in a temporary eclipse whenever tyranny becomes mighty on earth and vents its barbarism in afflicting the Jewish people.

Survivors who remained religious and continued with their Jewish traditions were a testament to the fact that it was possible to emerge spiritually whole from the Shoah.

Psychologists say that there is no need for concern about negative effects of teaching the Shoah to youngsters. Let them learn from the past how to cope in the future. Indeed, there are many Holocaust experiences in which children can take pride. Here are some examples of personal courage with which children should be familiar.

Little *Shmulik,* Samuel, was brutally whipped by a Polish guard for sneaking out of the ghetto to buy extra food for Shabbat. He suffered quietly and hid his pain from his parents. Against his father's orders, he made his way to the subterranean *shul*, the Synagogue, where his father had gone for *Kabalat Shabbat*, welcoming the Shabbat. Participating in public prayer was punished by death by the Germans, so parents refused to let their children go to pray. Shmulik knocked on the door. Thinking it was the Gestapo, the men opened the door fearfully, ready to face death bravely. When they saw Shmulik, they became enraged and his father slapped him. Unable to endure more pain, Shmulik said to his father, "You are also beating me? Haven't I had my share of blows? I, too, am a Jew. I, too, want to pray."

Rabbi Shem of Cracow, Poland, was among those chosen at random to be tortured in jail. He began comforting his fellow Jews by asking them, "If each of us were given the choice at this moment to be the victim or the victimizer, which would you choose?" He lifted his eyes to heaven and said, "*Ribono Shel*

Olam, Master of the universe, there is not one Jew who would like You to turn him into a murderer."

The Jews of Lublin were sentenced to become the victims of S.S. Commander Odilo Globocnik, a sadistic murderer, who herded them against a barbed wire fence. Their flesh was torn by the barbed wire. He ordered them to sing while Nazi troops beat them savagely with batons. The Jews began falling and trampling each other. Suddenly one of them freed himself and began singing: *Mir velen zay iberleben avinu she ba shamayim*, "We shall outlive them, O Father in Heaven, we shall outlive them, O Father in Heaven." The bruised and bleeding Jews rose one after another and joined the singing. Globocnik roared with laughter, until he realized they weren't pleasing him. They were defeating him. He ordered them to stop, but they continued. He panicked and pleaded with them to stop, but the singing and dancing continued. The S.S. troops plowed into them with swinging clubs and whips and still the singing continued.

Our children today should know the whole truth of the Holocaust. Let them know that the Catholic Church gave its tacit approval to the Final Solution. Indeed, the entire world was silent; the democratic, enlightened society of Europe and America alike. Why was humanity silent when the smoking ovens were fed with Jewish bodies? Where were the so-called Liberals when the fat of the Jewish bodies was made into soap? Where were all the decent people, the Gentile world and all humanists? Our children must know this aspect of the human race, and prepare themselves for healthy aggressiveness and courageous self defense.

Just as we teach about the destruction of the Temple in Jerusalem and about *Tisha B'Av*, we must teach about the *Churban Shlishi*, the third destruction, the Shoah from which we can learn inspiring lessons of *teshuvah* and *emunah*, repentance, faith, and belief. Indeed, it is a hard task, especially when we lack adequate materials correlated with established traditional curricula.

Many of us don't know where our dear ones perished, or on what day they returned their souls to the Creator; therefore the Knesset, the Israeli Parliament has established the 27th day of the Hebrew month of *Nissan* as *Yom Hashoah*, or a day for remembering the Holocaust victims. Although our national *Yahrzeit*, the memorial day, is observed once a year, we should teach our children that every day is a *Yizkor*, a day for millions of Jews who perished without survivors in the Nazi concentration camps. It is a Yahrzeit for all of us to remember them, not once a year, on Father's Day or Mother's Day. It is a Yahrzeit which teaches our children to affirm the unbeatable bond of continuity that joins our generation with the previous one. *Yisrael arevin zeh bazeh*. (Tractate

Shavuot 39A) "Jews are responsible for one another." We are all our brother's keepers.

The Shoah, therefore becomes a lesson in *Ahavath Yisrael*, in the love and devotion to our fellow Jews. As long as there is one Jew who is oppressed or persecuted, or whether Israel is in danger from its Arab neighbors, we must be on guard and act vigorously and in a unified manner. Otherwise there is always the danger that we shall be caught in another tragedy.

There is indeed great value in transmitting the testament of the *Haruge Malchut,* the 6,000,000 martyrs. If the echoes of the voices of the Holocaust martyrs weaken, we will not survive either. We must therefore teach this tragic chapter to every Jew, especially to our youth and thus preserve the future of our people.

The lessons of the Holocaust must be transmitted as a legacy to future generations. The memory of their lives must be bound up with our lives so their deaths will not have been in vain. Not to forget them is our moral obligation. It is a responsibility to our conscience, to humanity and to future generations.

Actually, every one of us, whether we were direct victims of the Nazi Inferno or not, teacher and student alike, are *udim mutzalim meaish*, survivors of the great inferno. We are the witnesses of the "wolf man;" of the existing pathology of a sick mentality, a mass psychology, which turned man into beast, love into hatred, effacing the *Tzelem Elokim,* the image of G-d through a Nietzschean philosophy devoid of G-dliness, mercy, and holiness.

A study has been made of the survivors and their children and it shows that the traumatic experiences the survivors suffered have been revisited upon their children. The children of the survivors of the Shoah are indeed themselves also victims.

The Director of the Shalvah Psychiatric Hospital in Tel Aviv, put it succinctly: "The trauma of the Nazi concentration camp is re-experienced in the lives of the grandchildren of camp survivors. The effects of systematic dehumanization are being transmitted from one generation to the next through disturbances in the parent child relationship." Most people tend to deny a problem exists. They want to avoid confrontation with pain of this extremity. Many survivors and their children refuse to talk about it.

Some children of survivors ask of their parents the following hard questions; "Who put the number on your arm? Why? Did it hurt? Why don't I have grandparents? Why did the Germans kill them? Where are they buried? Why aren't they buried? Then where are they?" Can one imagine this kind of conversation between a child and a parent survivor? Usually these discussions don't take place until the children start to grow up because the survivors try to give their children a normal upbringing without hurting them. Therefore, the subject is not discussed at all at home. Some children would like to share with their parents their experiences of those horrible years. But because they can't really share those experiences, it makes them feel helpless and guilty.

The ritual of Yizkor, the remembrance, therefore, is not only to remember those who perished in the Shoah, but also those who escaped and lived. As the Psalmist says, "I shall not die, but live and tell the wonders of the Lord." (Psalm 118:17) We have to continue to carry the banner of faith of Jewish continuity and survival.

Preparing To Teach The Holocaust

According to a recent survey, one out of every five Americans does not know or is not sure that Jews were killed during the Holocaust.

The solution to the problem of ignorance about the Holocaust is to provide serious and committed education about the Holocaust to high school and college students; the next generation of teachers, professors, researchers, museum personnel, and ordinary citizens.

For many years the Holocaust played a small role in the school curriculum and community activities because of the tendency to emphasize the positive in Jewish life and history. There is a need to place the study of the Holocaust within the broader historical and educational context. Efforts to bolster aspects of Jewish identity through the study of the Holocaust require a special sensitivity to the balance between the devastating negatives of the experience, and the positives which can be derived from resistance in all its facets and the demonstration of human dignity. For the Holocaust to be meaningful to Jewish identity, there is a need for the acquisition of knowledge as well as the emotional tug.

Up to the present time, hardly more than a tentative beginning has been made in teaching our youth the lesson of the Shoah. In the few textbooks in which some account of the Holocaust is given, the subject is treated in the most cursory and general terms. Many teachers admit that because of inadequate progress in teaching the history syllabus, many primary schools, and even post primary, classes never come to study the period of the Holocaust. Thus, in the course of the years, very little has been achieved. Most of our young people only come into contact with the Shoah on the 27th day of Nissan, the Day of Remembrance, when teachers tell their pupils about the significance of the occasion, during a memorial ceremony, which is not an integral part of the curriculum. The results are very meager. The older generation, especially the teachers, are convinced that our youth do not want to hear about the Holocaust. And, as usual, this void is filled somehow with immature opinions and misconceptions, with the results that many young people have come to hold various prejudices and mistaken notions.

For a number of reasons, parents and educators have tried to keep the knowledge and understanding of the Shoah from the youth. The reason, which is constantly reiterated, is that the equilibrium of the young person must be preserved, he must not be brought face to face with the atrocities perpetrated in some of the darkest years in human history. There is, of course, no question we have here a matter requiring prudence and sober judgment. The study material must be adjusted to the age of the pupils, to their emotional and intellectual grasp. But this does not mean that it is not a matter suitable for all to study. We cannot, after all, conceal from the youth the horrors that were perpetrated. The daily newspapers, the literature our children read, are full of accounts of facts of violence and bloodshed. The young people do not grow up in an ivory tower.

It is not uncommon for parents to shield their children from any discussion of death, and thus try to protect them from attending funerals, houses of mourning, or even riding through cemetery grounds. I still recall vividly the emotional reaction of parents when I presented the Holocaust in the school where I was the principal in the 1960s. Many parents were shocked that we educators could present to the children such a *traumatic experience*, for youngsters should not be exposed to these horrors. If we cannot face the truth and reality of the Holocaust, no matter how frightful, shocking, or depressing, its evil will become blurred and will be ready to reappear in a new generation, in another place, when society goes awry. Youngsters cannot be kept ignorant of certain facts that are part and parcel of our daily lives.

It seems to me that the subject of the Holocaust, when discussed in the proper spirit, can strengthen the young person and foster his moral values. We cannot ignore the fact that this subject is full of pitfalls and for that reason the educator must be equipped with adequate knowledge if he is to be successful in his task. Above all, some suitable method of study, of imparting information, must be found.

The subject of the Holocaust is becoming, as of late, one of the most popularly chosen courses among our young people at the high school and college levels. Students today seeking relevance in contemporary events see in the subject of the Holocaust, an opportunity of further searching out the meaning of their Jewish identity. In this regard, the Holocaust affords an excellent educational occasion, which justifiably demands a good teaching approach to make the learning experience a satisfying one.

At what age level should the teaching of the Shoah be introduced? Many educators are reluctant to introduce the subject under ages 10-12. However, there is an overwhelming agreement among all streams in Jewish education that courses on the Holocaust might be introduced at the 13 to 14-year-old level.

It is not an altogether easy task. However, it is my conviction that one can start introducing the subject gradually, even on the elementary level. The Holocaust curriculum in the Jewish school should be subdivided into three cycles of learning; from kindergarten through grade five; grades six to eight; grades nine to twelve.

Isaac Berez

Moshe Avital conducted the National Bible Contest in 1977 in New York.

In the first cycle one should concentrate on specific incidents close to the life of the child, mostly on stories about children of the Holocaust or about personalities such as Anne Frank, Chanah Senesh, Mordechai Anilevitch and others.

Encourage students to read the following stories: *The Diary of a Young Girl*, by Anne Frank; *Young Moshe's Diary*, by Moshe Flinker; *A Touch of Earth, A Wartime Childhood*, by Janina David; *The Children of Mapu Street*, by Sara Neshamit; and *The Forest, My Friend*, by Donia Rosen.

One can also find a number of worthwhile stories in the *World Over* magazine. The *World Over* put out a special issue with selections of stories on the Shoah that was published by the Board of Jewish Education, New York.

Another approach may be to invite survivors of the Holocaust to tell the young children about some of the experiences they encountered during their years of captivity.

In the second cycle, grades six to eight, the teachers should build another layer on what has been already accomplished. The educational objectives for this age group should include the following components:

It is essential to approach the children in terms of reality. Questions of life and death, good and evil, are inescapable. Because of the emotional ramifications of the study, parents should be involved in some of the organizational aspects of the program.

The concept of remembering is basic and should be reinforced. Aspects of resistance, in addition to the physical, should be emphasized, as well as the value of passive resistance through maintaining faith and tradition, and love and concern for fellow human beings.

The concept of cruelty and innocence, as they apply to the victims of the Holocaust, should be discussed.

The special meaning of the Shoah to Jews should be taught, rather than its broader applications. In general, one can say that teaching such a unit to young children should move gradually from the specific incident close to the life of a child, to the more universal concepts. The principal should also involve the entire school. The faculty should be fully briefed and the program must be part of the curriculum of all classes. There would be a long lasting effect upon students exposed to the Holocaust experiences in a sustained program.

Day Schools have a special advantage in that they have the student five full days a week for both Hebrew and general studies. The program can therefore be molded as a core into history, social studies, language arts, and other subjects. In the Hebrew division, the subject can also be approached through literature, using storybooks such as: The *Lador* series, The *Gesher* series, and *Gesher Lanoar* series, to mention a few.

Every effort should be made to elicit programs and ideas from the students. The students should be given a chance to do research, create filmstrips and tapes, produce their own dramatic program and become personally involved, thus giving the study of the Holocaust a much greater impact on

Isaac Berez

Moshe Avital conducted the National Contest on Zionism in 1978 in New York.

their lives. Some schools utilize the days of the counting of the Omer, the semi-mourning period between Pesach and Shavuot for the Holocaust unit, since it includes four special days: *Yom Hashoah (27 Nissan), Yom Hazikaron (4 Iyar), Yom Haatzmaut (5 Iyar),* and *Yom Yerushalayim (28 Iyar)*, all of which lend themselves for such study. Some Yeshivah educators feel that by creating a Holocaust unit for this period, you build from the tragic events of the Shoah to a period of sunshine and hope of the reborn and reunited Israel.

The third cycle, grades 9 to 12, should include a more intellectual approach to the issues of the Shoah. Proper study is not possible without basic knowledge in the history of the period.

However, when we are discussing the fate of our own people, of a human tragedy, which is without parallel in the history of mankind, we must put the accent on the emotional and moral aspects. Compilation and study of statistical material provide an excellent example of the sort of latent danger. The murder of millions conveys nothing to the young person. The figure is beyond his grasp. One can identify oneself with the fate of an individual; one can understand the feelings of an individual, justify his surrender, participate in his struggle. The *Diary of Anne Frank* has proven more eloquent than the infinite number of articles and essays written on the Holocaust. The individual must be the main subject in any attempt to explain and study the problems. From the individual case, we can deduce the wider implication.

Our teachers must evoke in their pupils a real admiration for the individual Jew, for his great power of endurance and continued steadfastness under the gravest conditions. The teachers should also arouse in the pupils an attitude of optimism that no matter what, *we shall overcome.*

The overall objective should be the survival of the Jewish people and to remember never to forget what happened.

The following should be among the important goals:

To convey an idea of the development of events which made up the horror of the Holocaust.

To express the anguish of individuals caught up in the enormity of world events over which they exerted little control; to have the students begin to understand and, if possible, experience that anguish, through reading diaries and eyewitness accounts.

To develop a sense of *Klal Yisrael*, of identification with the world Jewish community.

To gain an appreciation of the dimensions of the Holocaust by comparing Jewish life in Europe before and after the tragedy.

The course should consist of four units. Suggested lesson plans for each unit follow:

Unit One

Pre-War European Jewish Culture

The first unit should be a study of the Jews of Eastern Europe, examining the various facets of life which made Jewish existence unique, including the culture of the *shtetl* and the peculiarities of its people and events.

As part of the culture of the Eastern European shtetl life, it is essential that students be exposed to the religious intellectual aspect of that life.

A very important aspect of a people's culture is its music. For this reason the class should hear Yiddish and Hebrew music both from the period before and during the Holocaust.

In addition, a project should be suggested for the class to prepare a map of Europe before World War II, with cities of large Jewish centers filled in, along with approximate numbers of Jews in each country at that time. These numbers will assume greater importance later when compared with figures of Jewish survivors in each of the European countries.

Unit Two

The Holocaust – The Destruction Of European Jewry

The background of anti-Semitism, racism, and Nazism in Germany and other parts of Europe should be examined in this unit. An all encompassing study will be made of its historical beginnings, its psychological impact on the German people and the mechanisms of social, physical, religious and political control it exercised to dominate the German people.

The unit should include the growth of anti-Semitism in Germany, the Nazis' first years of power, the Nuremberg laws, the Kristallnacht, the period of restrictions and internment of the Jews from 1939 to 1941, Nazi expansion all over Europe, the Final Solution from 1941 to 1945, life under Nazism, Nazi techniques, and the silence of the Gentile world including the Pope and the Catholic Church.

Unit Three

Jewish Resistance

In this unit, emphasis should be put on the various kinds of resistance the Jews exhibited during the Shoah. The teacher should point out that there was massive Jewish psychological, spiritual, and moral resistance. They refused to be brutalized; they kept up their human image under the most horrible conditions. They continued with their children's education against the strict German orders to abolish all educational and cultural activities. And finally when they realized the Germans planned to annihilate all Jews, armed resistance broke out in many places, in ghettos, concentration camps, and in labor camps. Jews fought in all the undergrounds of Europe, they joined the partisan units of Eastern European nationalities and even formed their own units, since in many cases the local inhabitants hated the Jews and sometimes even surrendered them to the Nazis.

Unit Four

Rehabilitation Of Survivors And The Establishment Of The State Of Israel

The few who survived the camps refused to return to their former homes. Those lands had become graveyards for them and they could not face the prospects of resuming life in those countries.

The very few survivors who returned to their native cities and villages in Eastern Europe were received with anger and hostility. The survivors, unwanted in their former homes and weary of a life of tribulation and adversity, waged a stubborn struggle for the right to immigrate to the Land of Israel.

Those D.P.'s, (Displaced Persons) insisted on their right to immigrate to their land and constituted a powerful force in the political campaign waged for the establishment of Israel.

The subject of the D.P. Camps should be mentioned as a glorious chapter in American Jewish involvement in helping with the rehabilitation of the Jewish survivors.

We should point out the tremendous contribution the Holocaust survivors made to the establishment of the State of Israel. Their devotion and contribution can be found in almost every aspect of life in Israel.

Pedagogic Assumptions And Techniques

Focusing on issues, rather than confining oneself to descriptions of brutality (or, simply recounting experiences of oppressed Jews) will decrease tensions and increase insights. Sensitivities aroused by the study of traumatic experiences can be more effectively channeled in a classroom where tensions are reduced by thought provoking involvement. It does not mean, divorced from emotion completely, but rather a certain mood can be established in each lesson.

The flexible teacher, in utilizing discussion freely, will reduce unwarranted class tensions. Anxieties will inevitably arise from the topic but relaxed interpersonal relationships in class will lead to concern without nervousness.

The Approach To Teaching The Holocaust

In order to implement multi-level experiences about the Holocaust, one can choose one of the two methods: The integrated method, or the separate formal course.

In the Jewish school, especially in the day school, the subject lends itself to be integrated. This could be done in history, social studies, literature, prayer, music and song, the arts, holiday observances and others. The integration into the other subjects could be accomplished while at the same time the uniqueness of the Shoah is maintained.

There are some educators, especially those who have survived the Shoah, who advocate the teaching of the Holocaust as a separate formal course in order to emphasize the uniqueness and the enormity of the tragedy. They also feel that by using this method, they can better utilize all resources of all subject material and multi media aids.

The overall objective should be to contribute to the survival of the Jewish people and to help our youth to remember and never forget. Each school according to its needs and ability should decide which method to use. Some schools might find it difficult to allocate time for a separate formal course, due to the limited time available to teach all the Jewish subjects.

The Instructor's Role

The instructor's role is not to preach hostility and not to propagandize. Very often, careful selection of materials will itself create a moral climate. One does not have to justify the study of the Holocaust in the Jewish school since there are students who are interested and want to know and understand. The student's interest before instruction may be grounded on personal involvement; he might be aware that the lives of his relatives were affected by World War II; or he may be searching for his own Jewish identity by asking about Jewish-Christian relations during World War II.

Whether all Jewish students should be required to study the Holocaust in depth is a separate question. Perhaps the Holocaust should be offered in certain schools as an elective.

However, it is my feeling and belief, that there are many gains for the student of the Holocaust. After a close examination of the Holocaust issues, he will gain new perspectives, which very few students obtain in public schools or colleges. The student will experience a renewal of Jewish identification and concern.

The course material can be presented as parts of a seminar series in a classroom setting. The sessions may be one or two hours per week. The students who study the Holocaust can be informed about good and optimism in a matrix of evil and despair. Such learning can cause an indifferent person to become a good human being.

Activities – Involve The Students

If the Holocaust is to have meaning, it must be brought out of the realm of facts and figures and be made into a personal, tragic part of our lives and those of the children we teach.

Have the children find out such facts as:

From what part of Europe their ancestors came.

The names of members of their family if any who died in the Holocaust.

Have each child report and then discuss the possibility that, "but for the grace of G-d," they might not be here today.

Have students write to various Jewish organizations for material.

Have students write to survivors and ask specific questions concerning their life during and after World War II.

Ask students to prepare a scrapbook of letters and responses from the various sources contacted.

Utilizing a bulletin board of clippings is another method of enlarging the sphere of class learning activities and awareness of the relevance of the subject.

By asking students to look for pertinent material from newspapers and magazines and establishing the search on a rotating basis among the students, it will be possible to bring in the added dimension of current events.

Students ages 13 to 15 react more attentively and more favorably to printed material when it is an emotional or first person account. Traditional lectures or historical narratives, no matter how well written, cannot compete with the immediate reaction evoked by the personal writings of people who were there. Retention will be increased by the use of eyewitness reports and strong impressions will be conveyed which will most probably prove lasting and indelible.

In order to attune and sensitize the students, selections from literature should be discussed, each of which will emphasize a primary symbol of the Holocaust. Experience has shown that poems have been most effective. Students react quite well to novels. It is worthwhile to make available or assign complete books.

No single work is more capable of conveying the horror and nightmare of Nazi brutality in an appropriate manner for youngsters as Eli Wiesel's *Night*, a novel written in the first person. Students are usually incapable of reading this book without reacting deeply to the experience. All find themselves caught up in another person's emotions, and the experience pulls them through. Many students have requested the name of another Wiesel book after they return to report that they have read *Night* in one sitting.

As excellent as written material may be, films frequently go far beyond words in conveying an impact. Among the many fine films which are available on the subject, three should be utilized for the purpose of the course: *The Shop on Main Street*, portrays the Nazi anti-Jewish brutality in Czechoslovakia and illustrates the German economic policy towards the Jews; *Memorandum*, deals with the guilt of all who served Nazism in any capacity from the giants of industry to the clerks who signed papers and *The Pawnbroker*, which illustrates how the Nazi defeat has not ended the nightmare for the concentration camp survivor.

Additional films could also be used include *Let My People Go*, a powerful documentary covering the length and breadth of Jewish history from the perspective of the Holocaust; *Triumph of Will*, presenting shocking captured Nazi war films; *Night and Fog*, an eerie look at a concentration camp during the war and a present day walk through on a clear and sunny day, with the echoes of the past reverberating cruelly in the wind past the barbed wire and into the sun lit surrounding fields of green grass and flowers; and *The Illegals*, a profound documentary on the illegal voyage of displaced persons to Palestine on unseaworthy vessels in the years immediately following the war, *The Voyage of the Damned*, *The Eighty-First Blow.*

Recordings are also far more effective than written words. One such recording, whose effect is overpowering is of Nazi songs and marches interspersed with the actual voices of Hitler and other prominent Nazis, all accompanied by the narration. The record is called *Hitler's Inferno*, and is available in two volumes by Audio Masterpiece/Audio Rarities.

Have the students read aloud some of the many dramatizations that deal with aspects of the Holocaust, Jewish heroism of the period and the like, for example; *Behind the Ghetto Wall, Parachutists and Partisans*, *Israel Dream and Fulfillment*, and *His Brother's Keeper.*

Invite a guest speaker, a survivor of the Holocaust who will describe some aspects of his experiences to the students. Let the students ask questions on topics that bother them. This can be a most effective and moving dialogue.

Prepare exhibits of books, recordings, pictures, maps, posters, yellow badges and other symbols, diagrams on European Jewry, cassettes, films, slides, magazines and other material that deals with that period.

Create a special corner or room in the school or Synagogue, which will serve as a memorial for the 6,000,000 martyrs. This room can also serve as a library on the Holocaust. A special wall could be prepared with the names of the major Jewish communities, which have been destroyed. It could also become an archive of all materials collected over the years.

Music of the Shoah, the songs of desperation, songs of hope, songs of the ghetto and partisans are a very effective media of involving the student cognitively and emotionally. Songs of the Holocaust should be taught and their content explained. Later on these songs should be utilized at special observances. There are a number of useful recordings which should find a permanent place in every Jewish school library. For instance, Kibbutz *Lochamei Hagetaot* in Israel prepared a collection called *Songs of the Vilna Ghetto*. These songs, composed during the Holocaust, recall the Shoah and *Gevurah*, the destruction and heroism of the Jewish people. Cantor Shalom Katz put out liturgical recordings memorializing this period called *Lest We Forget*, Westminster Hed Arzi. Equally impressive are Eli Wiesel's dramatic readings from his own writings, which are based on his own Holocaust experiences. An excellent source is the recordings of *Voices of History*, recorded interviews with narrative by people who survived the Holocaust.

Organize panel discussions within a class or at an interclass session and finally at an intercommunity assembly. This can be in the form of a trial against the nations who collaborated with the Nazis.

Organize a quiz program on the Holocaust. Have a student committee prepare the questions and plan the entire event.

Of special interest should be the discussions of moral problems.

One should bring out the contrasts and extremes that existed during the Holocaust. On the one hand, the Nazi machine and on the other, the resistance... The indifference by most of the Gentile world and the special efforts by the Scandinavian people and the Danes in particular.

To show the real image of the Catholic Church when, not only did the Pope keep silent, but also when the Church did save Jewish children from the Nazis, it did it for a purpose. Such children were converted to Christianity. After the war when surviving relatives wanted these children back, the Church refused.

The contrast between German doctors who used Jews as guinea pigs and Jewish doctors who tried desperately to save lives wherever they could.

What the difference is between the Nuremberg Trials and the Eichmann Trial in Jerusalem.

What should be the Jewish attitude to the German people? Should we forgive them? Should we do business with them? Should Jews go to Germany for any reason?

How should we look at the Judenraete leaders? Were they traitors? Were they heroes? Did they have any choice?

What is the difference between the Jewish ghetto in the middle ages and the ghetto during the Nazi era? Or the ghetto of blacks today in the United States?

In the cases when the Germans demanded that certain Jewish leaders be surrendered to them, what should have been their actions? To surrender the victim? To refuse? Should the victim himself surrender? Should the victim take revenge against the Jews? Is there a justification to endanger an entire community for one person?

Should the survivors accept reparations from Germany? If yes, how much should they receive?

Additional Activities And Materials

Jews In Distant Lands is a series of ten newspapers, describing Jewish life in ten countries. Among them there are at least three, which have very good material on the Holocaust. They describe the dramatic rescue of the Jews of Denmark in 1943, a description of Anne Frank and the secret annex where she and her family hid, and a moving story from Rumania about the ship *Struma*, which in 1942 the Russians sank when it was on its way to Eretz Yisrael. A filmstrip and a guide accompany each newspaper.

In order to involve the student more intimately with the Shoah, it is suggested assigning students to record interviews with survivors. The student prepares the questions to be asked of the survivors, arranges for an appointment, and conducts the interview. This personal touch has great educational and emotional value.

Students of Ramaz Day School and the Solomon Schechter School in White Plains interviewed me about my experience during the Shoah. It was quite a unique experience for them and also for myself. These recordings can become an oral history of the Holocaust which the school can keep in the library for future use.

In honor of the 30th anniversary of Israel, the Jewish National Fund came up with a marvelous educational idea. A Jewish child in the Diaspora and one in Israel will plant three trees, one for himself, one for his counterpart, and the third one for a Jewish child who perished in the Holocaust. This can be repeated year after year.

Educators should take their students to the various Holocaust museums that have been established so our youth can better understand what happened during the Shoah, especially when we hear more and more voices of Germans and other anti-Semites who take the authentic Nazi line, who claim, "There is no real proof that the Holocaust did happen." The non-Jewish world has quickly forgotten about the greatest Jewish tragedy and many today are denying that over 6,000,000 Jews were murdered in the Holocaust.

Organizing pilgrimages like the March of the Living for Youth to European sites where some of the Holocaust events took place, to Ghetto Warsaw, to Auschwitz and other places. From Europe, the pilgrimage continues on to Israel where they visit Yad Vashem, Kibbutz Lochamei Hagetaot, Yad Mordechai and other institutions that memorialize the Shoah. The climax being the impact of Israel, the rebirth of the Jewish State after the destruction of European Jewry.

Organize special weekend retreats and seminars for youth on the Shoah. This is very popular in Israel. Thousands of youth take part in a four-day seminar on the history of the Holocaust at the *Massua* Institute, at Kibbutz *Tel Itzhak*. The seminar includes eyewitness reports on pre-war Jewish communities in Europe, on the Holocaust itself, and on the heroism of the ghetto and resistance fighters. They view films, pictures and examine documents of that era. The students and teachers attempt to understand how such a tragedy could occur in the 20th century in the heart of civilized Europe. The seminar concludes with a visit to Yad Vashem, the Israeli Holocaust museum in Jerusalem and a visit to the museum at Kibbutz Lochamei Hagetaot, the Ghetto Fighters.

~~~~~~~~~~~~~~~~~~~~~~~~~~~~~~

To teach the Holocaust is not an easy task, but we must strive towards realizing our goals. For, as teachers and educators, we have the duty to emulate our teaching forefathers. We are called upon to do as they have done; to eternalize our history by structuring living links of ritual.

The Holocaust should be remembered as a uniquely Jewish tragedy, highlighted by spiritual heroism, which should serve as an inspiration for future generations to preserve their Jewish heritage. The Holocaust cannot, however, be treated as an event only of past history, but rather must be presented as a subject of contemporary relevance. The events of the Holocaust mark such a major turning point in Jewish history, as well as in the history of mankind, that it has to be regarded as a subject of vital importance in the curriculum of our schools.

Because the Holocaust is a historical crossroad, the impact of which we have yet to fully realize even in our times, raises profound questions of values and attitudes facing us today as parents, teachers, Jews, and human beings. We must therefore teach this tragic chapter to our youth and thus preserve the future of our people.
~~~~~~~~~~~~~~~~~~~~~~~~~~~~~~

Tell It To Your Children

This is the scroll of agony and heroism which I have tried to unravel for you. The Holocaust must be studied with awe and reverence and as we study it, we should take to heart the words of the Prophet Joel:

> *Listen to this, you who are old, hear this all you inhabitants of the land! Has the like of it ever been in your day or in the days of your fathers? Tell it to your children, and your children to their children, and their children to the coming generation.*
>
> *(Joel 1-2)*

Glossary

Aliyah Beth: Illegal immigration of Jews to the land of Israel against British orders.

Anti-Semitism: Anti-Semitism denotes all forms of hostility manifested towards Jews.

Antlousung: Getting rid of lice.

Apell Platz: A plaza where the entire camp lined up for roll call.

Auschwitz: The most notorious concentration camp where millions of Jews and other nationalities were put to death in the gas chambers.

Blockaeltste: Block elder, head of a dwelling barrack.

Bricha: Flight, the name of an organized underground operation which moved Jews out of Eastern Europe on the way to the land of Israel.

Burger Meister: A Mayor.

Concentration Camp: The place of imprisonment for Jews during the Holocaust. The camps of imprisonment for Moshe Avital were Auschwitz, Plaszow, Gross-Rosen, Bolkenheim, Reichenau, and Buchenwald.

Crematoria: Special ovens in which the Nazis burned the corpses of their victims.

D.P. Camps: The survivors of the death camps were placed in displaced persons camps in Germany and Austria before they were able to find a new home.

Einsaatzgruppen: Mobile units of the Nazi S.S., S.D. and local collaborators who were involved in killing Jews.

Final Solution: The code name for the organized mass murder of the Jewish people.

Gas Chambers: Chambers which looked like regular showers. The deadly gas was emptied into the chamber through the showers.

Genocide: The partial or entire destruction of a religious, racial or national group.

Gestapo: The Nazi secret police.

Ghetto: Usually the Jewish quarter in a city or town which was separated and closed off by walls from other parts of the city. Jews were concentrated in the ghetto and were not allowed to leave its premises.

Heftling: Prisoner.

Hitlerjugend: Hitler Youth - the youth of Germany was organized in youth battalions. They helped in implementing the Nazi philosophy.

Holocaust: The Shoah. Also known as the Catastrophe. The most tragic period of Jewish Diaspora history and indeed of modern mankind. It represents the 12 years of Nazi atrocities against the Jewish people.

Judenraete: Council of Jewish representatives set up in Jewish communities and ghettos under the Nazis to carry out their instructions.

Judenrein: A locality from which all Jews had been eliminated.

K. Z. Camps: Concentration camps like Auschwitz, Buchenwald, Dachau, Majdanek, Mauthausen, Bergen-Belsen, and many more.

Kapo: Prisoner in charge of a group of inmates in Nazi concentration camps, extremely feared by the inmates.

Kiddush Hashem: The sanctification of the Divine Name. Jews during the Holocaust suffered and died as religious martyrs and thus sanctified the Divine Name.

Kristallnacht: Crystal Night, meaning night of broken glass. Organized destruction of Synagogues, Jewish houses and shops, accompanied by arrests of individual Jews that took place in Germany and Austria under the Nazis on the night of November 9-10, 1938.

Lageraelteste: A prisoner in charge of the entire camp inside the camp.

Labor Camps: Jewish men ages 18 to 50 were put into labor camps. These men were forced to work for the Nazi war effort. Many of these camps were later transformed into concentration camps.

Luftwaffe: The German Air Force.

Madagascar Plan: Nazi plan to deport 4,000,000 Jews to Madagascar, an island in the Indian Ocean, over a period of four years. It was shelved after the Nazis decided to carry out the Final Solution.

Mein Kampf: My Struggle, title of work written by Adolf Hitler setting forth his political program.

Munko Tabor: Hungarian forced labor camp.

Musselman: Nazi camp slang word for a prisoner on the brink of death. A prisoner who has despaired and lost the will to live.

Nazis: National Socialist Party of Germany. Their belief, nazism, was based on racism and on the idea that the German people were superior to all other people.

Nuremberg Laws: Laws enacted in September 1935. This legislation comprised two basic laws; only persons of German blood were German citizens, which made Jews second class citizens, and forbade marriages between Jews and Germans. There were also many other discriminations and restrictions.

Nuremberg Trials: First international military tribunal, in the fall of 1945. This court tried the 21 men who had occupied important positions in the Government of Nazi Germany.

Obermench: Superman - The Germans thought of themselves to be supermen.

Partisans: Jewish resistance fighters who took part in guerrilla warfare against the Nazis during World War II. Their bases were located in the forests of Eastern Europe.

Righteous Among The Nations: Term applied to those non-Jews who saved Jews from Nazi persecution, often at the peril of their own lives and of their loved Ones.

Shoah: The Holocaust

Shtetl: Small towns or villages where Jews lived in Eastern Europe

Stubenaelteste: The person responsible for a section within the barrack.

S.S. Troops: "Schutzstaffel," Nazi elite formations which carried out central tasks in the Final Solution. They operated the concentration camps in occupied Europe and Germany.

Va'ad Ha-Hazalah: Jewish rescue committees that functioned in different countries in Europe during the Holocaust.

Wachman: East Europeans from Lithuania, Latvia, Estonia, Ukraine, Poland, and other countries who volunteered to guard the concentration camps.

Wehrmacht: The German regular army.

Yad Vashem: The National Israeli Remembrance Authority in Jerusalem.

Yellow Badge: A yellow six-pointed star outlined in black with the word "Jude" (Jew) written in black. The Jews had to wear the star either on an armband or on the front and back of the outer garments. It also appeared in various languages.

Yom Hashoah: Day of Remembrance and observance for the martyrs who perished in the Holocaust. It is observed on the 27th day of the Hebrew month of Nissan.

CPSIA information can be obtained at www.ICGtesting.com
Printed in the USA
BVOW04*0849141115

426110BV00003B/6/P

9 781936 778577